# More praise for *The School Psychologist's Survival Guide*

"Taking up where grad school leaves off, smart and savvy Rebecca Branstetter has written a practical, thorough, and truly helpful guide that will ease the nervousness of newbies and provide a revitalizing refresher for experienced school psychologists. An invaluable book for getting started, keeping up and ultimately finding satisfaction in this whirlwind of a career."

—**Katherine A. Briccetti, Ph.D.,** school psychologist, Piedmont (California) Unified School District, author of *Blood Strangers: A Memoir*

"In the first book of its kind, Dr. Branstetter provides an invaluable resource for school psychologists both new and veteran. Her easy humor, reproducible charts and letters, and on-the-job personal experiences help translate classroom and textbook learning into real-life application."

—**Aimee Koehler,** author of *Musings of an Urban School Psychologist* blog

"In *The School Psychologist's Survival Guide*, Dr. Branstetter provides a wealth of helpful hints in dealing with the breadth of activities that school psychologists engage in. From the practical to the pragmatic, these ideas and the summary tables will be useful for both new and experienced practitioners as well as for school psychology trainers and interns."

—**Frank C. Worrell, Ph.D.,** director, School Psychology Program, University of California at Berkeley

# *Jossey-Bass Teacher*

Jossey-Bass Teacher provides educators with practical knowledge and tools to create a positive and lifelong impact on student learning. We offer classroom-tested and research-based teaching resources for a variety of grade levels and subject areas. Whether you are an aspiring, new, or veteran teacher, we want to help you make every teaching day your best.

From ready-to-use classroom activities to the latest teaching framework, our value-packed books provide insightful, practical, and comprehensive materials on the topics that matter most to K–12 teachers. We hope to become your trusted source for the best ideas from the most experienced and respected experts in the field.

# Other titles in the Jossey-Bass Teacher Survival Guide Series

First-Year Teacher's Survival Guide: Ready-to-Use Strategies, Tools & Activities for Meeting the Challenges of Each School Day, Second Edition
Julia G. Thompson    ISBN 978-0-7879-9455-6

The Art Teacher's Survival Guide for Elementary and Middle Schools, Second Edition
Helen D. Hume    ISBN 978-0-470-18302-1

The Classroom Teacher's Survival Guide: Practical Strategies, Management Techniques and Reproducibles for New and Experienced Teachers, Third Edition
Ronald L. Partin    ISBN 978-0-470-45364-3

Writing Workshop Survival Kit, Second Edition
Gary Robert Muschla    ISBN 978-0-7879-7619-4

Special Educator's Survival Guide, Second Edition
Roger Pierangelo Ph.D.    ISBN 978-0-7879-7096-3

The English Teacher's Survival Guide: Ready-to-Use Techniques & Materials for Grades 7–12, Second Edition
Mary Lou Brandvik and Katherine S. McKnight    ISBN 978-0-470-52513-5

School Newspaper Adviser's Survival Guide
Patricia Osborn    ISBN 978-0-7879-6624-9

Play Director's Survival Kit: A Complete Step-by-Step Guide to Producing Theater in Any School or Community Setting
James W. Rodgers and Wanda C. Rodgers    ISBN 978-0-87628-565-7

Math Teacher's Survival Guide: Practical Strategies, Management Techniques, and Reproducibles for New and Experienced Teachers, Grades 5–12
Judith A. Muschla, Gary Robert Muschla and Erin Muschla.    ISBN 978-0-470-40764-6

A Survival Kit for the Elementary School Principal: With Reproducible Forms, Checklists & Letters
Abby Barry Bergman    ISBN 978-0-7879-6639-3

The Reading Teacher's Survival Kit: Ready-to-Use Checklists, Activities and Materials to Help All Students Become Successful Readers
Wilma H. Miller Ed.D.    ISBN 978-0-13-042593-5

Biology Teacher's Survival Guide: Tips, Techniques & Materials for Success in the Classroom
Michael F. Fleming    ISBN 978-0-13-045051-7

The Elementary/Middle School Counselor's Survival Guide, Third Edition
John J. Schmidt Ed.D.    978-0-470-56085-3

Discipline Survival Guide for the Secondary Teacher, Second Edition
Julia G. Thompson    ISBN 978-0-470-54743-4

The Substitute Teaching Survival Guide, Grades K–5: Emergency Lesson Plans and Essential Advice
John Dellinger    ISBN 978-0-7879-7410-7

The Substitute Teaching Survival Guide, Grades 6–12: Emergency Lesson Plans and Essential Advice
John Dellinger    ISBN 978-0-7879-7411-4

The Classroom Teacher's Technology Survival Guide
Doug Johnson    ISBN 978-1-1180-2455-3

# *The* SCHOOL PSYCHOLOGIST'S SURVIVAL GUIDE

### Rebecca Branstetter

JOSSEY-BASS
A Wiley Imprint
www.josseybass.com

Published by Jossey-Bass
A Wiley Imprint

One Montgomery Street, Suite 1200, San Francisco, CA 94104-4594—www.josseybass.com

Jossey-Bass books and products are available through most bookstores. To contact Jossey-Bass directly call our Customer Care Department within the U.S. at 800-956-7739, outside the U.S. at 317-572-3986, or fax 317-572-4002.

Wiley publishes in a variety of print and electronic formats and by print-on-demand. Some material included with standard print versions of this book may not be included in e-books or in print-on-demand. If this book refers to media such as a CD or DVD that is not included in the version you purchased, you may download this material at http://booksupport.wiley.com. For more information about Wiley products, visit www.wiley.com.

*Library of Congress Cataloging-in-Publication Data*
Branstetter, Rebecca.
    The school psychologist's survival guide / Rebecca Branstetter.—1st ed.
        p. cm.—(Jossey-Bass teacher survival guide)
    Includes bibliographical references and index.
    ISBN 978-1-118-02777-6 (pbk.)
        1. School psychologists—United States—Handbooks, manuals, etc.   2. School psychology—
    United States—Handbooks, manuals, etc.   I. Title.
    LB3013.6.B74   2012
    370.150973—dc23                                                                    2012001571

Printed in the United States of America
FIRST EDITION
PB Printing        V10010878_060619

# Contents

*Exhibits, Forms, and Figures*                                    *xv*

*Acknowledgments*                                                 *xix*

*About the Author*                                               *xxi*

*Preface*                                                       *xxiii*

*Introduction*                                                   *xxv*

**1**  WEARING MANY HATS: THE ROLES OF THE SCHOOL
       PSYCHOLOGIST                                                 1

    Assessment                                     2

    Consultation                                   3

    Prevention and Intervention                    4

    Counseling                                     5

    Pulling It All Together                        6

    Key Points                                     6

    Discussion Questions                           7

**2**  FINDING WHERE YOU BELONG: LOGISTICS AND
       BUILDING RELATIONSHIPS IN YOUR SCHOOLS                       9

    Getting Situated at a New School Site          11

    Building Relationships with Key Staff Members  12

        The School Secretary: Your New Best Friend   12

The Principal: Captain of the Ship 12

Counselors and Other Support Staff 14

Special Educators 14

General Education Teachers 17

The Custodian 17

Beginning-of-School Logistics 17

What to Do in the First Few Days and Weeks of School 18

Managing Multiple Sites 18

Finding a Work Space at Your School Site 22

Getting Needed Materials 23

Other Considerations in the First Few Weeks 23

Once You Are Settled In: Introducing Yourself 24

Introducing Yourself to Staff 25

Introducing Yourself to Families and Students 27

Pulling It All Together 28

Key Points 28

Discussion Questions 29

**3** HELP! I'M DROWNING IN PAPERWORK!
HOW TO TAME THE BUREAUCRACY MONSTER 31

Managing Your Assessment Caseload 32

Completing Your Assessments Within Timelines 34

Check Your Assessment Caseloads for Accuracy 35

Make Your Yearly Assessment Calendar 35

Documenting and Tracking Interventions,
Counseling, and Crisis Counseling 39

Documenting Interventions 39

Documenting Counseling and Crisis Counseling 39

Documenting Child Protective Services Calls and Reports 40

What's Next? Time Management Tips for
Balancing Assessment Caseloads with Other Roles 40

Scheduling Your Week 41

Scheduling Your Day 43

What to Do When You Are Drowning in a Sea of Assessments 44

Pulling It All Together 45

Key Points                                                                46
Discussion Questions                                                      47

## 4   INTERVENTION AND PREVENTION     49

How to Be Preventive When You Have No Time                               50

Being Effective on Leadership and Prereferral
Intervention Teams                                                       50

Schoolwide Support Teams                                                 51

Student-Focused Support Teams                                            53

Developing and Supporting Academic Interventions                        56

Developing and Supporting Social, Emotional,
and Behavioral Interventions                                            57

Developing Your Own Prevention Activities and Programs                  59

Common Pitfalls and What to Do About Them                               60

When Special Education Intervention Is the
Only Game in Town                                                       60

When Your School Is Sending You Inappropriate Referrals                 61

Pulling It All Together                                                  62

Key Points                                                               62

Discussion Questions                                                     64

## 5   RESPONSE TO INTERVENTION (RTI): CHANGING YOUR ROLE FROM SPECIAL EDUCATION GATEKEEPER TO KEYMASTER OF INTERVENTIONS     65

School Psychologists' Roles in RtI                                       66

Academic RtI: Data-Based Decision Making                                 68

Tier 1 Interventions                                                     68

Developing Individual Intervention Plans and
Data-Tracking Tools                                                      69

Behavioral RtI: Data-Based Decision Making                               73

Universal Screening                                                      73

Assessment and Intervention Audits                                       74

Monitoring Tier 1 Effectiveness                                          74

Tiers 2 and 3: Gathering Baseline Data and
Using Progress Monitoring Tools                                          74

How to Track Individual Student Progress with Your RtI Team    75

Navigating Your Role Change    76

Pulling It All Together    76

Key Points    77

Discussion Questions    78

## 6   SPECIAL EDUCATION ASSESSMENT    79

The Assessment Process: From Parental Consent
to Report Writing    80

     Determining Timelines and Informing All
Involved Parties of the Assessment    80

     Reviewing the History and Gathering Environmental Data    83

     Conducting a Developmental History with
Parents or Guardians    89

     Deciding If You Need to Do a Full
Social-Emotional-Behavioral Evaluation    92

     Selecting Appropriate Testing Instruments    98

     Selecting Your Testing Tools    99

     Beginning Your Testing with the Student    100

     Writing Quality Reports    101

A Note About Other Types of Evaluations    102

Pulling It All Together    103

Key Points    103

Discussion Questions    104

## 7   THE INDIVIDUALIZED EDUCATION
PLAN (IEP): FRIEND OR FOE?    105

Before the IEP Meeting    106

     Learning About Your Role and Presentation
Style in IEP Meetings    106

     Building Consensus on Your IEP Team    106

     When to Share Results with Parents
Before the IEP Meeting    108

     Collaborating with Outside Team Members in the IEP    109

During the IEP Meeting    110

Laying the Groundwork for Presenting Results 110

Other Helpful Tips When Presenting at an IEP Meeting 117

After the IEP Meeting 118

Pulling It All Together 119

Key Points 119

Discussion Questions 121

**8 DO YOU HAVE A MINUTE? HOW TO BE AN EFFECTIVE CONSULTANT** 123

Where Theory Meets Real Life 124

Behavioral Consultation 124

Social-Emotional and Crisis Consultation 128

Academic Consultation 130

Consultation During the IEP-Writing Process 131

Dealing with Negative Nancy and Naysayer Ned: Working with "Involuntary" Consultees 133

The Uncomfortable Teachers' Lounge Consultation 134

Pulling It All Together 134

Key Points 135

Discussion Questions 136

**9 INDIVIDUAL COUNSELING** 137

Counseling Roles 138

Types of School-Based Individual Counseling 139

Psychodynamic ("Insight-Oriented") Therapy 139

Play and Art Therapy 140

Cognitive-Behavioral Therapy (CBT) 142

Solution-Focused Brief Therapy 143

Beginning Counseling 145

During Counseling: Documentation and Sticky Situations 149

Documentation 149

When You Need to Call Child Protective Services (CPS) 151

When a Child Is a Danger to Himself or Others 152

Sticky Confidentiality Issues 152

Terminating Counseling                                            153
Pulling It All Together                                            154
Key Points                                                         154
Discussion Questions                                               155

## 10   GROUP COUNSELING                                          157

Starting a Group: Factors to Consider                              157
  Conduct a Needs Assessment at Your School              158
  Deciding What Type of Group to Run                     158
  Deciding Who Is in Your Group                          159
  Choosing a Cofacilitator                               167
  Deciding on When and Where to Hold Your Group          167
  Deciding on the Level of Structure in the Group        168
What to Do When Things Get Messy                                   172
  A Student Wants to Drop Out of Group                    172
  Group Members "Gang Up" on Another
  Group Member or Members                                 172
  The Group Is Out of Control                             173
  A Student Leaves the Group Without Permission           173
  A Group Member Does Not Participate                     174
Pulling It All Together                                            174
Key Points                                                         175
Discussion Questions                                               176

## 11   THE DREADED LATE-NIGHT PHONE CALL: HOW TO
DEAL WITH A CRISIS AT YOUR SCHOOL                                  177

Preparation for a Crisis                                           178
Types of Crises                                                    179
  Individual Student Crises: Danger to
  Self and Danger to Others                               179
  Schoolwide Crises: Determining the
  Ripple Effect and Implementing Psychological First Aid  185
Pulling It All Together                                            195
Key Points                                                         196
Discussion Questions                                               196

12  PUT ON YOUR OXYGEN MASK BEFORE
    HELPING OTHERS: HOW TO MANAGE
    THE STRESS OF THE JOB                                      197

    Practicing Self-Care                                       198
        Moments of Zen                                         198
        Flocking                                               199
    Maintaining Healthy Work-Life Boundaries                   200
        Your Role and Saying No                                200
        Know When to Say When                                  202
    Pulling It All Together                                    202
    Key Points                                                 203
    Discussion Questions                                       203

    *Bibliography and Resources*                               205
    *Index*                                                    207

# Exhibits, Forms, and Figures

EXHIBITS

Exhibit 2.1   Sample Multiple-Site Work Schedule   20

Exhibit 2.2   Sample Letter to Staff   26

Exhibit 3.1   Sample Master Assessment Log   33

Exhibit 3.2   Sample Master Triennial Calendar   37

Exhibit 3.3   Sample Weekly To-Do Calendar   42

Exhibit 5.1   Sample Individual Intervention Plan and Tracking Form   71

Exhibit 9.1   Resources for Counseling   144

Exhibit 9.2   Sample SOAP Notes   150

Exhibit 10.1   Sample Group Referral Form   160

Exhibit 10.2   Sample Group Counseling Permission Slip (English)   163

Exhibit 10.3   Sample Group Counseling Permission Form (Spanish)   165

Exhibit 10.4   Sample Group Reminder   168

Exhibit 10.5   Sample Ten-Week Agenda for Talent Group   170

Exhibit 10.6   Sample Daily Agenda for Talent Group   171

Exhibit 11.1   Sample Crisis Intervention Handout   187

Exhibit 11.2   Sample Crisis Letter to Parents   192

FORMS

Form 2.1   Confidential IEP Summary   16

Form 2.2   School Psychologist Schedule   21

Form 3.1    Master Triennial Calendar                                    38
Form 5.1    Individual Intervention Plan and Tracking Form               72
Form 6.1    Psychological Services Memo: CONFIDENTIAL                     82
Form 6.2    Cumulative and Special Education Review Checklist             85
Form 6.3    Classroom Observation Form                                   88
Form 6.4    Developmental History                                        90
Form 6.5    Survey/Rating Scale Memo to Teacher(s)                       93
Form 6.6    Teacher Feedback Survey                                      94
Form 6.7    Survey/Rating Scale Memo to Parent(s)                        97
Form 9.1    Consent for Individual Counseling                           146
Form 9.2    Consentimiento para Consejería Individual                   147
Form 11.1   Suicide Assessment                                          181
Form 11.2   Threat Assessment                                           184
Form 11.3   Crisis Counseling Referral Form                             190
Form 11.4   Crisis Referral Tracking Sheet                              194

## FIGURES

Figure 4.1   Response to Intervention Pyramid                            52
Figure 6.1   Assessment Flowchart: Initial Referral                      81
Figure 7.1   Normal Curve (English)                                     112
Figure 7.2   Normal Curve (Spanish)                                     113

*To my husband and greatest supporter, Steven Branstetter*

# *Acknowledgments*

Writing this book has been a journey. I have had many people come along with me, encouraging me to keep going, and giving me great advice and guidance. First and foremost, I want to thank my husband, Steven, for all the encouragement and support. Your advice to "just write thirty minutes a day" paid off, especially in the final stretch of getting the book completed while I was nine months pregnant with our baby girl! I couldn't have finished it without you by my side.

Thanks to my family—my parents, Ann and John, and my sister, Sammi, for your support and encouragement as well. Having educators in the family to consult with has certainly been to my advantage as I write about ways to support teachers and students.

I also want to thank my editor, Margie McAneny, for finding me among a sea of bloggers and supporting this book idea. I have enjoyed the process and appreciate your giving me creative license to write a book with a personal narrative. I hope that readers find the book more accessible as a result. I also want to acknowledge my fabulous peer reviewers—Danielle Nahas, Kelley Pursell, Lainie Sgouros, and Kate Perry. Your input was invaluable in making sure the book captured a range of experiences for school psychologists. Thanks so much!

I wouldn't even be writing this acknowledgment section if it weren't for my good friend and PR guru, Jennifer Parson. You encouraged me to start my blog and Facebook page in the first place and coached me every step of the way, and for that, I thank you.

# *About the Author*

Rebecca Branstetter is both a school psychologist and a clinical psychologist in the San Francisco Bay Area. She graduated from the University of California, Berkeley, school psychology program with her doctorate in 2004. After graduating, she conducted her postdoctoral work at the University of California, San Francisco Autism Clinic. She has worked as a school psychologist in both the San Francisco and Oakland school districts for the past ten years. She is the founder of Grow Assessment and Counseling Services, a private practice agency that works with children and families in the San Francisco Bay Area.

Rebecca also writes the blog Notes from the School Psychologist and is the editor of *The Teachable Moment: Seizing the Instants When Children Learn* (Kaplan, 2010), an anthology about reaching the difficult-to-reach child.

# *Preface*

When I started my career as a school psychologist ten years ago, I was ridiculously unprepared for the challenges that lay ahead of me. Armed only with optimism, pluck, and a few years of practicum and coursework, I thought I was ready to work in a large urban school district. I fancied myself the school psychologist version of Michelle Pfeiffer in *Dangerous Minds,* changing the world, one student at a time. Little did I know, there were on-the-job skills I didn't have, and I learned something new every ten minutes. I was fortunate to have a fantastic supervisor, Minoo Shah, who guided me through my traumatic first few years, when I made mistake after mistake. I felt for school psychologists who did not have the great mentoring I did. I couldn't believe all the things I was never taught in graduate school. This is not my alma mater's fault: there are some things you just have to learn when you are on the job for the first time.

One thing no one ever told me going into this profession was that it could be isolating. Even though I am surrounded by educators, children, and parents every day, I only get to see my school psychologist colleagues once a month at staff meetings. The support and input you receive from your colleagues is instrumental in preventing burnout and becoming a better practitioner. So in 2007, I began my blog, Notes from the School Psychologist (www.studentsgrow.blogspot.com), in an effort to connect with other school psychologists and share knowledge I wish I had starting out. Whether I was talking about how to deal with nasty advocates at meetings or giving advice about how not to accidentally form a gang in group therapy, I felt good about helping other school psychologists learn from my mistakes. Little did I know, my blog and subsequent Facebook page for the blog would connect me to colleagues across the country, all of whom have great information to share, insights to learn from, and emotional support I didn't even know I needed. I love hearing from colleagues about how to improve our skills, our profession, and our experience in day-to-day life as school psychologists.

I began to receive e-mails asking me to recommend a resource for school psychologists to learn the on-the-job skills needed to be successful. I knew of no such resource—one that provided practical, real-world advice about how to be an effective school psychologist. That is how this book came to be. I hope you find it useful, entertaining, and practical. I have enjoyed consulting with many of you to make sure the book captures the wide range of experiences we have in this profession. Thank you all for your input, and enjoy!

# Introduction

School psychologists are professionals who provide mental health and educational services within school districts, typically for students with special needs. School psychology was named one of the top twenty careers in 2009 by *U.S. News and World Report,* and represents a growing field. The U.S. Department of Labor cites employment opportunities in school psychology at both the specialist and doctoral levels as among the best across all fields of psychology.

Much has been written about the technical aspects of performing the job of a school psychologist, such as theories of learning, principles of cognitive assessment, and counseling theory. However, there is little so far about the nuts-and-bolts practical side of the profession—what school psychologists experience once they are in the field. There is a growing need for a survival guide for navigating the day-to-day challenges of working in the bureaucracy of a school district, managing large caseloads, dealing with legal and ethical challenges on the job, and crisis management. There is a dearth of materials for school psychologists with regard to how to bridge the theories learned in graduate school and the practical challenges experienced during the workday.

The purpose of *The School Psychologist's Survival Guide* is to bridge that gap between research and reality. School psychologists just entering the field are often lacking the day-to-day practical advice they need to survive in the job, and the theories they learned in graduate school about how to deliver high-quality services in the schools often do not match the reality of the job. This guide will give new school psychologists ready-to-use tools they need to streamline their work flow and overcome the challenges they face every day. School psychologists who have already been working in the field will also profit from fresh ideas about how to improve their practice and prevent burnout.

*The School Psychologist's Survival Guide* takes on the top challenges school psychologists face every day and provides real-world solutions. Instead of a dry textbook about the profession and a school psychologist's job duties, it brings to life how to bridge the gap between best practices according to the research, and the realities of working in school district bureaucracies, often with limited resources. The purpose is to give new school psychologists a go-to resource with ready-to-use strategies and time-saving reproducible materials they can use every day.

Although I've taken great care to represent school psychologists' experiences across the country, there are differences in how laws and policies are interpreted by states, districts, and school sites. You will want to stay current with your local and state guidelines and laws, and consult with your supervisors and site staff about the application of these hands-on tools and strategies in your local setting.

This guide begins with a big-picture overview of the job of a school psychologist, including the many roles that we play on a daily basis. Chapters Two and Three focus on the day-to-day logistical challenges that we face—from heavy caseloads to working in janitors' closets to battling with unnecessary paperwork—and how to deal with them. The subsequent chapters are organized by the roles that school psychologists frequently assume in the schools. These chapters do not necessarily need to be read sequentially, as school psychologists' jobs are often different depending on the particular schools to which they are assigned. Chapters Four through Seven detail ways to become more efficient in working with students experiencing academic and behavioral challenges. Chapter Four discusses practical ways to become involved in prevention and early intervention; Chapter Five outlines strategies for being effective in schools implementing a Response to Intervention (RtI) framework. Chapters Six and Seven highlight how to be more efficient in the special education referral and assessment process and how to be an effective presenter at Individualized Education Plan (IEP) meetings.

In addition to providing advice and resources for the assessment and intervention process, this guide describes nuts-and-bolts techniques for being an effective consultant (Chapter Eight) and providing counseling services (Chapters Nine through Eleven). Specific strategies as well as ready-to-use forms are available in these chapters, which discuss individual counseling (Chapter Nine), group counseling (Chapter Ten), and crisis counseling (Chapter Eleven). The guide concludes with an important chapter on preventing burnout and increasing job satisfaction (Chapter Twelve).

Overall, *The School Psychologist's Survival Guide* aims to help new and veteran school psychologists become more efficient and effective service providers, improve and hone their skills in the multitude of roles they assume in the schools, and increase their job satisfaction. With practical ready-to-use forms and time-saving suggestions, this guide will be your go-to resource for dealing with the situations that were never covered in graduate school. Sprinkled throughout the guide is a touch of school psychologist humor, which is of course a necessary ingredient for survival in this profession!

# *The* SCHOOL PSYCHOLOGIST'S SURVIVAL GUIDE

# chapter 1

# WEARING MANY HATS
## The Roles of the School Psychologist

I've been told that you should be able to explain your career to a stranger in the time it takes to ride an elevator for a few floors. I have been working on my school psychologist "elevator speech" for years now, and I think I need to be in a high-rise elevator in order to fully explain my duties. That is because school psychologists may be responsible for many different tasks, and their roles vary considerably from school to school, district to district, and state to state. I have finally settled on saying, "School psychologists are like if a teacher and a psychologist had a baby. We do interventions to prevent school failure, test struggling students to uncover reasons for learning problems, and provide them with appropriate interventions. Those interventions could involve special education services, counseling, or consulting with teachers and parents to help students with their areas of need." Then, inevitably, someone responds with, "Oh, so you're a counselor?" Sigh. It really is a difficult profession to explain.

In general, school psychologists have four main "hats" they may wear in the schools: assessor, consultant, prevention and intervention specialist, and counselor. Each graduate school program places different emphases on these roles, but once you are working in the schools, you are often expected to fulfill many, if not all, of these roles in some capacity. There will also be unofficial roles in your job as well, depending on your school sites. These could range from supervising traffic during afternoon dismissal to serving on administrative committees. This chapter outlines the four most likely roles of the school psychologist and helps you identify chapters in this guide that will help you improve your skills and bolster your effectiveness in each role.

## ASSESSMENT

Assessing students is often seen as the primary role of the school psychologist, though this varies among districts and schools. Historically, school psychologists came on the scene in 1975 as a part of the first special education law, PL94-142. Under this law, school psychologists were identified as the professionals responsible for testing students to evaluate their school functioning related to special education disability criteria. Even now, for many school psychologists, assessment of students suspected of having disabilities and of those students already in special education continues to be the primary role in many districts.

In graduate school, the first courses I completed were in psychoeducational assessment, which covered the history of tests and how to administer them, and in applied statistics, which covered in part how to interpret the information that the test administrations produced. It was exciting learning all the new tools, practicing administering IQ tests (mostly on the children of professors and friends), and perfecting the art of the standardized assessment. I remember borrowing my first testing kit, then housed in a 1980s-style briefcase that weighed almost as much as I did. I felt so fancy clicking it open and administering the tests with my brand-new stopwatch that I had rigged to be nearly unnoticeable by removing its beeper. It was so exciting.

Ten years later, the luster and excitement of administering these tests has faded, my iPhone has replaced my cute little timer, I've ditched the circa 1982 briefcase, and I've administered IQ tests so many times that I have them memorized. I would estimate that I have given the same test about seven hundred times since becoming a school psychologist. Although this has the potential to become extraordinarily boring, one thing that keeps it fresh is the challenge of figuring out how to help a child learn more easily and efficiently. Each child is like a puzzle, and each test we give is a piece of the puzzle in understanding how the child learns best and what gets in the way of learning. No two children approach testing the same way. You can learn a lot about kids just from their reactions to the words, "Today we are going to do a series of activities to see how you learn best!" From "Go away, I'm not special ed!" to "Yay! Let's go!" you can learn a lot about students that the numbers won't be able to tell you. There are many tricks of the trade for making the evaluation process meaningful, in terms of both the numbers you get and of the qualitative observations of how kids tackle problems. Chapter Six outlines how to gain information from your assessments that is useful for helping students, their parents, and their teachers.

Your testing caseload will vary tremendously according to the size of your school district, the area of the country in which you are employed, the type of setting in which you work (rural, suburban, or urban), and the policies of each school district regarding your responsibilities in general education (intervention and prevention) and special education. As a school psychologist, you are often assigned both new referrals (often called "initials") and legally mandated three-year assessments (often called "triennials" or "reevaluations").

Each of these assessments has its own legal timeline for completion, which is an added pressure for a school psychologist. The first year I was employed by a large urban school district, I was assigned three schools of approximately five hundred students each. The list of mandatory three-year evaluations I had to complete that year numbered about seventy-five. In addition, I was employed only three days per week! I couldn't fathom how I would get through it all within the timelines, and many of the cases were already overdue when I walked in the door my first day. Even without any new referrals, I felt that my caseload was almost impossible if I wanted to do a thorough job with each student.

I learned more about the dramatic differences in caseloads through my blog, Notes from the School Psychologist (www.studentsgrow.blogspot.com). I asked the online community of school psychologists who follow the blog to report their testing caseloads on the blog's Facebook page. The reported yearly caseloads for full-time psychologists ranged from 4 to 120, with the median at about 60. One of the main factors that determined caseload was whether or not the district had adopted the Response to Intervention (RtI) method of identifying and responding to learning difficulties, which heavily emphasizes prevention and early intervention. Regardless of your caseload and whether or not your school has adopted RtI, in Chapters Four and Five you will learn more about how to infuse a preventive model of intervention into your daily work to reduce the amount of time you spend doing individual assessments.

Another key factor in determining caseload is school placement. School psychologists at the elementary level tend to have more initial evaluations, and school psychologists at middle and high schools tend to have more triennial reevaluations. Psychologists assigned to preschool diagnostic centers, bilingual assessment teams, charter school teams, and nonpublic school teams tend to have the most restrictive roles; evaluation responsibilities make up nearly all of their daily activities.

Your role may also be more complex if your student population has a high proportion of students learning English as a second language, if your school has a large homeless or transient student population, or if a significant number of students qualify for free and reduced lunch due to living in poverty. In these schools, assessment cases tend to be lengthier, and they are more challenging in terms of teasing out environmental and situational factors that contribute to learning and emotional challenges. Chapter Six details these specific roles within school districts. One of the great things about school psychology as a profession is that there are opportunities to mix it up in terms of the ages and types of students you will see.

In assessment-heavy school placements, one of the most challenging aspects for all psychologists is completing quality assessments within legal timelines. Fortunately, there are a few things that will help you streamline this process. Chapter Three will help you with a structure to organize and effectively complete your assessments within timelines.

## CONSULTATION

One of the services that principals, teachers, and parents value the most is consultation with you. Once you establish yourself as a resource, you will have plenty of "customers" knocking on your door, calling you for advice, or e-mailing you about their concerns for their students. In my experience, I often get a ton of little notes in my school mailbox with requests to talk about particular students. Given all the other obligations you have and the limited time available to talk to teachers during the day, you will probably find it challenging to carve out quality time to consult about students. At times it can feel as though you're doing "psychological triage"—sorting all the calls, notes, e-mails, and requests by urgency of need.

School psychologists are expected to be knowledgeable in many areas, including but not limited to child development, disabilities, assessment, teaching, parenting, learning, special education law, general education law, discipline, district procedures, classroom management, relationships, intervention, prevention, data analysis, crisis management, and counseling. Tall order! I remember when I was in my school psychologist internship, people would come to me all the time with really difficult questions that I would have no idea how to answer. Even now, after nearly ten years of experience, I still get stumped by some of the situations that arise.

Learning to be an effective consultant is not about knowing all the answers. In many ways, it's about knowing the right questions. Effective consultation also requires an understanding of the relationships between you, the consultee, and the student or students in question. Despite its complexity, consultation offers many rewards. When you effectively consult with a staff member about how to work with a child in need, you educate him or her on working with similar children down the road, and all the kids in the teacher's class benefit from the new knowledge. Depending on your graduate school program, you may or may not have been explicitly taught how to consult, especially how to consult with staff who seem unwilling to consult with you. There are many different models of consultation as well, and finding one that is a good match for you is important. Chapter Eight discusses how to be an effective consultant, and Chapter Eleven talks about ways to use consultation in crisis situations.

## PREVENTION AND INTERVENTION

Even before special education law first introduced the term *Response to Intervention (RtI)* in the revision of the Individuals with Disabilities Education Act (IDEA) in 2004, school psychologists understood the importance of prevention in increasing positive student outcomes. Whether or not your school has existing structures to support prevention and early intervention activities, you can often carve out a role for yourself in providing prevention services. The benefits of dedicating your time and energy to prevention include reducing your assessment caseload and keeping students from falling so far behind that they give up.

School psychologists will often face discrepancies between research-supported best practices and the realities of the school district policies and legal guidelines regarding eligibility for special education services. Many times I have heard myself say ridiculous things, such as "He is below grade level, but he's not far enough behind to be considered disabled, so he doesn't qualify for services." What? That doesn't make sense. The idea behind early intervention and prevention is that kids receive targeted services *before* they fall behind or give up on school. A student shouldn't be forced to fail in order to receive much-needed assistance.

The school psychologist plays a key role in developing appropriate interventions for struggling students. Since the change in IDEA law, there are more and more opportunities to prevent students from struggling in the first place. Your role will depend on what your district's policies and funding structures are, and whether your state or school district has adopted RtI. Unfortunately, it is still the case that many school psychologists are put in the difficult position of adhering to policies that don't make intuitive sense and aren't backed up by the robust research on the power of prevention and early intervention. Some school districts have followed the research about prevention and adopted an RtI model of service delivery. The general concept of RtI is that prevention and early intervention are better than remediation—financially, ethically, and practically speaking. However, the traditional role of the school psychologist has been to intervene when things become so difficult for a student that a disability is suspected and special education may be warranted. This "wait to fail" model is not supported by research or common sense. School psychologists are often in need of practical suggestions on how to navigate a useful course between best practices and district policies. Chapter Four talks about ways to infuse a prevention model of delivery into your day-to-day work schedule, and Chapter Five details the array of school psychologists' roles in RtI.

## COUNSELING

When I first heard about the profession of school psychology, I had this fantasy of sitting in a cute little office full of play therapy materials, sipping herbal tea and waiting for little friends to come by for a warm, cozy session where we talked about feelings. Doesn't that sound great? Little did I know, most days would involve my frantically trying to prioritize and tackle my to-do list, which grew exponentially by the minute. I never thought my only counseling time would be spent doing crisis counseling. Colleagues across the country have reported on the Notes from the School Psychologist Blog Facebook page that they are not even *allowed* to do counseling at their school sites. So sad! Counseling is one of the most rewarding parts of my job because it allows me to have direct, ongoing contact with the students. Carving out this quality time can be a challenge, though.

As I became more efficient with my other obligations (assessment, report writing, attending and leading IEP meetings), I liberated more of my time to devote to counseling. I started a few counseling groups at lunchtime so that I could provide direct services to students and feel more preventive. Your counseling caseload will likely vary by school site, funding structures, physical space, and district priorities. Counseling might not even be a permitted role for you, or you may not have the training to feel comfortable with a counseling role. In some states, school counselors are responsible for counseling services, particularly at the elementary school level. In other states, there is a distinction between school psychologists and school psychologist examiners, and only the school psychologists can do counseling. It should be noted, however, that counseling is not for everyone, even if you are permitted to do it. For those of you who share my love of counseling and are permitted to do it in your current role, Chapters Nine (individual counseling) and Ten (group counseling) discuss in detail the counseling roles you may assume.

As a note of encouragement for those who enjoy the counseling role, when I changed districts, there was funding in place for two full days a week of counseling and prevention activities. I finally got to talk about feelings with my little friends on a regular basis, just as I had imagined. Sure, I shared my cute little office with three other people, I had to buy my own therapy supplies, and there was no electrical plug for a teakettle for my herbal tea, but I still love the regular direct contact with students.

## PULLING IT ALL TOGETHER

Reading the list of all of our responsibilities as school psychologists can be daunting. That list is not even exhaustive! There are days when I am alternately on yard duty, consoling crying teachers who want to quit, getting icepacks for kids who have fought on the yard, searching for a lost file, tracking down paperwork, fighting with Human Resources about inaccurate pay, putting on parent education nights, attending school events, driving to a school to test a kid who won't work with me, driving to a child's home to locate a parent to sign documents, or even searching for a stapler or a functioning printer. These are the days when I feel stretched in too many different directions to be functional or efficient. The good news is that most school psychologists love the excitement, challenge, and ever-changing environment, and often thrive in the chaos. We adapt, learn amazing executive functioning and planning skills, and feel empowered to make a difference in the lives of our students.

We also need strong, reliable coping skills to manage the stress and chaos. You cannot help others effectively if you do not have a deep bag of tricks for managing your own stress. Burnout in this profession can be high, and, as for any job, you need to learn how to tackle the daily stressors and cope with the challenges of the job. It is often the challenges of managing your time, enforcing emotional boundaries, and dealing with bureaucracy that cause burnout rather than the direct work with the children. Chapter Three details practical tips on taming the "Bureaucracy Monster," and Chapter Twelve discusses the importance of self-care in becoming an effective and emotionally healthy school psychologist. You might want to bookmark those chapters!

---

## Key Points

- As a school psychologist, you will wear many hats and have many different roles. Your roles are often defined by the school district, school site, or state in which you work.
- The four main roles of a school psychologist are most likely to be assessor, consultant, prevention and intervention specialist, and counselor.
- Graduate school programs emphasize different roles, and your training and confidence in serving in each role may vary.

---

- Once you are employed by the school district, you will be expected to fulfill many different roles, often dictated by district procedures and priorities. It is important to keep in mind that your role can change from district to district as well as from school to school.
- Navigating multiple roles can be stressful. You need both practical skills as well as coping skills for managing stress.
- This guide offers information about all four roles, and you can choose to read the chapters most germane to your current job description. You can also read chapters about roles outside your current job description to help you open a dialogue with your supervisor or site administrators about expanding your role.

## DISCUSSION QUESTIONS

1. What are the current roles of a school psychologist in your school or district? How are they defined? Is there flexibility in roles, or are they prescribed for you?
2. If you are not yet working in a school, which role is most appealing to you? Which is least appealing? Why?
3. How do you set role boundaries at your school site? It can be challenging to say no to extra duties, especially when you are a new employee or your duties are ill defined at your school site. What are some strategies for defining your role without appearing rigid or unwilling to take on more work?
4. At times, a school psychologist's roles are defined by those of his or her predecessor. How do you renegotiate your role with employees at your new school site?
5. In which of the four roles do you think you need the most support in developing your skills? What supports are available to you for professional development and practical advice?
6. If you were in an interview for a job in a school district, what key questions would you ask about roles expected of school psychologists?

# chapter 2

# FINDING WHERE YOU BELONG

## Logistics and Building Relationships in Your Schools

There is something so exciting about receiving your school site placements at the beginning of the year. When you are a new school psychologist or new to a school district, you may know nothing about the school(s) you are assigned, and wonder if you got "good" schools. You may work in a small district where you only have one school, or you may be in a large school district where you have many schools.

During my first year as a school psychologist, I was assigned to one elementary school, one middle school, and one high school. They were all in the same part of town, which was primarily low income, and the schools all received Title 1 funding. I was excited about my schools. I imagined myself as the school psychologist version of Michelle Pfeiffer in the movie *Dangerous Minds,* and dreamed I could transform urban education just by listening to kids and doing a home visit or two. I couldn't wait to get started! I thought the principals would welcome me with open arms, usher me to my darling private office space, and hand over the keys to everything I needed. I had a vision of a warm, cozy, private space where kids could come to seek refuge from their suffering.

I went to each school psychologist who had the schools before me to get the scoop—something I would definitely recommend doing. However, if you do this, know that each person has his or her own perceptions of the school that may not match up with your experience. So take their observations with a grain of salt. Some schools are better matches for certain personalities. My elementary school was described as "sweet," my middle school was described as "a nightmare," and my high school was described as "challenging." As for office space, each psychologist said something along the lines of "good luck" or "stake your claim right away." Hmm.

School psychologists do not always have choice about which schools they are assigned, particularly early in their careers. In my experience, most supervisors will try to take your preferences into consideration. Some larger districts have a formal bidding process for schools that is organized by seniority. You may have one site or fifteen sites. You may work out of offices in each school or have a work space in the central district office. You may have an alternative placement doing preschool assessments or nonpublic school assessments.

You can start to prepare in advance for the process of school assignment by asking, when you interview with a school district, about how it works. If hired, would you have any choice of which ages, levels, locations, or types of school you are assigned? How often are school psychologists moved between school sites? I didn't have choice in my first few years, and I experienced changes in my school assignments every year, but now, in another district, I have gotten all the schools I've wanted, year after year.

One thing that is consistent across districts I have worked for is that it can be challenging in the first few weeks and months of being the "newbie" at a school site. Your first challenge is to build relationships with the staff, parents, and students. They may have preconceptions about your role and abilities based on their prior experience with school psychologists or based on your appearance or age. For example, when I began my first practicum in schools at the age of twenty-two, one principal remarked upon meeting me, "Oh great. You're so young, you look like you need a hall pass!" Another principal had the opposite reaction: "Oh great!" she enthused, "I love young people in the profession! They have such fresh ideas and great energy!" In other words, be aware that you are something of a walking Rorschach inkblot to school staff members.

There may be staff you have to work with who have difficult personalities. If one of those staff members is the principal, it might be a long school year for you! The principal often sets the tone and climate of a school site, and if you are in disagreement with his or her philosophy and policies, you may be facing a challenge. However, there are many ways to collaborate with staff members who have different visions of how to work with students or who have difficult personalities. Most of us go into school psychology because we like to work with kids, but I'm here to tell you that much of your job will be forging positive working relationships with the adults in the building.

Another challenge for new or new-to-a-district psychologists is finding a "home" within the school. Prepare for the process of becoming comfortable in school to be a lengthy one. The first steps in finding your place within a school culture are building relationships with school staff, navigating the logistical challenges of finding a space to work, managing multiple sites, determining your work schedule, and introducing your-self to the students and parents.

## GETTING SITUATED AT A NEW SCHOOL SITE

Before beginning my first practicum in graduate school, I was told to take note of my experience when I first walked into a school building. My instructors informed me that I would gain powerful information about the overall school climate. Is the building invit-ing? Do you feel welcome? Do people smile at you or ask you who you are? Do the staff seem friendly? Are the students orderly? These are all clues to what your experience working at the school may be like.

The middle school that was described as a nightmare did not have a welcoming feel to it at all. I eagerly bounded up to the front door for a staff meeting, and it was locked and bolted. There was not a soul in sight, despite the fact that I was there during school hours. I rang the doorbell, and an incredibly grumpy woman opened the door, not even bothering to make eye contact or greet me. Everyone was late to the first staff meeting, and when I introduced myself, a staff member murmured, "Wonder how long she'll last." The classrooms and the walls were beige and barren, except for the occasional graffiti. Staff morale was low, to say the least. No one ate lunch together, or if they did, there was a toxic environment of complaining. This made my work there all the more challenging. It took me four months to get a work space, which ended up being a tiny janitor's closet with chemicals and mops and such everywhere. It took me over a year to get a bathroom key. At my "challenging" high school site, I never did get an office space. Instead, I carried my purse, lunch, and testing materials all year long, each day hoping for a free space to spend a few hours. As pitiful as it sounds, my excitement overflowed one day when I found an empty elevator shaft that I could use as a testing space. I defi-nitely got the shaft at that school (pun intended).

As for my third school, the "sweet" description proved to be apt. I arrived to an open door and a hanging banner that said "Welcome back staff!" Snacks were laid out, and busy staff chatted happily with one another. People introduced themselves right away, and I was given a full tour by the principal of the school, during which he explained all the pro-grams he had nurtured to support students. Posters on the wall had positive messages, and the classrooms were cheerfully decorated. Staff ate lunch together and shared strategies for improving their teaching. I had my own little office that I would share with the special education teacher and speech pathologist. Best of all, the secretary immediately gave me a key that worked in every door at the school (including the staff bathroom!).

Strategies for making yourself feel at home at a new school will differ depending on the school site. However, the universal first step toward a successful school year will always be to begin the slow process of building rapport. Just as you do not expect a child to cooperate with testing until you have developed some rapport with him or her, you should not expect to achieve collaborative relationships with staff without first making an effort to earn their trust. Making relationship building a priority in the first few weeks of the school year allows you a golden opportunity to set the stage for collaboration when things get rough down the road.

# BUILDING RELATIONSHIPS WITH KEY STAFF MEMBERS

The most important part of getting acquainted with a new school site is building relationships. School psychologists who are assigned multiple school sites are in a dual role of being both an insider (because you are a part of the school staff) and an outsider (because you may not be there every day). Staff may perceive you as that person who breezes in and out to test kids on Tuesdays, or you may be seen as part of the core staff. The more that staff perceive you as an insider, the more success you will have in your role. People tend to be more cooperative and pleasant to work with when they know who you are and know what to expect of you. Building relationships early on in the school year will pay off down the road when you are asking a teacher to complete a survey, interrupting a class to remove a student for testing or counseling, or asking for support from an administrator. The first order of business is to get acquainted with key staff members in the building.

## The School Secretary: Your New Best Friend

The best advice my mentor gave me during my first year in the schools was to make the school secretary my best friend. This person is on the front line of every interaction at the school. He or she is a rich source of valuable information and is often the best resource for getting your questions answered. My school secretary gave me a key to the bathroom, showed me where the cumulative folders were, gave me the inside scoop on the attendance issues of students I was testing, knew the families so well that she could get them to meetings when no one else could, and even let me practice my Spanish with her during the day, including teaching me important new words and phrases. For the majority of my school assignments, I have been blessed with great secretarial staff.

Unfortunately, you will also occasionally get a supergrumpy secretary who seems annoyed every time you ask for something. I had one secretary who always forgot my name and why I was there, even though I reintroduced myself almost every week. These are busy people who deal with tons of people coming in and out all day long, interrupting their work flow. Some secretaries love the interaction, and some have burnt out on the job. It is even more important to make an effort to get to know a disgruntled secretary before you start asking for any favors. Small gestures of appreciation, such as thank-you notes, cards on important days, and the simple act of acknowledging how busy he or she is and saying "thank you" go a long way toward establishing a positive environment in the school office. School psychologists often have great people skills; use them with your school secretary, and you will have a much more pleasant experience at your site.

## The Principal: Captain of the Ship

Your relationship with the principal can make or break your experience working at a school site. Principals have a wide variety of leadership styles, visions for their school, interpersonal skills, and personalities. The principal is possibly both the busiest person at the school site and the one who gets the least recognition. She is the person who handles all the crises and complaints, but no one thinks to stop by her office simply to make the observation that things are going really well at the school. It is sometimes difficult to get a solid chunk of consultation time with the principal to introduce a dialogue about your role. However, such a conversation helps you start the year on the same page with her about how you will make the most of the time you have at her school.

Without a good working relationship with your principal, you could be asked to take on a role that is inconsistent with your expectations or experience. For example, at my first assignment at a middle school, the principal found out I used to teach hip-hop dance. For the entire school year, she was fixated on encouraging me to teach dance to a group of troubled students during their lunch period. Although this is something I would have loved to do, I was busy running from crisis to crisis and consulting with teachers during lunch. Another principal sent me all the kids who were acting out so that I could "fix them up" and send them back to class. Another wanted me to sit in on all expulsion hearings and supervise the in-house suspension classroom because that is what the previous school psychologist had done. All of these duties were assigned to me in addition to an overwhelming testing caseload. Ongoing discussions with your principal about your roles and responsibilities will go a long way toward saving your sanity in situations like these.

One of the big challenges early in the school year is finding time to meet with your new principal to introduce yourself, get acquainted with his or her expectations, and define your role together. Some principals are fine with the "drop by and chat" approach, and others will want you to make an appointment for a block of time. Ask your secretary (your new best friend!) what the principal at your school prefers. Here are some key questions to ask your principal at your first meeting:

- How much time do we have to chat today? Is this a good time? [This shows respect for his or her busy schedule.]
- What was your experience with your previous school psychologist? How would you like my role to be similar or different? [This one is great, because you can get a sense of his or her expectations of you. Pay attention to nonverbal information being conveyed as well as what the principal tells you about your predecessor. This will clue you in to the quality of the relationship with the previous school psychologist.]
- What traits did you appreciate the most in him or her? What role did you find most helpful to you as a principal? What do you wish the previous psychologist had done differently?
- What roles would you like me to take on at the school? [At this point you can bring up your supervisor's expectations of your role and discuss how to best allocate your time.]
- What is the best way to communicate with you? Notes? E-mail? Calls? "Stop and chats"? A formal meeting time?
- Are there any students currently on your radar who you perceive to be in need of immediate attention? [This shows you are ready to collaborate around the needs of the principal and possibly serve the most at-risk students right away.]
- What is the process for special education referrals at the school site? Referrals for counseling or special services?

- What days would be most helpful for me to be here at this site? Will there be space available on those days? [Often, principals prefer for you to be on-site on days when they have special meetings or on days when other support staff are not on-site, so that there isn't conflict over office space. You may or may not be able to accommodate the principal's preferences, but it shows good faith that you will make an effort to do so.]
- Is there anything else I should know about this school site that you think will be helpful for me in working with staff, parents, or students?

You may not be able to get through all of these questions with your principal in the first meeting, especially in the first few weeks of school. One of the best lessons I have learned about the first few weeks and months of school is to be comfortable with ambiguity. Each time you meet with your principal, you can further clarify your role. Even after many years at the same school, my role continues to evolve each year. Needs change at a school site, and your role will not be static.

## Counselors and Other Support Staff

Depending on the type of school you are working in, there are a variety of support staff with whom you will regularly interact. There may be counselors, intervention specialists, outside mental health professionals, speech pathologists, occupational therapists, parent liaisons, and in-house mental health professionals to get to know. Use the time before students arrive to learn about the duties and roles of the various support staff. Conduct informational interviews about their roles and take notes! You may be able to combine efforts with some of them or cross duties off your list that they are already completing.

## Special Educators

If your role is primarily assessment at your school site, you will definitely be getting acquainted with your special education teachers right away. You may have anywhere from one teacher to a whole group of them to get to know, depending on your school site. If there are multiple special education teachers at your site, start with the department head or lead teacher, if there is one. The most important thing you can do early on in the school year is define your role, clarify your expectations and procedures with each other, and set a plan for the school year. Chapter Six provides details on how to set a course for the year to keep up with assessment timelines.

I have found that the more helpful you are to your special education teachers early in the year, the better collaboration you will have throughout the year. For example, I often spend a good amount of time helping special education teachers set up their classrooms. This gives you an opportunity to get to know the teacher as a person, get a sense of her teaching philosophy, and learn how she delivers services to the students. The side benefit of doing some grunt work (for example, moving desks around, helping put up new bulletin boards, throwing away junk that was left over from the previous year or summer) is that your special education teacher will see you as a hands-on kind of school psychologist, rather than as an outside person who breezes in and out of meetings. This goes a long way toward building rapport with your special education team.

Reviewing the teacher's caseload (for example, IEP documents, previous psychoeducational reports) together provides another opportunity to get to know special education staff. You can sit down together and review a yearly calendar, as these teachers often have a list of when their students are due for annual IEP meetings and triennial assessments. In smaller schools, I often work with the special educator to create a "cheat sheet" of key information about each student to distribute to the general education teachers (see Form 2.1). Let's face it—general education teachers are unlikely to have the time or access to read every kid's IEP and psychoeducational report. A "snapshot" of the kids that outlines their learning strengths and weaknesses, goals, and supports is an incredibly useful tool for a busy teacher. The general education teachers appreciate the "heads up," and the special education teachers appreciate that you are getting to know the students. You will want to ensure that the general education staff know that this cheat sheet is a confidential document, so that they protect the student's private information.

# CONFIDENTIAL IEP SUMMARY

Student: _____ Language(s) of Student: _____

Grade/Teacher(s): _____

Exceptionality Category (e.g., SLD, ED): _____

Special Education Services: _____

Parent(s)' Name(s): _____ Language of Parent(s): _____

Parent(s)' Contact Information: _____

Learning Strengths: _____

_____

Learning Areas of Need: _____

_____

Key Accommodations and Modifications: _____

_____

| Summary of Goal | Present Levels | Notes About Supporting Student |
|---|---|---|
|  |  |  |
|  |  |  |
|  |  |  |
|  |  |  |
|  |  |  |

Case Manager's Contact Information: _____

School Psychologist's Contact Information: _____

## General Education Teachers

Depending on the size of the school you have, you may find it's not possible to meet all the general education teachers in the weeks before school starts. However, it is extraordinarily important to establish yourself as a member of the school team in any way you can. In the first few weeks of school, I often offer classroom support in many different forms. In my elementary schools, I like to spend the first day of school with the kindergarten classes, consoling the criers (parents and kids!) and helping the little ones adjust to their new rooms and routines. In the days that follow, I circulate to every classroom at least once and offer to help. Often the teachers are doing fun "getting-to-know-you" activities that you can join or observe. You can also start informally observing the students and teachers and the dynamics among them.

Some teachers are more comfortable than others with having visitors in the first few weeks of school. New teachers may be nervous to have you in there, and fearful that you are judging them. I usually get to the class a few minutes before it starts or at a natural break time, and ask if it is okay to observe the students and help out. Keeping the focus on the students is the key to lowering anxiety. I have yet to have a teacher turn me down; they will probably just want to know your purpose in being there. Establishing that you are someone who will be spending time in the classroom also sets the stage for being an "insider" in the school, and teachers will feel more comfortable when you have to go in there to observe a student later on in the year. An added bonus is that the students too get to know you and will feel more comfortable in accessing you or working with you later on in the school year.

## The Custodian

Like the school secretary, the custodian at your site is also a really helpful person to know. I have had dead rats, mice, and other disasters in my office. You will want to know the person who can help you clean that up! Also, the custodian has keys to everything. In the beginning, you might not have keys to anything. Trust me—it is worthwhile to get to know the custodian. The custodian also might have relationships with the students and, at times, can share interesting and important information that will help you learn more about the students you work with.

# BEGINNING-OF-SCHOOL LOGISTICS

The beginning of school can be an exciting time. Most school psychologists report to work a week or two early, just like the teachers and administrators. This is the perfect time to build relationships and navigate logistical concerns, such as finding a work space and securing needed materials. If your district allows you to visit your school sites before school starts, take advantage of this! I have often participated in the school sites' professional development activities. They offer great opportunities to bond with staff. These professional development days often include icebreakers and getting-to-know-you activities. There may also be strategic planning; you may be able to participate in that planning, or at least observe as a way to become familiar with your school's overarching plans and goals for the year.

If you are doing your own "in-house" professional development activities in your school psychology department, you may not have this opportunity to join your school sites in theirs. In this case, you can visit your schools after you are done with your staff development. Chances are, teachers and staff are still there, setting up their rooms and preparing for their students.

## What to Do in the First Few Days and Weeks of School

The first order of business is often locating your schools and trying to work out a schedule if you have multiple school sites. Although it is important to create and share your school schedule at the beginning of the year, don't get too attached to it. It is likely to change several times throughout the year! I remember one year when I crafted the perfect schedule, and two weeks into the school year, I was reassigned to an entirely different school and had to start over again. Again, did I mention that key traits for being a successful school psychologist are to be comfortable with ambiguity and to be flexible? After you have set a tentative schedule, you will need to scout out a confidential work space, obtain needed materials, and continue to engage in relationship-building activities along the way.

## Managing Multiple Sites

As much as possible, you want to establish a regular schedule at multiple sites. That way, people will know when to expect you and when you are not available, and hunting for office space will take up less of your morning routine. For school psychologists with many school sites, it may not be possible to establish a regular routine. Hey, maybe you thrive in chaos and like it that way! Personally, I like to plan ahead, and having a regular schedule helps me do that. Here are some practical considerations when planning how to divide your time among sites:

- Start with learning the schedules of other district personnel with whom you will work. These are the people with whom you will need to meet on a regular basis. These could be special education teachers, educational diagnosticians, RtI coordinators, school counselors, school social workers, and so on. You will want to be at the school on the same day or days as these folks if at all possible, to ease the scheduling of IEP meetings.
- What days do your schools have important meetings, such as leadership team meetings, support staff meetings, and student support meetings?
- When is there office space available at your site?
- If you have to split one day between two or more schools, which of them are in close proximity to each other?
- If you job-share with another school psychologist, what days does he or she plan to be on-site?
- Does your principal have a preference for which day you are on-site?
- Is your schedule balanced so that you have mornings at each of your school sites? Often kids work better for testing in the morning, so you want to have at least one morning a week at each school if possible.

- If you have a placement that allots you half a day per week at one school, you can either go to the school one morning or afternoon a week, or alternate full days every other week. (For example, you go to the school for the whole day every other Wednesday.)
- If you are working in an urban area, what days are marked for street sweeping? You don't want to have to hunt for parking or have to move your car to avoid getting a ticket.

Once you have answered these questions, you can make a visual schedule to distribute to your principals and special education case managers at your site. Exhibit 2.1 is a sample multiple-site work schedule, followed by a blank schedule (Form 2.2) for you to fill out for your own sites.

EXHIBIT 2.1. SAMPLE MULTIPLE-SITE WORK SCHEDULE

# *SCHOOL PSYCHOLOGIST SCHEDULE*

## Rebecca Branstetter, School Psychologist

## Voicemail: XXX-XXX-XXXX

## E-mail: rbranstetter@districtemail.com

Greetings from your school psychologist! The following is my schedule for the school year 20XX–20XX. I will make every effort to be on-site on the appointed days. However, there are sometimes unavoidable scheduling conflicts, and I may need to make some minor changes throughout the year. I will notify each site if there is a schedule change. Feel free to e-mail me or call my district voicemail if you need immediate assistance on a day I am not on-site. Thanks! Rebecca

|  | MONDAY | TUESDAY | WEDNESDAY | THURSDAY | FRIDAY |
|---|---|---|---|---|---|
| **MORNING (8–12)** | Sunny Elementary | Happy High School | Merry Middle School | Happy High School | Nonpublic School Team (variable sites) |
| **AFTERNOON (12–4)** | Sunny Elementary | Merry Middle School (arrive at 12:30) | Merry Middle School | Happy High School | Nonpublic School Team (variable sites) |

# *SCHOOL PSYCHOLOGIST SCHEDULE*

_____, **School Psychologist**

**Phone/Voicemail:** _____

**E-mail:** _____

Greetings from your school psychologist! The following is my schedule for this school year. I will make every effort to be on site on the appointed days. However, there are sometimes unavoidable schedule conflicts, and I may need to make some minor changes throughout the year. I will notify each site if there is a schedule change. Feel free to e-mail me or call my district voicemail if you need immediate assistance on a day I am not on-site. Thanks! _____

|  | MONDAY | TUESDAY | WEDNESDAY | THURSDAY | FRIDAY |
|---|---|---|---|---|---|
| **MORNING** <br><br> **Time:** |  |  |  |  |  |
| **AFTERNOON** <br><br> **Time:** |  |  |  |  |  |

One final note about managing multiple sites: you will need to think about your organization system for keeping track of student files. If you don't have a system, you will end up dragging all the student files to each of your sites unnecessarily. I recommend color coding your student folders by school site (for example, elementary school students in yellow, middle school students in red, high school students in blue). That way, each morning, if you are off to your middle school, you can just grab all your red folders and know you won't be at your middle school cursing yourself for forgetting a student's folder you needed. Another quick tip about paperwork at multiple sites: have a folder (maybe a small accordion folder) of all the forms you frequently use, and bring it with you or keep it in your car. That way, if you need to whip out a developmental history form, you will have it handy. I would also recommend using a yellow highlighter to indicate which is your last form. Just write "last copy" in yellow highlighter on the last form. Yellow highlighter does not show when you photocopy it (other colors do!), so you will never inadvertently use up that last form and be stuck without one when you need it on the spot.

## Finding a Work Space at Your School Site

One of the most frustrating and challenging aspects of having a new school site can be finding a confidential space, which may involve sharing space with other support staff members. If you are one of the lucky few who have their own designated space, count your blessings! If you arrive at your site and your principal muses, "Hmmm . . . where are we going to put you?" prepare for some creative problem solving in finding a place to work! Many old school buildings do not have a lot of private spaces. I have worked with students in janitors' closets, supply closets, cafeterias, teachers' lounges, libraries, courtyards, art rooms, hallways, bathrooms (gross), and yes, as I mentioned earlier, even an elevator shaft.

Finding a space can be a tricky business, and you may have to use your very best negotiating skills. Ask your principal these questions to get you started in locating your space:

- Where did your previous school psychologist work with students?
- Where do other support staff members work with students, and are there days that they are not on-site?
- Which room do you think would be best for ensuring confidentiality and getting accurate results in testing? [Now is a good time to explain that kids won't open up to you if there are others in the room, and that your results on auditory processing tasks can be inaccurate if testing is done in a noisy environment.]
- How have you solved the issue of limited space in the past?

If all else fails, consult with your supervisor about not having a designated work space. At one site where I had found no space after multiple attempts, one of my supervisors needed to meet with the principal. She said the things I couldn't say, like "We are pulling your school psychologist until you find her a space. Let us know when you find one." I hated bringing in the "big guns," but I hated lugging forty pounds of materials around all day and wasting all my time getting evicted over and over even more.

## Getting Needed Materials

If you have finally scored a private space, congratulations! The next step is to gather all the materials you will need to do your job efficiently. Let's hope you will be working in a school district that has ample resources for all your needs! However, the odds are that at some point in your career, you will have to do some scrounging around for supplies, a working printer, paper, pencils and pens, keys, business cards, and locked cabinets for confidential files.

Remember your BFF, the secretary? He or she is a great person to start with for getting keys. Sometimes the previous school psychologist just hands over his or her keys to you; sometimes there are no spare keys, and they have to be ordered for you. At one school, I had to borrow the secretary's keys every morning to unlock my space and then go back at the end of the day to lock up. I have also been at sites where I never did get a key and had to ask the custodian (my other BFF!) to unlock a door or two to get to where I needed to be.

Become a detective at your site. Ask where other staff members print their work. Bring a memory stick (flash drive) with you so that you can easily transport your files to a working computer or printer. Find out from your secretary how people get paper and folders and other such supplies. The secretary and custodian often know of secret closets full of materials such as extension cords, old filing cabinets, and other goodies. Many schools also have a form to fill out to request supplies.

In less resource-rich districts, be prepared to have to purchase some or all of your own supplies. In some situations, you may be given minimal supplies at the beginning of the year (for example, a few reams of paper) and are then expected to buy your own when you run out. In some districts, school psychologists are in the teachers' union and therefore qualify for educator discounts and tax write-offs for supply purchases. For me, sometimes it is just easier to buy a bunch of pencils than to spend time hunting them down every day. I also ~~steal~~ borrow pens from local businesses who have extras to spare, collect promotional pens at events, and grab a bunch of leftover pens and highlighters from conference attendees after a conference. I finally bought my own printer and ink for one of my schools so that I didn't have to waste time hunting down a working printer. It was worth every penny. There are also Web sites now with very cheap or free business card printing services. The free ones sometimes print their Web site on the back, but I say that beats writing down your contact information on a sticky note every time you want to give it out. Finally, you might check out donorschoose.org, a nonprofit organization that accepts donations of money or supplies to educators who request materials for their students.

## Other Considerations in the First Few Weeks

This is the stuff no one tells you in grad school. I know, this sounds silly, but I wish someone had been explicit with me about some of the little things to consider in the first few weeks. They may apply only in certain districts, but if you are in a large urban school district, they may be tips you'll want to consider.

### Wardrobe

Why didn't anyone advise me on my wardrobe choices when I was working in an urban school district? It took only a few weeks of kids calling me a Norteño, Crip, Surreño, or Blood before I realized that red and blue were poor choices for my wardrobe given the location of my school and the neighborhood gang activity. Sure, they didn't really think I was in a gang, but believe me, kids notice the colors you wear. Mostly, I eliminated red and blue from my wardrobe because I was tired of kids asking me why I got to wear gang colors and they didn't, and getting teased about which gang I was representing that day.

As a young woman, I also eliminated most skirts and dresses, deep V-neck shirts, and any tight pants from my wardrobe within my first few years of working at the secondary level. I'm not saying I'm "all that" in the looks department, but I am saying that some clothing can invite unwanted comments. I'll save the comments I've gotten when wearing a skirt for my memoir. This book rated PG-13!

### The Neighborhood

I was supernaïve about the dangers of the neighborhood at some of my school sites when I first started. I was told that if I stayed late, I should have someone walk me to my car, and I didn't really do that. Then a teacher was robbed at gunpoint outside my school, and I changed my mind. Play it safe, people; don't let your *Dangerous Minds* complex get you into trouble.

Also, don't leave anything visible in your car. Not an iPod cable, not a single file, nothing. In particular, never leave confidential materials or testing materials in your car. I know what you're thinking! Your car is your mobile office, right? I used to have crates in the back of my car with all my test kits, protocols, play therapy materials, and so on. Then my car got stolen. It wasn't fun to tell my supervisor that I needed thousands of dollars' worth of test kits replaced. I do sometimes wonder if the thief put the materials to good use and assessed himself to find out if he had conduct disorder or impulsivity. I sought comfort in the thought of the thief giving himself a behavior rating scale, playing with the anger management game, and making a change for the better. Yeah, probably not. So just don't keep anything in your car, if possible. If you have no other option, keep items in the trunk, but no matter what, don't ever put confidential folders in your car, as they are irreplaceable.

## ONCE YOU ARE SETTLED IN: INTRODUCING YOURSELF

One of the other things that is not explicitly taught in grad school is how to introduce yourself to staff, parents, and students. I remember the first few times I tried to introduce myself as the school psychologist: I was uncomfortable and unversed in describing my complex role. In part that was due to my not really knowing the full scope of my role, but it would have been nice to have some ideas about how to introduce myself to the school community.

## Introducing Yourself to Staff

Ideally, in the first few weeks before the kids arrived or in the first few weeks of school, you have had a chance to make your rounds to get to know the staff. There are some situations where there are too many staff members to meet personally in those first weeks of school. This is often the case at large middle and high schools. In these cases, and even if you have personally met the staff, I suggest that you introduce yourself in writing to the staff so that they are at least familiar with your name and your role.

Exhibit 2.2 is a sample letter you might write to your staff. Some school psychologists are superfancy and create their own Web site for staff and parents. Someday, when I have the free time, I will learn how to do that! In the meantime, here is one possible way to introduce yourself to staff the old-fashioned way. You can also transfer the content of the letter to a welcome page on your school's Web site if you're more technologically savvy than I am.

EXHIBIT 2.2. SAMPLE LETTER TO STAFF

Rebecca Branstetter

School Psychologist, Happy Unified School District

Voicemail: XXX-XXX-XXXX

E-mail: rbranstetter@districtemail.com

Dear Happy High School Teachers and Staff,

Hello from your school psychologist! I'm excited to be working with the Happy High School staff this year. I am new to the school district and look forward to collaborating with you all to help support the students of Happy High School academically and with their social-emotional needs. I work with general education students doing prevention and intervention activities, as well as with students receiving special education services. In this role, I collaborate frequently with teachers about how to support struggling students.

I am on site at Happy High School Tuesday mornings (8–12) and all day on Thursdays. My office is in Room 101, next to the counselor's office on the 1st floor. My phone extension is 1234. If I don't answer, you can leave me a voicemail at XXX-XXX-XXXX, which I check frequently. You are also welcome to send me an e-mail at rbranstetter@districtemail.com.

The following information may be useful for your questions about special education assessments and behavioral/learning difficulties for a particular student:

If you have concerns about a student's learning, behavioral, or emotional needs, please bring it to the attention of your grade-level colleagues in your grade-level meetings to consult about interventions that other teachers may be using with success. The grade-level team is also welcome to make a referral to the SAP (Student Assistance Program) team, which meets weekly to discuss referrals. Referral forms are available in the counseling office.

If you receive a parent request for special education evaluation, please forward the information to the respective grade-level counselor. He or she will then follow up on scheduling a Student Success Team meeting to address the parent's concern and will forward the referral to the appropriate case manager.

If you have any questions or concerns about a particular student, feel free to find me on Tuesday mornings or on Thursdays. You may also leave a confidential voicemail or e-mail about your concerns and set up a consultation meeting.

I look forward to getting to know each of you and your students!

Sincerely,

*Rebecca Branstetter*

Your letter will likely vary from the sample depending on your role and referral procedures. It is a good idea to run a draft of your letter by your principal, key support staff members, and case managers to ensure that you have accurately described how teachers and staff access your services. At some school sites, everything is filtered through a support staff team meeting; in other schools, people will contact you directly.

You also want to consider what contact information to give out. Some school psychologists are okay with distributing their personal e-mail address and cell phone number to all staff, others do so only to select staff, and others have strong boundaries about work and personal contact information. What information you give out may be contingent on your district's resources. In one district where I worked, we didn't have access to voicemail, and people were supposed to leave messages at the district office; we then had to drive there to collect them! I ended up having to give out my cell phone number, or my messages would be weeks old. You can also research if your cell phone company gives discounts to educators, to offset the cost of using your cell phone for work.

In terms of work and personal contact information boundaries, I fall somewhere in the middle. For general staff, I give out only my district e-mail and phone numbers, and then key people, like the principal and special education staff, get my cell phone number. I ask those individuals to whom I give my cell phone number not to distribute it to others without my permission. Trust me—if a few anxious staff members have your personal contact information, you just might get a call at eight on a Saturday morning or at nine at night asking you to consult.

## Introducing Yourself to Families and Students

When I first started out, I often gave shoddy "elevator pitches" to parents and students about who I was and what I did. You will need to develop your "introduction to families and students" speech early on in your career. I often say, "I'm the school psychologist, and I work with students who need additional support at school" or something vague to start. Some families are scared off by the word "psychologist" and conjure up images of you taking their kid to a room where the child lies on a couch and talks about his or her parents. After I say "I am the school psychologist," I tend with parents to emphasize the school and learning part of my job by saying things like, "My job is to figure out how kids learn best and see what is helping them and what is getting in the way of their learning."

With students, I find that the "I work with kids to see how they learn best and help them become better students" line works pretty well. Older kids will ask follow-up questions like "So, you do therapy with kids?" or "Aren't you the lady who puts people in special education?" I respond with the truth, because older kids know better anyway. I tell them that "therapy" in the school is basically learning how to be better students and make school more enjoyable or easier for them, or learning how to cope with everyday issues that come up for all teenagers.

The term *special education* is often seen as a stigma, so I frame it by saying something like "I work with students in general education as well as students receiving special education supports. Usually, in middle and high school, special education is for students needing extra academic support, which they get in Ms. Jenkins's class [resource room teacher's name]. She helps them learn study skills and ways to make school easier and more enjoyable."

## PULLING IT ALL TOGETHER

Getting situated in a new district or new school site can be an exciting and challenging experience. Although most of us got into this profession to work with students, the fact is that much of our job is building working relationships with adults—teachers, parents, administrators, and other support staff members. The first few weeks of school are a time of great opportunity to set the stage for a successful school year.

School psychologists understand the power of a positive relationship and are well equipped to build these relationships early on. It is important to avoid getting so wrapped up in your beginning-of-year to-do list that you skip the step of making personal connections with the adults in the building.

In addition to joining school activities, introducing yourself, and negotiating your role, you are also faced with logistical challenges at the beginning of the year. Finding a private work space and needed materials, working out your schedule at multiple sites, and communicating your role to others are important tasks that you can do in the context of building relationships and becoming familiar with your schools' unique cultures.

## Key Points

- As noted in Chapter One, your roles will vary depending on your school site. Understand that initially, the previous school psychologist's roles might determine the expectations for your activities at that site.
- Key staff members with whom to build relationships are the principal, secretary, support staff, special education teachers, general education teachers, and custodial staff.
- Spend the first few weeks conducting informational interviews with each of these key staff members so that you can better understand their roles and how your job will interface with theirs.
- Finding a private work space can be challenging. Ask the previous school psychologist and the current principal where in the building there may be space for you. Negotiate with other support staff: find out which days and times a space may be available, and coordinate schedules with them.
- If you are assigned multiple school sites, consider creating a consistent schedule and disseminating it to your school staff so that people will know how to reach you each day. Things to consider when making your schedule include when space is available, when important meetings are scheduled, what days

other support staff are on-site, and other factors, such as parking, morning versus afternoon needs, and whether you want to spend time at more than one school on the same day.

- Introducing yourself formally to your new school staff is important in defining your role and making your presence known at your new school. Be sure to run a draft of your formal letter of introduction by key school staff to ensure that you are accurately representing your role and describing proper referral procedures for working with students.
- Practice your "elevator speech" about what a school psychologist does and get comfortable with describing your role to parents, teachers, and students of different ages.
- Building relationships and defining your role are ongoing processes. Much of the groundwork can be laid down in the first few weeks of school, but recognize that schools are dynamic, changing systems that require adaptability and constant effort to ensure positive working relationships with others.

## DISCUSSION QUESTIONS

1. Imagine you just received your school placements from your supervisor. What do you see as your first order of business in getting acquainted with your new schools and staff members?
2. The beginning of the year is often a time of ambiguity and uncertainty. How do you plan to navigate the logistical and relationship-building tasks in your first few weeks?
3. What concerns do you have about relationship building with staff members? What ideas do you have for overcoming these concerns?
4. What are three to five specific tasks that you think are most important for building relationships at a new school site?
5. What is your "elevator speech" about your role at your new school site? Does it vary by who is asking what a school psychologist does?

# chapter 3

# HELP! I'M DROWNING IN PAPERWORK!

## How to Tame the Bureaucracy Monster

Knock knock. Who's there? It's the Bureaucracy Monster! In the day-to-day life of a school psychologist, it's always there. It always knocks on my door and has me fill out a piece of paper I already filled out four times. It has me write the same thing in three different places and then file it in three different files. It makes me painstakingly complete unnecessary forms. Like the Weight Watchers Hunger Monster, that little orange monster in the commercials who is lurking everywhere and ready to attack you, the Bureaucracy Monster is alive and well in school districts. Only instead of attacking your self-control with donuts (yum), it attacks your working time with paperwork that you are required to complete. It steals time away from your interactions with students. It keeps you from having a working electrical outlet, an office, or a key to the building so that you can get in every day to do your job. It often prevents you from having a nice, quiet space to work that contains a functioning phone, computer, printer, and voicemail. Oh, my kingdom for voicemail and a working printer! Boo on the Bureaucracy Monster! Mind you, the Bureaucracy Monster is much bigger in size and power in larger school districts than in smaller ones. However, it is your involvement with special education, rather than the size of your district, that is most responsible for bringing the Bureaucracy Monster to your door.

Another hazard of our job is its resistance to the efficacy of traditional time management skills. When you have a never-ending to-do list and no real way to prioritize one kid over another, you occasionally end up being frantically paralyzed by the size and complexity of that list. And unlike poor time management in a corporate job, not getting to your action items has effects on students' lives rather than on a budget or a profit margin.

One of the most difficult tasks for a school psychologist is keeping organized and on top of logistics, paperwork, procedures, referrals, caseload, and report writing. These challenges, which can be responsible for an enormous amount of the stress associated with our jobs, are scarcely addressed in most graduate programs. Sadly, the gap between our job descriptions and the actual makeup of our days is so large at times that I have often wondered if there is a conspiracy in graduate school to hide the horrible part of this job so that people will still enter the field! I do recall professors mentioning the paperwork aspect, but I thought that because I was superorganized in graduate school, such bureaucratic and time management tasks would not have a big impact on my work. Ha! It is the single biggest challenge in my day-to-day work life. Then again, maybe your district is a well-oiled machine of efficiency, but I highly doubt that. If it is, please let me know the name and location of your district so that I can submit my job application.

Thankfully, there are many practical tools and ideas for taming the Bureaucracy Monster. Some of these tools were developed from my own attempts (and failures!) to get organized, others were provided by the great school psychologists I have worked with, and some have been offered by the readers of Notes from the School Psychologist. This chapter compiles the best of the best in terms of managing your caseload, completing your work within timelines, and documenting and tracking interventions.

## MANAGING YOUR ASSESSMENT CASELOAD

Perhaps you have only one school and a supermanageable caseload. In that case, I am beyond jealous, and I advise you to thank your lucky stars and hop on over to the next section of this chapter. The truth is, most school psychologists have heavy testing caseloads, and some have large counseling and case management loads as well. Case management responsibilities vary by district and by school. In one district where I worked, I was responsible for tracking all referrals, completing all the referral and assessment plan paperwork, informing all parties of their roles, setting the Individualized Education Plan (IEP) meeting dates, and filing all the completed paperwork. In another district, the special education teacher completed all those activities, and I was responsible only for mental health referrals. Your role in managing paperwork and student case management will vary, but odds are, you are likely to have some case management obligations. Better and more efficient case management will help you with meeting your deadlines and freeing up time for other roles.

Whether you have a role in case management or are simply tracking students in your own caseload, you will need some sort of log. In one school district, there was a template in a Microsoft Excel spreadsheet already created that we all used to track our students. In another, I had to create my own and then *handwrite* the names of students with whom I had worked and what the outcomes were—in three different places, one of which was on a card catalogue. Yes, even in the new millennium, I still had to use an archaic card catalogue to track student files. (For you young ones who don't know what a card catalogue is, find a movie from the 1960s that shows a librarian sorting through a bunch of alphabetized index cards to find the book she wants.)

Even if you have a district with an archaic system, you will probably want to use technology to your advantage. I recommend using a spreadsheet—what I call my Master Assessment Log—for tracking assessment cases. For counseling and intervention tracking, refer to Chapters Eight and Nine on counseling and Chapters Four and Five on interventions and RtI, respectively. For assessment cases, the benefit of making a spreadsheet are that you will have documentation of your timelines, as well as the ability to sort by school or by due date (for example, the sixty-day legal timeline), depending on your need. I often sort by due date for my own tracking, and then if I need to provide data to my individual school sites, I can sort by school and do a different printout. The data can also be used to track the percentage of referrals that end up qualifying for services, as a consultation tool or feedback for your school site. The cells you use in your spreadsheet will vary depending on how involved you are in the referral process, but in general, you will want to include the following basic categories across the top cells (see Exhibit 3.1).

EXHIBIT 3.1. SAMPLE MASTER ASSESSMENT LOG

| Last Name | First Name | DOB | Date Assessment Plan Signed | Due Date | Type of Assessment | Eligibility Code | Date IEP Held | Outcome |
|---|---|---|---|---|---|---|---|---|
| Jenkins | Phil | 4/4/98 | 10/5/10 | X/X/XX | Triennial | SLD | X/X/XX | Resource Program; referred for counseling |
| Steele | Jessica | 6/3/03 | 3/5/10 | X/X/XX | Initial | Not Eligible | (1) X/X/XX (parent no-show) (2) X/X/XX | Referred to after-school tutoring |

You can always add columns that make sense for you, such as testing dates, dates reports were written or turned in, dates you contacted parents, attempted IEP dates, and so on. At minimum, though, you want to be able to easily reference your log when you get the inevitable inquiry about where you are with testing so-and-so, and what happened at so-and-so's IEP meeting. It becomes even more handy if you are at a school site for multiple years. Your log then serves as a useful source of information for special education reevaluations, tracking the progress of students you tested who did not qualify, and documentation of the size of your caseload.

At times, I have also had to show to parents, administrators, and advocates that action was taken when they complain that "nothing has been done, and I requested testing two years ago!" It's a lot easier to show that you followed through on your part as a case manager when you can whip out your log and say, "I sent an assessment plan home on X date and followed up with a phone call on Y date, and another assessment plan on Z date, and did not receive anything back. That is why we were not able to complete testing two years ago." I know, I know, it's not fun to sound like a Bureaucracy Monster in training, but it is better than not remembering what happened two years ago, which makes you look as though you are incompetent or out of compliance.

Now let's imagine you have a meticulous case management log, full of all the students you are going to work with in the year. You look at your fabulous log, and if it is lengthy, you might think, "Wow! How am I going to get to assessing all these students by my timelines?" Yes, as every good to-do list maker knows, making the to-do list is the easy part. Getting to all the tasks is the hard part. The next section will help you with streamlining some of your paperwork and with tracking and managing your time well.

## COMPLETING YOUR ASSESSMENTS WITHIN TIMELINES

One of the most time-sensitive tasks of a school psychologist is to complete assessments for special education within the legal timelines. If you are in an assessment-heavy school district (or if you are a school psychometrician or a school psychologist examiner), assessment may be your main role, and you will have an ongoing challenge of juggling and prioritizing testing, report writing, and holding IEP meetings, all in the midst of your other obligations and crises that pop up. In one sense, the legal timelines make it easy to prioritize which students you will be working with; however, you might find that some students move up in priority because of the urgency of their particular circumstances. In order to develop an efficient system, you will need to tap into the untaught skills of case management. In graduate school, we are rarely explicitly told how to organize our caseloads and deal with the unfortunate reality of sometimes having more students in our caseload than we can manage. Fortunately, there are organizational tools you can implement early on in the year to get and stay organized, and several tips you can follow for managing your workload when you are in the midst of the year, wondering how you're going to get to all of your students.

## Check Your Assessment Caseloads for Accuracy

At the beginning of the year, most school psychologists get a printout or log of all the students who are due for a triennial assessment for the year. If you do not automatically receive this, ask for it! If you are in an assessment-heavy school district or you work at the high school level, there can be many, many pages of names. Some of them may already be ominously marked "overdue," and some may be due within the first few weeks of school (when you are trying to bond with your staff and get situated). At first, you might have your very own panic attack. Before you do that, be sure to check the log for accuracy.

There are many reasons a case log can be incorrect (besides my fantasy of the Bureaucracy Monster hacking into the district database and changing dates, as he drops donut crumbs on the computer and laughs maniacally). First, the students may have already been assessed the previous year, and the printout does not reflect that. Second, many students may no longer attend the school. Third, there may just be a plain old typo, and the student is not really due for reevaluation during the current year.

If you are new to a school, sit down with the previous school psychologist and ask if he or she has tested any of the students. Next, sit down with the case manager(s) at the school site (usually the special education staff) and cross-check your list with their list and with the actual student files. It's laborious, to be sure, but not as laborious as doing a full assessment when you don't need to! If the Bureaucracy Monster has stolen the student's file or it has not yet been moved up from a prior school (for example, new sixth graders at the middle school, new ninth graders at the high school), then you can help the case manager track them down. Or if you are the case manager of the files, then you can recruit the special education teacher(s) to help you track them down.

## Make Your Yearly Assessment Calendar

One of the best tools my mentor gave me in my first year was a very simple yearly calendar for my triennial assessments, which I call my Master Triennial Calendar. I keep it in addition to my Master Assessment Log spreadsheet that tracks everything I do with students. I do this because it is a one-pager, so I can easily see in which months all my assessments cluster, and do some advanced planning. I can also post it or keep it handy for a visual snapshot of my caseload. For example, for some reason, every year, I have tons of triennial assessments in September and October and in March and April. I don't know what's magical about those months, but if I see the year in snapshot form, I can move up some assessments to less impacted months and save myself from an impossible month. I also put all my school sites on this one page so that I can see how the assessments cluster together across schools.

Another benefit of creating a one-page Master Triennial Calendar is that you can reconcile dates with your special education teachers. It is sometimes the case that your triennial due dates do not match up with your special education teachers' annual IEP due dates. In ideal circumstances, these dates should match up or be very close together in time. However, for whatever reason (I'm looking at you, little orange monster), sometimes they are way off from each other. This can result in not meeting timelines or the need to hold two separate meetings. The way to reconcile this is to negotiate moving up the triennial to the annual date. The other way around is possible, but not preferred. In most districts, your performance (and that of your district) can be partially measured by the completion rate of triennials within legal timelines. If you move your triennial assessment to a later annual due date, you will be out of compliance. Most special education teachers understand this and have no problem moving up triennials. If you and your teachers can reconcile the date differences at the beginning of the year, you will avoid a frantic rush to finish an assessment right away when you discover the discrepancy in annual and triennial dates a few weeks before the annual IEP is due.

The following is an example of my Master Triennial Calendar (Exhibit 3.2), followed by a blank one for your use (Form 3.1). In the example, I would likely move up a few of the students in March and April to the less crowded months. I would also move up any students due in June, as by that time of year, I am usually frantically trying to finish all the initial evaluations that come right at the end of the year.

EXHIBIT 3.2. SAMPLE MASTER TRIENNIAL CALENDAR

# *SCHOOL YEAR: 2012–2013*

| Overdue | September | October |
|---|---|---|
| 4/8: Javon Smith (High)<br>5/12: Harry Jenkins (Elem) | 9/12: Steven Ellison (Middle)<br>9/13: Cosme Martinez (Middle)<br>9/15: Sebastian Ratigan (Elem) | 10/1: Judy McAllister (Middle)<br>10/5: Leigh Lamont (Elem)<br>10/6: Amber Jones (Elem)<br>10/22: Karen McGee (High) |
| **November** | **December** | **January** |
|  | 12/8: Beth Tennison (High)<br>12/9: Mary Brookdale (Elem)<br>12/12: Victor Martinez (High) | 1/5: Sabrina Gonzales (High)<br>1/7: Monica Almaguel (Elem)<br>1/10: DeAngelo Jones (Middle) |
| **February** | **March** | **April** |
| 2/1: John Roscoe (Middle) | 3/3: Samantha Hoyt (Elem)<br>3/5: Jack Banks (High)<br>3/7: Allie Murphy (Middle)<br>3/14: Dalia Martinez (Middle) | 4/1: Esmeralda Yee (Middle)<br>4/4: Diego Vasquez (High)<br>4/6: Marquez Baily (High)<br>4/8: LaShandra Smith (High)<br>4/30: George Lee (Elem) |
| **May** | **June** | **July/August** |
| 5/15: Oliver Meyers (Elem) | 6/4: Ava Banks (Elem)<br>6/7: Dylan Riff (Middle) |  |

# *Master Triennial Calendar*

## *SCHOOL YEAR:* _____

| Overdue | September | October |
|---|---|---|
|  |  |  |

| November | December | January |
|---|---|---|
|  |  |  |

| February | March | April |
|---|---|---|
|  |  |  |

| May | June | July/August |
|---|---|---|
|  |  |  |

When you make your own Master Triennial Calendar, use pencil or make it into a word processing document if you work in a district like mine, where kids move around a lot. You can also expand your Master Triennial Calendar to include initial evaluations as they come up, so that you can balance the triennials and initials; or you might prefer to create an initial evaluation log using the same template. If you are in a district where you have other roles besides assessment, you will likely have other case management obligations.

The next section introduces another way to help you properly document your work with students. Although at first glance it may seem as though I have developed a case of Bureaucratic Obsessive-Compulsive Documenting Disorder, these organizational activities are really for your benefit and the benefit of your students. In my early years as a school psychologist, I prided myself on having a tremendous memory for the details about each student. My mom even bought me a book bag that said, "My head is full of children!" with adorable drawings of a bunch of different kids. Ten years into the profession, my head is so full of the hundreds and hundreds of children I have worked with that there is no human way to remember all the details about each of them. I would need a gargantuan book bag to represent all the students I have encountered. Write it down, people. In addition to jogging your memory about the progress of each student and your plans for intervention, writing everything down also covers you legally if down the road there are inquiries or (gulp) subpoenas. Take comfort that in ten years, I have had only two subpoenas, but trust me—I was happy with myself for documenting everything.

## DOCUMENTING AND TRACKING INTERVENTIONS, COUNSELING, AND CRISIS COUNSELING

During my first week as a school psychologist, my supervisor handed down this very useful piece of advice: remember that in a school district, if you don't write it down, it didn't happen. At first I thought that perhaps she was just a bit paranoid, but over the past ten years, that advice has really paid off for me. Trust me—if you get involved in a legal mediation or are subpoenaed to testify, you are going to thank yourself for writing everything down!

### Documenting Interventions

Chapter Four details specifics for serving on prereferral intervention teams, and Chapter Five provides information about the various intervention roles in the Response to Intervention framework. For this chapter, which focuses on taming the Bureaucracy Monster, it is sufficient to say that my supervisor's mantra about documentation should stay with you throughout your school day. If you are part of a team that tracks interventions or you are implementing an intervention, you need to document it. More specifically, keep your own intervention files for each student you work with one-on-one (for example, daily check-ins for behavior, thirty-minute read-togethers for reading fluency, binder reviews for organizational skills).

### Documenting Counseling and Crisis Counseling

Keeping case notes for individual counseling clients is a must. Crisis counseling meetings or simple check-ins with students require less documentation than formal case notes, but these services should be reflected somewhere in your files. Examples of these occasions include when a child has experienced a traumatic event, when a student reports wanting to hurt himself or herself (perhaps in a class journal entry or to a trusted teacher), when a student makes a threat, or when a student is out of control in class. Each of these scenarios is talked about in more detail in Chapter Eleven on crisis counseling. One simple way to keep track of such services is to maintain a single confidential file for all the crisis counseling and emergency situations, in which you write down what happened, what the child said, and how you followed up. Chances are, you may never have to look at these notes again, but if you do, you will be thankful you took detailed notes.

While we are on the subject of record keeping, let's address the importance of having a locked file cabinet. This is an essential, and you should talk to your principal about getting one. In situations where I have had to wait for a locked cabinet to be ordered and delivered, I have gone to the office supply store and gotten my own locked filing case to use in the interim. Then, each summer, either I find a secure place at my school site or, if I anticipate that I will not be at the same school the following year, I clutter my closet or garage at home with the files of the students I worked with. I know it's not ideal to clutter up your own home, but it's necessary. Check your state guidelines for when it is okay to destroy records. It is often when the child has reached adult age, but it can vary. I label the outside of the folder with the child's birthday in bold print and then sort alphabetically. Then, some day down the road, I can easily see which kids are adult age and which files I can shred. I think I have another decade or so until I can hold my personal shredding party, but I do look forward to that day.

## Documenting Child Protective Services Calls and Reports

If I could rewind time, I would ask my supervisors in graduate school to spend more time on how to properly document reports to Child Protective Services (CPS). The chapters on counseling will go into detail about these reports, but for the purposes of managing the paperwork behind them, my mantra persists: document everything. Document when you called, whom you spoke with, what his or her recommendation was, and when you filed the written report. If the child welfare workers at CPS say that the event is not reportable, still document what you told them and their response. I have a folder in my confidential files for all CPS consultations and reports. Keep them forever. Or at least until the legal date you have to keep them, according to state law. Your supervisor might be helpful in figuring out how long you must keep these records. Also, most of my school principals ask for a copy of the report for their school file as well.

## WHAT'S NEXT? TIME MANAGEMENT TIPS FOR BALANCING ASSESSMENT CASELOADS WITH OTHER ROLES

So now you have a system for documenting interventions with students and a pretty log of all your triennial assessments. Congrats! We'll hope that the assessment logs you receive at the beginning of the year are mostly accurate, but you will also have to see which kids show up in the first few weeks. Sometimes new kids pop up, and sometimes kids have moved away and you can drop them off your log. This is a working document that is subject to change! Perhaps you have also done some advance planning and moved some of your triennials up to months that aren't quite as busy, which will be helpful. Now the real work begins!

Over the years, I have learned a few tricks for completing assessments in a timely manner. Some of these may work for you, and some may not apply, so feel free to pick and choose the ones that make sense to you. These are tips that I have found to increase my efficiency in testing and report writing so that I can free up time to do other tasks I prefer. I mean, not that I don't love writing reports and all, but I find the one-on-one time with the kids to be much more fulfilling! Chapter Six is packed with tips about conducting meaningful and legally defensible assessments.

This next section is designed to help you manage your everyday time management issues. All of this emphasis on assessment timelines exists because the legal timelines take precedent over the other roles you may have. Even if you have a smaller caseload, I'd still recommend reading this section on how to prioritize students in general. This is because traditional time management doesn't work well in the helping professions. The mantra to "do what is most important first" is a bad match for school psychology, because all students are equally important. Your to-do list in working with students is also a moving target, because situations change rapidly in the schools.

A recent poll of school psychologists from the Notes from the School Psychologist Blog Facebook page revealed that the top trait that people think makes a good school psychologist is flexibility (followed closely by patience and sense of humor). I concur! Anyone who has been a school psychologist knows that each day is a brand-new surprise. You may wake up thinking you will be testing John and Ava and holding a parent meeting. In actuality, you end up having to deal with a crisis, Ava is absent, John won't work with you, and your parent no-shows. On the positive side, one of the things I love about this job is the variety and the excitement. Some people just thrive in chaos, and you may be one of those people. You also may be someone who is unaccustomed to the constantly moving target of to-do items on your daily calendar. Fortunately, there are some scheduling tricks and systems you can put in place to increase your odds of having productive days.

## Scheduling Your Week

Because your game plan is often changed in the middle of the game by circumstance, I suggest that you set up a weekly at-a-glance calendar. It's much more flexible than a daily to-do list, and you can easily change your plan when something unexpected happens. It also allows you to look at multiple school sites at once. You may have a better organizational system that works for you, and in that case, keep it up. But if you find yourself sitting at your school site with tons to do and no idea where to start, you might try this approach and tweak it to meet your unique needs. Exhibit 3.3 shows a sample weekly calendar.

EXHIBIT 3.3.  SAMPLE WEEKLY TO-DO CALENDAR

# Weekly To-Do List: September 5–9

| Elementary School | Middle School |
|---|---|
| *Assessment:*<br>1. Harry J. (TRI overdue)—observe, cognitive test, attention and executive functioning test<br>2. Sebastian R. (TRI due 9/15)—observe, parent rating scale, cognitive test<br>3. Leigh L. (TRI due 10/5)—set up parent meeting, locate missing cumulative file<br><br>*Other:*<br>1. Check in with Darius<br>2. Observe Michaela in Science<br>3. Counseling—Jim 10:30 Weds | *Assessment:*<br>1. Steven E. (TRI, due 9/12)—observe, call parent re: medication update, cognitive test<br>2. Cosme M. (TRI, due 9/13)—score cognitive test, administer auditory processing test (English and Spanish)<br>3. Judy M. (TRI, due 10/1)—call parent, get assessment plan signed<br><br>*Other:*<br>1. Student Success Team meeting for Julian 9/6<br>2. Get counseling permission slip to Mary's mom |
| **High School** | **Office Work/Other** |
| *Assessment:*<br>1. Karen M. (TRI, due 10/22)—review prior testing to see if a review or full evaluation needed<br><br><br>*Other:*<br>1. Meet with counselor re: Group Therapy referrals<br>2. Check in with Dimitri re: crisis at home<br>3. Consult with Beth T.'s special education teacher and parent to see if we can move up triennial from December to November | 1. Turn in timesheet by 9/15<br>2. Get protocols: visual-motor test, parent adaptive behavior record forms in Spanish, more cognitive test protocols<br>3. Turn in mileage reimbursement form<br>4. Enter new case management data on spreadsheet<br>5. Call Human Resources re: benefits |

In this example, I am assigned three school sites, and I have included an additional row to represent office work and administrative tasks that may not be associated with any particular school. Under each school in my example, there is a section for assessment and a section for "other." You can also further specify the "other" category by breaking it out for your other roles, such as counseling, consultations, meetings, or whatever category makes sense for you. Notice in the weekly to-do list that assessments are prioritized by due date. Of course, I don't expect to do all of the full assessment for each kid listed; I just have the next three or four "on deck" listed so that if a few kids are absent or unavailable for testing, I can still get some assessment work done that day. I usually put the kids for the current month and the upcoming month on the weekly to-do list. You may prefer only to put ones on there for whom you have current permission to test, and reserve the on-deck kids for the yearly calendar you made.

Note that I also put down some specific assessment tasks I need to do next for each child. That is not the exhaustive list, but the first two or three things I need to do for each child's evaluation. You can modify your list each week. This will remind you from week to week where you are in the assessment and what materials you may need to bring that day to finish up. Nothing is worse than having only one subtest left to give to finish off the testing and not have that booklet!

## Scheduling Your Day

Now that you have a gorgeous weekly to-do list, you may be feeling as though you know exactly where to start. Or the to-do list may start to have baby to-do lists, and extra things pop up each day for you to add! I know that when I first enter my school sites, I often can't make it to my office to put down my bags without at least one or two people giving me new information that may alter my plans. I also might get a new e-mail or note in my box that changes my day. That is why I spend the first twenty minutes of my day making a daily task list based on my weekly to-do list. To focus your efforts, you can also highlight or put a star on the weekly to-do list to mark the one or two items you must get to that day. Unless there is new information that a child is in danger or crisis, I make assessment a top priority for first thing in the morning.

To illustrate why I put testing first, I'm going to tell you a little tale of my first year as a school psychologist. I was so excited to be a part of the school, I just started my day with whatever presented itself to me when I walked through the door. I'd console a child, consult with a teacher, chat with the principal, talk to a parent, visit a classroom, return an e-mail, review a file, or follow up on a note in my box. Next thing I knew, it was lunchtime, and I had not begun testing any of the students in my caseload. By the time I got to testing, the kid had either been kicked out of class for bad behavior, was cutting school, was attending an assembly or involved in a special project going on in class, or was too tired to push through difficult items. I would finally get to testing kids here and there, and then have no time in the day to score protocols and write reports. This resulted in my spending almost every evening and weekend working on reports. I was doing important things all day, but not prioritizing well.

Situations like those I've described here are why I recommend spending the first two hours of each day either testing or writing reports. I am religious about it now, and teachers and administrators no longer come to me first thing in the morning because they all know I'm testing students. And because I have my weekly to-do calendar to look at, I know that if Harry is absent and Sebastian is taking a test, then I can just move down my list to Leigh and know that I am still making dents in my testing responsibilities. Of course there are days when all three kids I need are not available, and then it is report-writing time. I camp out with student files and write up the background section of my reports for all my students. Trust me—when it is a week before the IEP meeting and you are just finishing testing, you will be thanking yourself for having those sections of the reports already finished.

When I am able to test kids in the morning, I also make a point of quickly writing up my observations of their testing behavior right then and there. Trust me on this one: you will think you will remember the nuances, especially if you jot down notes in your protocols, but it is way easier to synthesize your experience of a child right after working with him or her. Again, your future self will thank you when you sit down to write the report in a few weeks and you can't remember if the student gave up on easy items, pushed through them, or started fidgeting when things got hard.

Now if assessment is not your primary role at a school site, you can just plug in your most important role in the beginning of the day, during the "sacred two hours" time block. I put assessment and report writing in that block only because assessment has historically been my primary role. That being said, I have had special assignments where counseling and intervention are my primary roles. At those schools, I put counseling and interventions in the first two hours of the day if possible.

Of course, there may be certain situations where school staff or parents prefer that you work with students during nonacademic times of the day. The beginning of the school day tends to be academic, so you might have a conflict in working with a student first thing. Or you go to get a kid and she's taking a test. At the high school level in particular, you may not be able to pull students for testing except during certain classes. So if you can't swing the first two hours of the day for testing, then find your own sacred two-hour block that works for your situation.

## What to Do When You Are Drowning in a Sea of Assessments

The reality of being a school psychologist in an assessment-focused district is that you may be the most organized and efficient school psychologist on the planet and still not meet your deadlines. If you have a perfectionistic streak, you may just find yourself in your own personal hell. This may involve a caseload too large to allow you to finish all your work no matter how efficient you are or how quickly you complete each task. If this sounds familiar, I'm here to say that you're in good company. I rarely meet a school psychologist who says, "You know, I'm just so bored all day because I have nothing to do!" You are not a psych robot. You have to accept your own limitations. Chapter Twelve will help you do just that, so that you don't get burned out and leave the profession.

I would also recommend being proactive if you are not meeting your timelines or if, after you've made your logs and to-do lists, you anticipate not meeting your timelines. Tell your supervisor and show him or her your list. There is no shame in trying to be proactive and alerting your supervisor that you foresee challenges in meeting deadlines.

Tell him or her that you are doing your best, but need assistance. I once worked in a district where I had twenty-five signed assessment plans and was killing myself to do them all. When I went to my supervisor to see how I could be more efficient, she sent out an e-mail to other psychologists in the department, and it turned out that a few had only one or two signed plans! Instead of having me try to be impossibly more efficient, she reassigned some of my cases to the less busy psychologists. Then, when I had a slow month, I picked up a few cases for my colleagues. Don't suffer in silence! Of course, all supervisors are different, and at first you may be hesitant to admit that you can't handle all your cases, but I strongly believe that most supervisors would rather you be honest about your situation than try to cover it up and end up having many overdue assessments.

## PULLING IT ALL TOGETHER

Some of the most difficult aspects of the job of a school psychologist are not always explicitly taught in graduate school—managing paperwork, learning how to document properly, and dealing with inefficient and ineffective district policies. Even if these topics are addressed, it is hard to anticipate the special quirks of each district and how the Bureaucracy Monster might rear its ugly head in your daily life. One of my school psychologist friends called the world of special education assessment the Department of Redundancy Department because you end up writing the same thing in a bunch of different places, requiring parents to sign virtually the same thing over and over, and then filing everything in a hojillion different places. (A hojillion is somewhere between a million and infinity.) You really have two choices when it comes to dealing with redundancy of paperwork and impossible caseload responsibilities: you can either fight the monster or dance with it.

Fighting with the Bureaucracy Monster might look like going to your supervisor or district higher-ups and pointing out inefficient policies and redundancies. This can be a dangerous task if not done carefully. I remember that the "great ideas" I brought to my principal and supervisor during the first year in my career were not received well. There was a policy that essentially dragged out the referral process so much that it often took months to get all the paperwork signed to work with a kid. When I pointed this out and proposed streamlining the process, I was essentially shot down in a blaze of glory. They scoffed at my ideas and said that I wasn't the district lawyer, so I couldn't make such changes. The school system is often entrenched in the ways things have been done for ages, or district administrators are bound by their higher-ups and cannot make changes.

That being said, there are some things you can do to fight the monster tactfully. You can volunteer to be on leadership committees within your psychology department or at your school sites. These teams often strategize ways to make systemwide changes. One of my colleagues even formed a technology committee of psychologists to figure out a way to get rid of our 1960s card catalogue and automatically log reports by uploading them to a database. The team then presented the idea to the district technology department, and it is working on the new system. Sure, it may be a while before it comes to fruition, but it would never have come to fruition without the leadership in the psychology department.

The other way to tame the Bureaucracy Monster is to dance with it. Instead of complaining about the redundant paperwork for parents to sign for assessments and trying to fight the huge system, I just reframed my role. Once I saw myself as a Bureaucracy Monster expert, I figured out a way to streamline the process on my own and cut through the redundancy. I just had parents sign all three forms at once instead of individually sending each form, which the district policy "suggested." I was still getting the signatures, but just doing it more efficiently, and it worked out. The parents I worked with appreciated my cutting through the red tape, and it actually helped build rapport quickly. I often have all the forms I need handy for every occasion, so if a parent is in front of me, I have my arsenal of forms that he or she needs to sign so that I don't later have to waste my time getting signatures.

Another way to dance with the monster is to implement some of the organizational strategies outlined in this chapter—creating a Master Assessment Log, a Master Triennial Calendar, a weekly to-do list, and a daily priority list. Increasing your efficiency within an often inefficient system can be easier than fighting the inefficiency daily. I just use the stupid card catalogue system and make it fun by pretending I am in an episode of *Mad Men*, the television drama based on life in the 1960s.

That being said, if your district has policies that are unethical, then fight away. Just consult with your colleagues about the issue and decide how to proceed as a group so that you don't have to be the lone whistleblower. I was the lone ranger fighting an unethical policy once, and it did not go well! Often the problem you are seeing is universally recognized, and you might be able to make systemic changes as a group of psychologists.

## Key Points

- The Bureaucracy Monster is my name for the organizational, legal, and systemwide challenges that are often present in the daily life of a school psychologist. The challenges include redundant paperwork, lack of needed supplies and physical space to work, ineffective systems for referrals to intervention or special education assessment, strict timelines, and legal requirements for documenting work with students.
- One way to work within an ineffective school system is to develop your organizational skills. Traditional organizing and prioritizing principles such as "do what is more important first" don't always work for a school psychologist, because it is hard to decide which student is "more important."
- There are some basic principles of organization that will assist in streamlining the inefficiency in your school district. Creating tracking systems is a good place to start.

- Managing your assessment caseload will be easier if you create two documents: (1) a Master Assessment Log spreadsheet that tracks all the assessments you do throughout the year with important details and (2) a yearly Master Triennial Calendar that details when all your students are due for triennials.

- The Master Assessment Log serves as an organizational tool as well as a way to document your efforts to complete your assessments within legal timelines.

- The Master Triennial Calendar helps you plan your year so that you can spread out assessments more equally in each month, ensure that your triennial dates and annual IEP dates coincide, and guide your weekly and daily to-do lists.

- Documenting and keeping confidential files of your work with students for one-on-one counseling, check-ins, crisis counseling, and other interventions is just as important as documenting your assessments. Good documentation can often guide your intervention as well as protect you down the road if there are informal or legal inquiries about your work with a student.

- Consider creating a weekly to-do list that captures all your assessment activities, other roles, and administrative tasks across school sites in one "snapshot" piece of paper. Because your list is often a moving target depending on circumstance, you will have more flexibility in finishing tasks on your daily to-do list because you will have given yourself several options to choose from. Consider marking one or two "must-dos" from your daily to-do list and focusing on those.

- To the extent possible, spend the first two hours of your school day working in your primary role. In most cases, this role is assessment and report writing. Carving out a sacred two hours for testing and writing will help you make progress in your primary role, or the role that is most time sensitive.

- If you are not meeting your timelines, or anticipate that you will not be able to meet timelines no matter how efficiently you plan your days, do not be afraid to admit you are struggling. Seek consultation from your supervisor and strategize an action plan together.

## DISCUSSION QUESTIONS

1. Which systemwide issues most affect your job as a school psychologist? What does the Bureaucracy Monster look like in your school district? If you are not yet in a school district, what do you anticipate to be your greatest challenge in taming the Bureaucracy Monster?

2. What organizational tools do you already use that help you streamline paperwork and deal with inefficient systems in the schools? What tools in this chapter can you see working for you in your particular situation?

3. Flexibility is seen as a core strength for school psychologists. Do you agree? How can you foster your own flexibility?

4. How does your school district document, track, and store or file assessment referrals and assessments? Do you think any of the tools provided in this chapter could fit into the current system? If so, how do you see them being integrated into your job?

5. Do you see yourself as someone who fights the Bureaucracy Monster, or do you dance with it? Discuss any specific situations where you did one or the other, and the outcome for you and the students you work with.

chapter $\boxed{4}$

# INTERVENTION AND PREVENTION

Most days, when I arrive at a school site, I am greeted with a ton of little notes in my mailbox and several e-mails and calls from parents, teachers, and administrators asking for help with students. Some want me to check in with them because of a crisis, and many of them are requesting consultation or sending written requests about how to proceed with an assessment for special education for a student. In some schools where I have worked, the consultation step is skipped, and I arrive to find signed assessment plans for special education of students I have never worked with or heard about in meetings. In those situations, I have felt frustrated that someone has legally bound me to a sixty-day project without even checking in with me. Sound familiar? If not, consider yourself lucky. At some point in their careers, most school psychologists will have the experience of being so overwhelmed with assessments for special education that they have no time to step back and see why so many students are being considered for evaluation of disabilities in the first place.

School psychologists are frequently so busy putting out fires (that is, addressing the urgent concerns of students, teachers, and parents) that they have little time to "look at the wiring" of the school system for the purposes of preventing such fires from occurring. If you'll allow me to mix metaphors for a moment, school psychologists need practical strategies for stopping the flood of referrals for special education assessments so that student needs can be met before they are so far behind that they are considered "disabled." Flood or fire, having an impossible caseload of testing obligations is a disaster for a school psychologist trying to do his or her job effectively.

School psychologists and educators have long known that prevention and early intervention activities are the keys to reducing the incidence of school failure. Long before the term *Response to Intervention* came into our vernacular, we have known that prevention works. In the olden days of school psychology (you know, in the 1990s, when I started out), we borrowed from our public health friends and thought of prevention in three terms: primary prevention (everyone gets it), secondary prevention (a small group "at risk" gets it), and tertiary prevention (a group already experiencing challenges gets it). Now we are fancy and call it Tiers 1, 2, and 3, but the principle is the same: you get the most bang for your buck with prevention, or Tier 1 interventions. It's hard to imagine any other field in the helping professions where the focus is only on Tier 3, or tertiary interventions. What if medical professionals didn't give medical service to people to prevent heart attacks, only treating them when they were having actual heart attacks? What if dentists wouldn't give patients toothbrushes and toothpaste and then turned them away at the first sign of a cavity because they weren't eligible for help until the patients needed a root canal? Unfortunately, school psychologists often begin working with students only when they are experiencing the heart attack–root canal phase of learning problems.

So how can we do what we know is best for students, given our time constraints? A recent survey of school psychologists on the Notes from the School Psychologist blog showed that there is wide variety in how much of our time is spent in prevention and early intervention versus in special education evaluation. Some school psychologists are at school sites where they are fully embedded in an RtI framework, and their time is spent mostly in prevention and intervention. Others are employed by districts or assigned to schools where people have never heard of RtI, and the school psychologists are essentially "testing machines." This chapter is for psychologists on both ends of the spectrum, but in particular for those whose principals say, "Response to what?" when you ask when your school will be adopting a Response to Intervention framework. Chapter Five will outline roles within the RtI framework, and this chapter will describe ways to help your schools shift their lenses to a more prevention-oriented focus when thinking about ways to help all students achieve academically and thrive socially and emotionally.

## HOW TO BE PREVENTIVE WHEN YOU HAVE NO TIME

I can almost hear the collective "But *when* am I supposed to do all these great prevention activities when I am swamped with testing obligations and legal timelines?" I have been there, and I get it. The logistical challenges of becoming involved in prevention and early intervention activities when your primary role at the school site is testing for special education are common and feel overwhelming. However, there are ways to infuse a prevention mind-set into your daily work that will actually help reduce your testing caseload.

### Being Effective on Leadership and Prereferral Intervention Teams

Each school has a team of professionals whose purpose is to organize and improve service delivery at their site. Some of these teams are schoolwide support teams, and some are student-focused support teams. At the schoolwide level, they are sometimes called RtI teams, positive behavioral intervention support (PSIS) teams, leadership teams, building intervention teams, instructional support teams, coordinated services teams, or care teams. Student-focused teams are most commonly referred to as student support teams or child study teams, though I have heard such variations as student success teams, student study teams, and student support committees. Sometimes there is one team that is responsible for both schoolwide and student-focused interventions. Regardless of the name of the teams at your schools, what distinguishes these teams is typically the level of focus—school or student.

## Schoolwide Support Teams

The basic function of these teams is to look at the school and student achievement from a systems perspective and put schoolwide supports, policies, and programs into place. Some examples of schoolwide team interventions include revising the school's discipline policy, starting an anti-bullying campaign, bringing in a program for targeting writing skills aimed at the entire student body, adopting a new curriculum for students below benchmark in reading, or developing a system to support teachers who are having classroom management difficulties.

I have found it very useful to sit in on these meetings once a month to hear what is going on and to consult with team members about research on child development, principles of learning, research-based instructional strategies, positive school cultures, or how to effectively track students and work with data. You may or may not have time to actually assist in the implementation of the programs put in place, but you will be able to provide the invaluable service of helping the team find developmentally appropriate and research-supported programs and policies. You will also likely be in the valuable role of advocating for the use of data and assessment to drive policy and program decisions. Schools need to make decisions based on data—not on whims. Is the current curriculum working? What are the referral rates for suspension compared to other similar schools? And so on. You can be helpful in looking at assessment data, choosing appropriate assessments, or doing an assessment audit with administrators. With data, you are all saving a lot of time that might have been spent "thinking," "feeling," and "guessing" about how students are doing.

You can also start using the lingo of RtI at these meetings to lay the groundwork for future change. The RtI pyramid graphic (Figure 4.1), probably old hat to you, can be a useful consultation tool at these meetings. Some of my schoolwide support teams have looked at the blank pyramid and filled in all the services we have at our schools for each tier. At other schools, we have made a giant poster of the RtI pyramid and kept it posted for us to change and reference as a team. This process helps us identify gaps and overlaps in our service delivery model. For example, we may have many social-emotional and behavioral interventions, but not as many academic interventions, or we may have very few Tier 1 programs. We may also find that we have a large gap in services for English Language Learners or other populations at our school. Having the graphic and using the language of RtI helps teams focus on the big picture of service delivery and use data to drive decisions, and the school psychologist is a key consultant in that process.

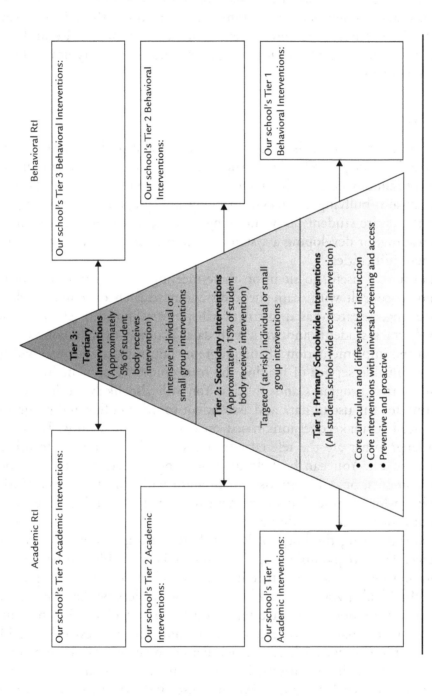

**FIGURE 4.1.** Response to Intervention Pyramid

*Source:* Adapted from *The Essential Guide to RTI* (fig. 2.1), by S. L. DeRuvo, 2010, San Francisco: Jossey-Bass.

## Student-Focused Support Teams

When the unit of analysis is a student rather than a whole school, it is very likely that the topic of special education assessment will come up at some point. This is one of the most important reasons why it is advisable to serve on the student-focused support team at your school site. Participation on this team will reduce (though not necessarily eliminate) the surprise assessment plan in your mailbox. For example, when I receive signed assessment plans (or written requests for an assessment plan) for special education testing, I often discover upon review of the files a variety of reasons why it was premature to generate a special education referral—the student was already assessed a year ago and didn't qualify; the student is on honor roll and is unlikely to need remediation; there have been no interventions in the general education environment; or the student needs help, but that help can perhaps be delivered in general education with accommodations.

The degree to which you are involved in the prereferral meetings will often determine how much control you have over the referrals that come your way. I know it can be hard to attend all student support team meetings, but an hour spent talking with teachers and parents can save you hours of cleaning up after an inappropriate referral or hours of unneeded testing and report writing. For example, I attend a 7:00 AM meeting once a week at one of my sites. Sure, I'd rather not get up and get to work that early! However, when I miss those meetings, I tend to get students referred for testing prematurely, or when I review the notes from the meeting, the interventions and supports generated are not meaningful or do not address the real issue for the student. Attending these meetings to consult about ways to access supports and interventions for the student without jumping to special education referral as the "intervention" is an hour well spent. If I have my coffee, I am usually able to guide the team toward appropriate interventions and to curtail inappropriate referrals. I have also been able to advocate for students who really need to move forward for assessment, and consult with parents who are reluctant to have their child tested.

Although the focus of this section is on stemming the tide of referrals, it is not to say that doing so is the entire goal of your participation in student support teams. The goal is to focus the team on effective, targeted intervention before jumping straight to trying to label a child as having a disability. I know that stemming the tide of referrals for special education has a "gatekeeper" feel to it, but it is an important gate to keep. At each of these meetings, you should be asking the team, "If we had a label for the child's challenges, would that change our intervention?" Often the team is just seeking help for the child to make progress, and you can facilitate the generation of intervention ideas. Your job is to help parents, teachers, and administrators make a mental shift from "There is something wrong with the student—figure out what it is and label it" to "There is something wrong with the match of curriculum, environment, or instruction, and we can alter it." Most people in the field of education believe in the internal model—that there is something wrong with the child. This is not helpful, as we do not have control over the child's disabling condition. But we can change the curriculum, instruction, or environment to match the student's needs, no matter the label.

So how do we as school psychologists focus the team on developing appropriate interventions without automatically jumping to special education assessment? There are many ways to help parents, teachers, and support staff use the early intervention lens for helping students. Here are some key questions to bring up at these meetings:

1. How long has this been a problem for the student?
   o Sometimes, particularly at the secondary level, we get so wrapped up in what is happening right now for the child that we forget the long view. Bring the student's cumulative folder to the meeting. This will help you see if this is a historical problem or a new problem. For example, if attention and focus issues are not mentioned in early report cards and emerge in middle school, then you have some clues about whether it is a pervasive or situational problem.
   o Review prior teacher comments and benchmark assessments on the report cards to see if there is a pattern of strength and weakness, or if challenges escalated over time.
2. What clues are there in the records about other reasons, besides a disability, for the student's challenges?
   o Review the student's second language acquisition assessments to see if his or her challenges academically or behaviorally may be related to difficulties with understanding and using English.
   o Review the records for attendance issues or bring a printout of the student's attendance record to determine whether poor attendance is contributing to the child's difficulties.
   o Ask the parents questions about the student's developmental, medical, and family history. If the referral is academic, then this can usually be done in the meeting. If the referral is social-emotional-behavioral, it is usually a more sensitive area to discuss. Make another appointment with the parents to discuss the history or ask if they can stay for a few moments after the meeting to discuss it. Then, if the student's case does move forward for assessment, you will already have some developmental information for your report and have built some rapport with the parents. Another option is to send the developmental history home with the invitation to the meeting. Chapter Six has a template for a brief but detailed developmental history that can be used.
3. What is the history of intervention?
   o Use the cumulative folder as a starting point for tracking interventions that have been tried already to help address the problem. Focus on the data, not the narrative. For example, if there is an intervention in the folder that is described as "Provided one-on-one assistance in reading," you would want to ask what was done during that one-on-one time and if it was implemented with fidelity.
   o Review the prior academic assessments done with the student (for example, standardized test scores, benchmark assessments, districtwide assessments) for patterns in the data.
   o If there is a social-emotional-behavioral challenge, what interventions have already been tried (for example, counseling, behavior support plans, teacher consultation) and for what duration? What was the outcome or effectiveness of these interventions? Were they implemented with fidelity?

o Ask pointed questions about what has been effective for supporting the student in the past. Sometimes we get so focused on the problem that we forget to identify strategies that have been successful that can be tapped into again. Also, to generate intervention ideas, ask the current teacher what has worked for him with other students he has taught who have similar differences.

4. What is the child's special education assessment history?

o Sometimes the child has already been assessed for special education and did not qualify for services. The psychoeducational report will often not be in the cumulative folder because it is confidential. There may or may not be an Individualized Education Plan (IEP) copy in the folder depending on how efficient your staff is with filing these in the cumulative folder. You may have to research the assessment history in the district's confidential special education or psychological services files or computer records to determine which students have been assessed before.

o Do not rely on parent report alone about whether or not a child has already been assessed. Sometimes children were assessed, but parents don't remember that it was for special education or didn't attend the IEP meeting. I've found that sometimes prior psychologists and teachers never use the term "special education assessment," so the parents don't know that the "screening for learning challenges" or similar euphemism was actually testing for special education.

o Be cautious about how notes are taken at this meeting. From Chapter Three we learned the documentation mantra: if you don't write it down, it didn't happen. The opposite is also true: if you write it down, it happened. If a note taker writes "special education assessment?" or "Attention Deficit Disorder?" as a concern or an action item, that can be considered legally binding, because then you have an area of suspected disability documented right there for a lawyer to see years later, enabling her to call the district negligent according to the child-find clause of IDEA. (The child-find clause states, basically, that a district is responsible for assessing students who have an area of suspected disability that may be impacting their academic performance.)

o Coach the meeting note takers to document the discussion about assessment carefully. For example, I tell them that instead of writing "special education?" as the intervention, they should write, "School psychologist will research if child has had prior assessment for special education and report back to team at follow-up" or "Team will review data to determine if special education referral is appropriate at this time and report back to team at follow-up meeting." Instead of their noting "Attention Deficit Disorder?" have them write, "Parent will take student to pediatrician to discuss possible Attention Deficit Disorder assessment referral" or "School psychologist will observe student during writing instruction for issues of focus, and take a baseline of time on task compared to a similar peer." Write what the *actual* action item is, not just the topic. Then people know what we all agreed to do at that time and how decisions about moving forward with testing or not moving forward were made.

It may be the case that your main role in the student support team meetings is to help the team use a wide lens when looking at a child's difficulties. You may also have a role in explaining data to them. (For example, a standardized score in the 50th percentile does not mean the same as an F or 50 percent on a test.) You can also guide them to factors other than a disability that could be causing challenges, help track data and interventions, and document discussions effectively.

The fact remains that the main purpose of these meetings is to develop actual interventions for struggling students, whether those interventions are in the general or special education realm. You also serve an important role in providing expertise on which academic and social-emotional-behavioral interventions would be most helpful to the student. Whether or not you actually help deliver the intervention will depend on many factors, but at minimum, guiding the team toward proactive and research-based intervention is important.

## DEVELOPING AND SUPPORTING ACADEMIC INTERVENTIONS

Regardless of their name or personnel makeup, all student-focused support teams involve brainstorming intervention ideas for struggling students. Many referred students need direct instruction in reading, writing, math, or study skills, and they need it delivered one-on-one or in a small group. Everyone on the team is likely to agree that these students need direct academic support. What people may disagree on or even shy away from is who will deliver this intensive academic support. The meeting often comes to a standstill when the team must decide who is responsible for implementing an academic intervention. I remember at one of my schools with limited resources, the "Who will implement the intervention?" part of the meeting was always met with a moment of silence, and the note taker would hold the pen above the notes, waiting expectantly for someone to respond.

At many school sites, there are very few academic interventions, or the academic interventions are delivered in a whole group setting, such as in an intervention class. This model of service delivery may work for some students, but many struggling students need more focused intervention. At other school sites, there are many targeted interventions, and it is an easy task to write in the type of support the student needs and actually provide it. Either way, we school psychologists are resourceful people, and an important part of our job is marshalling our resources to connect students with appropriate interventions. You can use the following tips to facilitate academic intervention for students:

1. Start your own personal resource binder of interventions and bring it to meetings to reference. (Or better yet, develop a resource binder with your team to empower all team members to be experts in interventions and supports.)
   o Make tabs in the binder for common academic challenges, and file the intervention information there. Some examples of section headings might be Reading/Decoding, Reading Comprehension, Math Calculation, Math Reasoning, Writing, Spelling, Homework Routines, Oral Language, Listening Comprehension, and English Language Learning. You could also make sections based on the RtI pyramid of interventions (for example, Tier 1 academics, Tier 1 behavior, Tier 2 academics, and so on) that your team has generated in the schoolwide support team meetings.

o Collect handouts for parents that explain or address these areas of need. The Web site of the National Association of School Psychologists (www.nasponline.org) is a good place to start with parent- and teacher-friendly handouts.

o Research free tutoring and academic support Web sites for parents and students to access. Develop a handout of the Web sites to provide to parents at the meeting for their reference.

o Have your school-specific RtI pyramid handy so that you can reference any Tier 1 or Tier 2 interventions that are available on-site for students (for example, math or reading programs the school has purchased, intervention classes, tutoring or homework help, peer tutoring, and the like).

o Research community-based organizations that provide tutoring. If you work with low-income populations, you might want to research low-cost or free programs for families.

o Contact a local university's school psychology or teacher preparation program and ask if their students need volunteer hours in the schools. If you're ambitious, you could train a small cadre of volunteers to deliver or support an academic intervention or provide homework assistance to students after school.

2. Familiarize yourself with the school's academic curriculum, assessments, and programs.

o Go through the curriculum with a few teachers at different grade levels so that you will know what is expected of students at each developmental level. Observe a few lessons and be familiar with what the benchmark assessments measure so that you will understand results when they are presented at meetings.

o Ask teachers if there are any supplemental materials for the curriculum that can be used as an intervention or a resource for parents or tutors to supplement instruction at home.

o Ask teachers about the assessments that accompany the curriculum and what type of information they provide. Ask teachers how they address content that is missed or misunderstood.

o Keep up-to-date with statewide changes in curriculum. When there are changes statewide, you will need to know if there are accompanying changes in expectations for students at each grade level in addition to the curriculum changes.

## DEVELOPING AND SUPPORTING SOCIAL, EMOTIONAL, AND BEHAVIORAL INTERVENTIONS

Another key role for the school psychologist in the student-focused meeting is to support students who are struggling behaviorally, socially, or emotionally. In addition to providing consultation about normative developmental challenges (for example, adolescents are striving for autonomy and independence and may challenge authority), the school psychologist serves as a consultant for connecting students, parents, and teachers to additional supports. Again, whether or not you will be delivering the service or facilitating the referral process, it is helpful to be prepared with a range of interventions that support the struggling student. The following tips may be useful when the referral question is in the social-emotional-behavioral domain:

1. Add tabs in the academic resource binder for social-emotional-behavioral challenges.
   o Make tabs for common challenges, such as anxiety, bullying, oppositional behavior, depression, study skills, test anxiety, divorce, grief, witnessing violence, gay and lesbian identity issues, acculturation issues, and school refusal. Include handouts that have tips for parents and teachers on how to modify the child's environment to support her with her challenges.
   o Collect handouts and useful Web site URLs (for example, support groups, informational Web sites) to distribute to parents and teachers. Again, the Web site of the National Association of School Psychologists is a good place to start for topic-specific handouts.
   o Evaluate your school's Tier 1 interventions for social-emotional and behavioral support (for example, schoolwide anti-bullying programs, social skills training) and accompanying assessments that may give information about the student's response to primary prevention activities.
   o Reference your school's RtI pyramid for Tier 2 and Tier 3 interventions available at your school site (for example, group counseling, peer counseling, individual counseling, participation in a mentoring program).
   o If the student is in a classroom where many of the students are having behavioral challenges, the issue may be better addressed by consulting with the teacher about classroom management and developing a classwide intervention. It may be the case that the student is acting the same way as his or her classmates, due to an unstructured or uncontrolled classroom environment. This can be the "elephant in the room," and it should be dealt with delicately. Chapter Eight on consultation provides some strategies for effectively consulting with teachers about classroom management.
2. Consult with the team about typical developmental reactions.
   o Sometimes teams can inadvertently pathologize normal development. It might be normal for a kindergartner to have some initial transition difficulties or for a student who has witnessed violence to show signs of inattention in the classroom, for example.
   o Sometimes teachers and parents have developmental expectations that are too high, and the child is reacting to the mismatch. (For example, most five-year-olds cannot sit in circle time or complete a worksheet quietly in their seats for thirty-five minutes.)
   o On the flip side, when a student's reaction to a crisis or situation is not typical in the developmental continuum (for example, regressive behaviors), then the school psychologist can consult about the next level of appropriate intervention.
3. Involve yourself in behavioral interventions.
   o School psychologists often have a wealth of knowledge about behavior management and developing positive behavior support plans. Whether a child is in special or general education, you can facilitate the team's development of a clear behavior plan for students experiencing behavioral challenges.
   o Helping the team focus on *one or two* specific behaviors to begin targeting for intervention may be the first step. Sometimes teams want to take on too much, and that sets the kid up for failure. We need to set behavioral goals that are specific, measurable, and within our reach.

o You can use tools from Chapters Seven on the IEP for developing behavior plans, and tools from Chapter Eight on consultation for gaining consensus and buy-in among team members for those plans.

o Sometimes students just need a point person with whom to check in every day before school, before recess, or after school to remind them of their behavioral goals. Identify staff members who might be able to fill this role and train them on how to do an effective "check-in" or "checkout." If you are at one school site or if the child can probably handle weekly check-ins, then you might be able to volunteer to fill this role.

4. Involve yourself in counseling services.

o Whether or not you have the time or role definition to do counseling is school, district, and state specific. Some school psychologists are contracted to provide counseling services as a direct instructional service on the IEP, or their schools have contracted extra hours for counseling time. Some school psychologists are not allowed to do counseling per state regulations, and some school psychologists are not trained or interested in having a counseling role. If counseling is a part of your role, Chapters Nine and Ten will be useful to you in developing your approach, managing your caseload, and monitoring student progress.

o When you cannot deliver counseling services or your school site does not have any counseling support, harness your inner social worker and look for community-based organizations that may be available. Make a list of all the free, low-cost, or sliding-scale organizations near your school for a reference. Call the agencies first and learn about their eligibility criteria before you refer a family. Accessing mental health services can sometimes be a lengthy and confusing process when it interacts with insurance companies and other social services programs. It is best if you have at least a basic understanding of the referral process so that you don't inadvertently send a family to an agency that can't help them.

o Begin to gather names of individual mental health providers in the community whom you respect and have found to be collaborative with schools. This way, if parents can pay for counseling and want a recommendation, you are stacking the deck for a collaborative endeavor between the provider and school. The more the provider understands the school system, the better. Provide two or three different names and contact information to the families so that they have a few options to choose from.

o Consult with your schoolwide intervention team about the possibility of bringing in a school-based mental health provider from a community organization. You may be able to involve yourself in writing a grant for your school to bring in outside support, or consult with your principal and key decision makers about the type of counseling support that is most needed.

## DEVELOPING YOUR OWN PREVENTION ACTIVITIES AND PROGRAMS

In addition to offering specific academic and social-emotional-behavioral interventions for particular students, you may also be able to involve yourself in more general prevention activities at your school site.

For parents, you can develop presentations on normative topics such as school readiness, homework routines, and supporting independent learning in adolescence, or on topics parents may be interested in for the student experiencing challenges, such as parenting a struggling reader, helping children with test anxiety, or dealing with bullying behavior. I have hosted evening workshops on topics of interest generated by the PTA or school leadership teams, such as bullying. I have also facilitated book club meetings for parents on hot new books on topics in child development. These evening workshops were helpful for disseminating information about child development as well as linking parents up to other parents for support. You may also be able to partner with another school staff member (for example, school counselor, intervention specialist, or teacher) to conduct presentations or ongoing support groups on a topic of interest to the school community.

Hosting professional development activities for staff in-service meetings is another way to disseminate information about how to prevent difficulties in your school population. Topics might include reaching students with special needs, classroom management, principles of learning and behavior, disability-specific information and interventions, understanding a psychoeducational report, supporting social-emotional growth, and fostering an inclusive classroom. You may even survey the school staff about topics that they would be interested in knowing more about and tailor your professional development to their needs. You don't have to do it alone, either! You can create a professional development workshop with another interested psychologist in your district and present it to a few schools to get the most out of your hard work. Or you can recruit a staff member at your school, such as a special education teacher or social worker, to collaborate with you. You can then establish yourself as a "go-to" resource for staff members on the presentation topic(s) to facilitate ongoing professional development, coaching, and training.

## COMMON PITFALLS AND WHAT TO DO ABOUT THEM

Being an active member of schoolwide and student-specific support teams is a great way to advocate for prevention and early intervention services. You may even be able to participate in some of the service delivery, depending on your situation. The degree to which your school is open to your ideas about prevention will vary depending on the leadership, staff, and school culture. I have worked in schools that have taken to prevention ideas like ducks to water; at other schools, I'm in a constant battle to explain that special education shouldn't be the go-to intervention for every struggling student.

### When Special Education Intervention Is the Only Game in Town

At resource-strained schools, it can be an unfortunate reality that the only "intervention" for academic and emotional support is special education. And when special education is the only game in town, your referrals skyrocket: every struggling student is sent to be evaluated, just in case he or she may qualify for that special attention and legally mandated monitoring and case management. This is not a sustainable way to deliver services at a school. It also puts you in the horrible position of being seen as a gatekeeper for interventions. At times, you may find yourself "gatekeeping" to avoid involving the child in what would be an ineffective intervention—at many school sites, special education is not always the best way to address students needs. So what do you do?

- Take the time to develop the resource binder. The more outside resources you have, the more you will have to offer at student support meetings as an alternative to special education testing.
- Be creative in getting outside support for your school. There may be a cadre of high school or college volunteers out there who need hours for internships that could be fulfilled by being tutors. Research your district's policies and procedures for volunteers and help facilitate the process of getting them on board working with students.
- Develop relationships with community-based organizations by visiting them and talking to their directors or outreach coordinators about opportunities for collaboration.
- Take a hint from our social worker friends and be the great connector for families and services. Often there are services out there, but the families need assistance in being connected to them.
- Adopt the mantra, "With every no, give them a yes." This is easier to do if you have your resource binder, outside referral base, and RtI pyramid of interventions at your school site. So instead of "No, we are not moving forward with a special education referral; thanks for coming," you get to say, "No, we are not moving forward with a special education referral, but yes, let's do X, Y, and Z to support the student."

## When Your School Is Sending You Inappropriate Referrals

A referral may be "inappropriate" for a variety of reasons: the student was already assessed, there is no area of suspected disability, the student is already meeting grade-level standards, or the student has not yet been given any intervention in the general education environment. The reasons staff send you inappropriate referrals can vary. Teachers and administrators may not yet be trained in the process, or they don't understand why certain referrals are accepted and others are not. In these cases, adopt the informational approach. Educate the staff on special education law and district procedures that follow that law. Validate their frustration that in districts that have not adopted the RtI framework, the process can seem like a "wait to fail" model of service delivery. Build relationships and rapport with those who are repeat offenders in sending inappropriate referrals your way. They probably are just seeking help for the child and heard somewhere to "just get the parent to put the request in writing" and the child will get an assessment. I once worked with a counselor who had a template on her computer for parents to fill in requesting an assessment, and whenever any parent even brought up the topic, she printed it out for them to sign; then our legal timeline started for following up with an assessment plan or a letter declining the testing request. In some cases, when I contacted the parents, they actually just wanted tutoring. Our school looked super-uncoordinated because one staff member was "approving" testing and the other denying it. I worked hard to consult with this counselor about the difference between support and special education and how to handle parent requests in the future, and that put a stop to the flood of referrals from her office.

Now it is quite another story if your staff knows the policy and procedures and tries to circumvent the process anyway. I have even had a teacher steal an assessment plan from my office and fill it out for the parent to sign behind my back! After my rage subsided, I was able to have a conversation with this teacher. She didn't do it again once I said to her, "I would never legally bind you to a three-month project without consulting you first. Please afford me the same professional courtesy."

If you have repeat offenders, particularly your principal, who has a lot of power and status in the school, then you will want to try to handle it "in house" first. Talk with the principal about the bind it puts you in when you have inappropriate referrals, and try to come up with an agreement about which students move forward for assessment and which do not. If you can't resolve this situation informally, you may need to consult with your supervisor about how to handle it. I have had supervisors come with me to work it out with principals and help them understand that there is a reason for the process. Sure, it's not a comfortable situation to be in, but sometimes it has to happen. Let's hope that most of you will not have to take it to that level and that educating your staff will be sufficient for developing a procedure for referrals.

## PULLING IT ALL TOGETHER

School psychologists often operate from within a prevention and early intervention framework, but work in schools where there isn't systemic support for intervening early to prevent school failure. Even in the absence of schoolwide supports for prevention and early intervention, you can infuse your workdays with consultation and activities that support students before they are so behind academically or so impaired emotionally that they are suspected of being disabled and in need of a special education assessment. By involving yourself in schoolwide and student-specific support meetings, you can be a partner in developing and harnessing resources for a student through general education and community supports. Intervening early and with fidelity not only is the best practice but may also have the added benefit of reducing your testing caseload for special education services.

---

### Key Points

- As a school psychologist, you are in the unique role of providing prevention, early intervention, assessment, and remediation of school problems for children. The proportion of time spent in each of these roles varies among schools, districts, and states.
- Research on the importance of primary prevention and early intervention serves to support current policies for Response to Intervention (RtI). However, your

---

school sites will vary in terms of their degree of familiarity with RtI and their phase of RtI implementation.

- For school sites where RtI has not been introduced or is in the very early stages, you may have a heavy caseload of referrals for special education. If you can involve yourself in prevention and early intervention at your school sites, you will be implementing best practices as well as possibly reducing your assessment caseload.
- The main way for you to be involved in prevention and early intervention is to serve as a consultant and participant on schoolwide and student-specific support teams.
- On schoolwide support teams, you can introduce and expose staff to RtI and the associated vocabulary in order to build a common language as well as to consult about system-level interventions that follow best practices and research about child development.
- On student-specific support teams, you have multiple roles: consultant, facilitator, educator, and advocate. In these roles, you can ask key questions to home in on the developmental nature of the problem as well as guide the team toward research-based interventions. You can bring the child's cumulative records and a resource binder to meetings in order to provide school- or community-based resources to support the student academically or socially, emotionally, and behaviorally.
- Depending on how you have to allocate your time, you may also be able to provide direct service to students. Some school psychologists provide counseling, behavioral support and check-ins, and consultation to parents and teachers about how best to work with a student. At times, school psychologists are involved in the data-tracking aspect of academic interventions in collaboration with the staff members who provide the actual intervention.
- You are also well positioned to provide workshops to families and professional development trainings to school staff on topics in child development and learning. These can serve as important prevention and education opportunities at your school sites.
- Common challenges in being preventive and intervening early for a struggling student include lack of intervention services and resources at your school, and dealing with staff who try to bypass or do not understand referral procedures for special education assessment. You can educate staff as well as collect outside resources for your schools as ways to take on these challenges. Doing so can result in a smaller assessment caseload, which in turn opens your schedule up for even more prevention and early intervention activities.

# DISCUSSION QUESTIONS

1. What does the service delivery model look like at your school(s)? To what degree have RtI principles made their way into your school culture?

2. How much of your time is currently spent in prevention activities, intervention activities, and special education testing? Are you satisfied with the proportions of your activities? If not, what is your ideal? What kinds of activities outlined in this chapter can you realistically see yourself engaging in to be more preventive?

3. What is the referral process for special education at your school? Is there common understanding of the process? If not, what can you do to educate staff and parents about the process?

4. Do you agree with the process for how students are referred to you? What changes would you make systemwide for improvement in the referral process for special education? What is one specific activity or action item you could do right away to improve the referral process?

5. What are a few topics about which you could see yourself making a presentation to a parent group or to a school staff? What is the area of need at your school in terms of systemwide education about a topic in child development or learning? Who can you identify in your school or among your colleagues to assist you in developing a presentation?

6. What activities do you now engage in that you see as preventive? What advice would you give to other school psychologists about how to make time for prevention?

# chapter 5

# RESPONSE TO INTERVENTION (RTI)

## Changing Your Role from Special Education Gatekeeper to Keymaster of Interventions

Anyone who has been at an IEP meeting where a student doesn't qualify for services but really needs an intervention knows that this is an uncomfortable place to be. In reality, school psychologists are often the ones who analyze the data and determine eligibility, even if it is supposed to be a "team decision." The fact is, in districts where the traditional model of eligibility is still in place (for example, the "discrepancy model" of SLD), you are often put in the position where you have to say ridiculous things that are counter to common sense and research, such as "The student is not significantly behind enough to qualify for help." The elephant in the room for school psychologists is also that sometimes, special education isn't all that great an intervention. Special education is good only to the degree that the special educator is a good teacher, goal setter, progress monitor, and intervention specialist. As I noted in Chapter Four, in some situations we are actually "gatekeeping" to prevent students from receiving an ineffective intervention, but are seen as the ones who are preventing the student from getting needed help.

This is where Response to Intervention (RtI) comes to save the day! It sounds so beautiful . . . solving problems, collaborating, setting goals, intervening, tracking progress, adjusting the intervention, monitoring progress regularly and consistently, and setting new goals to support the student, all without calling him or her "disabled." With RtI, we move the deficit out of the child and see the problem as a mismatch of curriculum, environment, and instruction. I can almost hear the prevention and intervention angels singing. And then my image of singing angels disappears, and I'm back to reality: RtI has its pitfalls too. A recent poll of readers of the Notes from the School Psychologist Blog Facebook page brought several problems to the surface: implementing RtI requires a *huge* mental shift for general education staff; the schools often grossly overestimate how much prevention and data-based decision making they do; people confuse tracking progress with implementing an intervention; the fidelity of the intervention is not always clear; or, worse yet, there isn't funding for the interventions needed. When the interventions are not implemented well, it can seem as though we exchanged a "wait to fail" model for a "watch them fail" model.

Historically, special education and general education have worked in separate spheres, but, thankfully, there is a movement toward inclusion, collaboration, coteaching, and joint problem solving. With RtI, the frame for working with students with challenges is moving away from a "my student–your student" mind-set to an "our student" one. To special educators and school psychologists, RtI makes sense because we love data, operationalizing behavior and goals, progress monitoring, and intervening early and with fidelity. That these all make a positive difference in a child's education is supported by an immense amount of research. The challenge is that because RtI is a general education function, not a special education function, and there is no systemic process outlined in the regulations for how to implement it, the role of the school psychologist and special educators in the process is amorphous at best. In those states and districts who are light-years ahead of others in the implementation of RtI, school psychologists' roles are more established and defined.

The degree to which the RtI framework is implemented varies from state to state, district to district, and even school to school. Your role in RtI may depend on the stage of implementation at which your school or district is currently functioning. You might be in the exploration or early implementation phase, or you might have progressed to a phase where RtI has been up and running for a while, and the staff are now making ongoing improvements. Chapter Four discussed the role of the school psychologist in the exploration phase of RtI. This chapter focuses on some of the challenges that arise once RtI is being implemented at your school, and some practical resources and suggestions for overcoming these challenges. For a state-by-state breakdown of where your state is in the implementation of RtI, check out the National Center on Response to Intervention at http://state.rti4success.org/index.php?option=com_chart.

## SCHOOL PSYCHOLOGISTS' ROLES IN RTI

So how can we facilitate and support the tectonic mind shift required to change the perception of school psychologists as special education assessors and gatekeepers to one of our being "keymasters" (or keymistresses!) of effective, data-based interventions? How do we get staff to see that RtI is just good teaching and that we shouldn't be thinking of RtI as a process with an end-goal of getting a child into special education? We need to be involved on many levels, as champions of the principles of RtI and as keymasters of interventions and data-based decision making. How do you get started?

First, enthusiasm can be contagious. Bring out your inner cheerleader. If you are enthusiastic, hopeful, and have "bought-in" to the principles of RtI, you are more likely to be able to "sell it" to your staff. This is not a one-time sales pitch! You will find yourself having the same conversation day in and day out to facilitate understanding about what RtI is and what it is not. The National Research Center on Learning Disabilities (NRCLD) has a great Web site full of materials explaining the core principles of RtI, ways to implement RtI, and case examples of the interplay between RtI and SLD identification (www.nrcld.org). It is a great place to start orienting yourself to the core features of RtI. In its manual *Responsiveness to Intervention (RTI): How to Do It* (Johnson, Mellard, Fuchs, & McKnight, 2006), the NRCLD identifies the core principles of effective RtI:

- High-quality, scientifically based classroom instruction
- Student assessment with classroom focus
- Schoolwide screening of academics and behavior
- Continuous progress monitoring of students
- Implementation of appropriate research-based interventions
- Progress monitoring during interventions (effectiveness)
- Teaching behavior fidelity measures

Your job as a school psychologist cheerleader for RtI is to know these principles and identify ways to get involved with the key stakeholders in RtI to be a champion for them. You also have a role in evaluating the degree to which your RtI program is meeting these core principles. For example, you might find a role for yourself as someone who can conduct an "assessment audit." I have found that there are many assessments being used at my school sites. Some are district mandated, and some are grassroots, teacher-driven assessments. In some cases, schoolwide assessments are conducted in a perfunctory manner, and absolutely nothing is done with the data. In other cases, the data are used right away for making adjustments in instruction. Being an assessment expert yourself, you might volunteer to do an assessment audit of your school and look at the following information:

- What district assessments are used?
- What classroom assessments are used?
- What type of information does each assessment give us (for example, about phonological processing skills, reading fluency skills, reading comprehension, math calculation, math reasoning)?
- Are there gaps in the assessment (for example, a reading assessment that measures phonological awareness and reading fluency, but does not give information about reading comprehension)?
- Do we have universal academic and social-emotional screenings?

- What is the purpose of each assessment (for example, screening, summative data, progress monitoring)?
- What are we currently doing with the data?
- What improvements are necessary in our assessment process?
- What questions do we want to answer with our data? (For example, What is our daily attendance rate? What percentage of freshmen are failing core courses? What are the "hot spots" in our school for behavior problems?)

Conducting an assessment audit is just one example of how a school psychologist might take on one part of RtI, focus in on one core principle, and take a leadership position on advocating for improvements. Depending on your time frame, you may also serve as a general consultant and cheerleader for all the core principles. This is where your consultation skills come into play. (See Chapter Eight for tips on how to be an effective consultant in the schools.)

In addition to being a cheerleader for the core principles of RtI, you may also find yourself in a role of explaining to the larger school community what RtI is and how it works. Your school district may already have produced materials that explain RtI to parents. If it hasn't, then you might find yourself having to explain RtI in parent-friendly language. There are a number of online resources for disseminating information about RtI to parents. For example, NRCLD offers a handout to parents called "The ABCs of RtI," a guide to understanding RtI in reading that is free to download at www.nrcld .org/free/downloads/ABC_of_RTI.pdf.

Another role that you may find yourself in is that of keymaster or keymistress of data-based intervention. Fortunately, school psychologists know data. This is one of our areas of expertise. We can be of great service to our colleagues in the RtI process by modeling, consulting, and interpreting data alongside them. I personally just love data. I love them even more if I can put them in a snazzy little graph to show people trend lines (nerd alert!). The good news is, RtI gives me the opportunity to work with data and train teachers and staff on how to interpret data for decision making. Be still, my nerdy heart!

## ACADEMIC RTI: DATA-BASED DECISION MAKING

There are a number of ways that school psychologists are involved in academic RtI. Some roles you may take on include consulting about Tier 1 interventions, conducting and interpreting schoolwide assessment data, and consulting about how to track individual students' progress.

### Tier 1 Interventions

The first step in effective data-based decision making in academic RtI is to know your core curriculum and data. You might start by looking at the core curriculum and instruction and at the accompanying assessments for the entire student body. For example, if 80 percent of students are below proficient in reading, RtI teams will be lost in doing individual interventions, because there isn't enough time or resources. It makes more sense to look at the curriculum or the school's instruction and implementation of the curriculum. School psychologists can help in this process by continually consulting about the "big picture" and helping team members focus the majority of their efforts on Tier 1 interventions. One way to consult about curriculum is to research instructional programs and their efficacy. Although you probably won't be able to change your school's curriculum, you may be able to play a role in exploring options available to your school if curricular changes are in the works or there are opportunities for selecting additional interventions. For example, the National Center on RtI has research on the efficacy of different reading interventions; see www.rti4success.org/instructionTools for a review of reading instructional programs.

## Developing Individual Intervention Plans and Data-Tracking Tools

Perhaps through your assessment audit, you may have discovered the key pieces of data you will have to work with as you track student progress. Depending on your school, you may have a standardized curriculum-based measurement program already in place, such as the Dynamic Indicators of Basic Early Literacy Skills (DIBELS) tracking system (https://dibels.uoregon.edu/) or AIMSweb, a computer program for benchmarking and progress monitoring that reports out results to parents, teachers, and administrators on the Web (www.aimsweb.com/). There are a number of online tools for data tracking. A good summary of these tools is available on the RtI Wire Web site: www.jimwright online.com/php/rti/rti_wire_5Jan06.php. Your school may also have its own common assessments or curriculum-based measures.

In order to integrate all the data sources, your school staff may also be interested in developing their own individual student tracking form that is specific to your school's needs. If you decide to develop your own form, there are a few key elements you will want to be sure to include:

1. *Problem statement and assessment data.* This statement should be a concise description of the area of academic or behavioral concern. The statement should be quantitative and data based, and it should possibly include peer comparison (for example, Student is scoring X on assessment where class average is Y or same-age peer is scoring Y). Include assessment data from district assessments as well as classroom-based assessments to serve as baselines.

2. *Strengths.* Identify student strengths that can be capitalized on or built on, using data if available.

3. *Goal(s).* Like IEP goals, intervention plan goals should be "SMART": **S**pecific, **M**easurable, **A**ttainable, **R**ealistic, and **T**ime bound. Also include the expected rate of improvement in quantifiable terms.

4. *Intervention plan.* Again, specificity is key. Ensure that your plan has at least one action item that is a research-based or at least research-informed intervention that matches the area of student weakness (for example, phonics instruction for a student struggling with decoding). It should go without saying, but a good intervention plan should have an *actual* intervention, not just accommodations, supports, or modifications. A question to ask to make sure it is an intervention and not a support is, "Is the

student being taught a new skill in the area of need?" If yes, it is an intervention. So "Allow extra time on written assignments" is a support because you're not really teaching a new skill, and "Teaching the 6 Traits of Effective Writing in Ms. Smith's small group intervention" is an intervention. Of course, you can add supports as action items as well, but just make sure there is an intervention.

5. *Start date, review date, and person responsible.* Make sure your intervention is time bound and that you know who is implementing the plan. Again, the more specific, the better. For example, "Classroom teachers will work one-on-one on Johnny's reading in the next month" is too vague.* Really nail down those details early on, or you will be at your review meeting and have neither a gauge of the fidelity of the intervention nor real data with which to make decisions when you review the intervention plan.

To illustrate, a sample intervention plan and tracking form with a fictitious student's data on it is provided in Exhibit 5.1; Form 5.1 is a blank version for your use and adaptation.

---

*Apologies to all the students named Johnny out there. You are always used in educational examples as the student with the problem. Sorry, but it's industry standard, so I'm using it.

EXHIBIT 5.1. SAMPLE INDIVIDUAL INTERVENTION PLAN AND TRACKING FORM

**Student:** Johnny    **Grade:** 7    **Case Manager:** Smith    **Team Meeting Date:** 01/16/2011

**Problem Statement:** Johnny's work production percentage on written assignments in his English class is at 40%, while a comparison peer is producing 85% of writing assignments. (See attached list of missing assignments and work samples.) On the last district writing assessment, he scored a 2.5 out of 6 on the grading rubric, which is scored based on the 6 Traits of Effective Writing Model.

**Strengths:** When Johnny produces written work in class, he scores between 3.5 and 4 on a 6-point rubric based on the 6 Traits Model.

**Goal(s):** (1) Johnny will score at least 4.5 out of 6 on the 6-point rubric of the 6 Traits Model. (2) When given a written class assignment, Johnny will initiate the task within a given time frame 4 out of 5 times with one prompt.

| Intervention | Implementer | Assessment Data | Frequency of Assessment Data | Start Date | Review Date #1 | Results/Data/Progress Made |
|---|---|---|---|---|---|---|
| **1. Tutoring:** Johnny will participate in the small group writing intervention group on Mondays to work on the 6 Traits of Effective Writing | Ms. Smith | Attendance record | Weekly | TBD | 2/27/2011 | |
| **2. Mentoring:** Johnny will participate in mentoring on Wednesdays to work on mini-lessons on self-advocacy and task completion | Mr. Jenkins | Attendance record | Weekly | 1/22/2011 | 2/27/2011 | |
| **3. Classroom Modifications:** Johnny will receive shortened writing assignments, paraphrase directions verbally, and use an "Initiation Timer" | Classroom teachers | Teacher checklist | Daily—per in-class assignment | 1/22/2011 | 2/27/2011 | |

*Source:* Adapted and reprinted with permission from Lainie Sgouros, Data Coach

# Individual Intervention Plan and Tracking Form

**Student:**          **Grade:**          **Case Manager:**          **Team Meeting Date:**

**Problem Statement:**

**Strengths:**

**Goal(s):**

| Intervention | Implementer | Assessment Data | Frequency of Assessment Data | Start Date | Review Date #1 | Results/Data/Progress Made |
|---|---|---|---|---|---|---|
| | | | | | | |
| | | | | | | |
| | | | | | | |

*Source:* Adapted and reprinted with permission from Lainie Sgouros, Data Coach

# BEHAVIORAL RTI: DATA-BASED DECISION MAKING

When we think of interventions for behavior, most of us think of support on the individual level. For example, we are trained to look at individuals and conduct functional behavioral analyses in order to figure out how to support a student in his or her environment. With RtI, we need to adjust our lens to focus on a more school-wide effort to support positive behavior. By focusing on these Tier 1 interventions, we get more bang for our buck, so to speak. Our role in behavioral RtI is to first consult with our RtI team members about universal screening. Then we can move to our assessment and intervention audits, and consult about ways to implement schoolwide positive behavioral and social-emotional support. Finally, we can consult about making improvements to progress monitoring for students receiving the next level of support in Tiers 2 and 3.

## Universal Screening

As in academic RtI, it is important to conduct universal screenings for social-emotional and behavioral concerns. School psychologists know all too well that the child who acts out often receives the intervention because he or she is disruptive to the school environment, and the ones quietly suffering with depression or anxiety may never be brought to anyone's attention. Universal screening measures will be able to identify the "internalizing" problems as well at the "externalizing–acting out" problems in a school environment. This knowledge will help guide intervention.

There are a number of "off the shelf" assessments and screeners that can be purchased and used for the purpose of gathering schoolwide data. These are great for screening for all kinds of behavioral and social-emotional problems, including the internalizing ones that tend to get overlooked. The added benefit is that they are already standardized and field-tested. However, if budgets are tight or there isn't administrative buy-in for a universal social-emotional screening tool, you may need to get creative. One technique is to conduct a classroom student study team (SST) meeting with each teacher at your school. Instead of focusing in on one student in depth, the level of analysis is the classroom as a whole. This works best at the elementary school level, where a teacher has a set class list, rather than at a traditional secondary school, where a teacher might see 100 to 150 students. (In the latter case, some schools have "advisory" teachers or "homeroom" teachers with whom students check in daily for a period of time, and these might be the staff to work with.) The classroom SST meeting is basically a process in which you sit down with the teacher and his or her class roster and identify three social-emotional or behavioral problems to target classroom wide (for example, work production, bullying, social withdrawal). You might ask, "What three behavioral or social-emotional problems that impede learning are present in your classroom?" With each teacher, you identify the top three concerns he or she has, then compile the data across the school. You may find, for example, that bullying is a big concern or that social withdrawal among English Language Learners is a schoolwide issue. Then your RtI team will know what Tier 1 interventions are likely to be the most beneficial to the most students.

## Assessment and Intervention Audits

You will want to be active in promoting the core principles of universal screening and providing research-based support for behavioral and social-emotional concerns, just as you are with academic RtI. You might review any current Tier 1 interventions that are in place. At times, schools have adopted off-the-shelf curriculum for building social skills, teaching tolerance, bullying prevention, and so on. You can investigate the research behind these programs, review what assessment tools are built into the curriculum, and consult with staff about implementation. In some cases, you might have time to train teachers or join in the implementation phase. I have found that joining in on the classroom lessons on building social skills is a great way to get to know the students in the class and gain hands-on experience with prevention. Another way to get involved is to train older students to be "helpers" in the classroom lessons or to be "conflict managers" outside the classroom, such as during recess time.

## Monitoring Tier 1 Effectiveness

Here is another chance to harness your data analysis skills. Depending on the intervention, you will have the chance to utilize and interpret schoolwide data about whether your intervention has been effective. In addition to the universal screener selected and assessments built into your curriculum or intervention, you can also use schoolwide data already gathered by your school site. Examples of data that can be used to monitor effectiveness of a behavioral or social-emotional intervention include discipline data (for example, detention numbers, suspension rates, and the number and type of discipline referrals) and attendance data. School psychologists have a huge role to play in turning the data into smart decision making. If programs are in place and have been for a while, there can be resistance to stopping them or choosing alternative programs. Why should we be implementing programs that don't work in the social-emotional and behavioral realm? Just because a program is called "Bullying Prevention" doesn't mean it's actually preventing bullying at your school. You have to get your team to look at the data to see if the program is effective.

## Tiers 2 and 3: Gathering Baseline Data and Using Progress Monitoring Tools

When students' behavioral and social emotional challenges reach the level of Tier 2 or Tier 3 interventions, your focus may shift to another core principle of RtI: effective progress monitoring. In order to monitor progress, you first need to get a baseline of behavior. You can do this as part of the development of the problem statement recorded on your Individual Intervention Plan and Tracking Form (Exhibit 5.1 and Form 5.1). There are a number of ways to track behavioral data. You can use data already collected by the school (for example, discipline and attendance data) or create your own. A good place to start with data tracking for behavior is online. One Web site that has a variety of resources to choose from is Intervention Central (www.interventioncentral.org). There are even tools to make fancy graphs of your data online, and tutorials on how to do so in a spreadsheet program, such as Excel. Even more fancy are online applications for your smartphone or tablet, in which you can electronically measure such behaviors as time on task. In my day (insert old-lady voice), we tracked data with a pencil and paper, and that worked just fine! We simply picked a target behavior (for example, time on task) for a target student and a comparison peer, marked every thirty seconds whether or not the target student and comparison student were on task, and calculated a percentage. But if technology makes progress monitoring easier, I say go for it!

# HOW TO TRACK INDIVIDUAL STUDENT PROGRESS WITH YOUR RTI TEAM

There are many tools designed to track individual student progress, whether they are online tools, tools you develop yourself, or tools the district provides. What isn't well defined is how you find time to make sure your team is effectively tracking the data and using it to guide decisions. One way that has been suggested is to have a monthly RtI team meeting to go over all the individual plans, using a master binder. It should also be noted that this master binder can also be created electronically on a private server, so that team members can access it, but parents and the public cannot.

The master binder or database of intervention plans is typically divided by month, not by student. That way, you don't accidentally forget to follow up with a student's progress when you said you would. Let's take the example in Exhibit 5.1 with Johnny's intervention plan. The RtI team met in January, and agreed to follow up with his progress in February. So this particular plan would be put in the February section of the master binder. Then, if at the RtI meeting the team decides to continue or change the intervention (or both), they can copy the intervention plan or add a new page to the plan and put it in the section for the month coinciding with the next follow-up date. This binder becomes a legal document, by the way, so it is important to document well and not lose track of the students whose progress you are monitoring. There is an added benefit of having a lot of data on students to make decisions down the road about special education assessment and eligibility.

Staff involved in the monthly RtI meetings will likely include you, the principal, special education teachers, intervention specialists and other support staff (for example, the speech and language pathologist, the school counselor), and general education classroom teacher(s). It is helpful if someone on the RtI team can meet with the general education teachers before the meeting, so that the time spent in the monthly RtI meeting is efficient and not spent developing a problem statement, looking through data, and so on. Some RtI teams divide up their members and delegate them to a grade level at which they will serve as a consultant and trainer on intervention plans and progress monitoring. At these grade-level meetings, you may also spot trends in the data, such as a small group of students that is experiencing similar academic challenges. Then you can consider putting students into small group interventions and discuss the feasibility of small group interventions at the monthly RtI meeting.

There are many ways your team can explore to make sure that time is built into the busy school day to hold your RtI team meeting. You will want to advocate for a whole day so as to be sure to get through all the students. One way to ensure participation for the general education teachers during the school day is to have a schoolwide substitute teacher to take over teachers' classes while they report out to the RtI team. You will also want to have a specific agenda and time frame for each student in the review process (for example, two minutes for problem statement, three minutes for new data, and so on) so that you don't get stuck discussing one student for a longer period of time. If follow-up conversations about students are required, they can be scheduled for another time. The key in these monthly meetings is to systematically and efficiently review all students with intervention plans. Doing so will not only benefit the students but also have a ripple effect in the school system as a whole. A school psychologist friend of mine relayed a story to me in which a principal shared the great academic results of the RtI team, and other principals got on board at their school sites.

## NAVIGATING YOUR ROLE CHANGE

Educational reform can sometimes move at a glacially slow pace, and sometimes we can get a directive from "higher up" that changes our educational system overnight. Some states are dipping their proverbial toes in RtI, which allows for a longer learning curve in becoming comfortable with the shift. Other states jumped into the deep end of RtI right away by eliminating the discrepancy model of eligibility, and required school psychologists to make the shift right away. Depending on when you were trained as a school psychologist, you may be ready for RtI or totally out of your comfort zone. If you were trained at a time when assessment for special education was your primary role, then you'll feel right at home with assessment but have some trepidation about an expanded role. If you are newer to the field, you may have been exposed to the research on RtI, or you may even have experienced it in a practicum or internship, and are more equipped to facilitate the process at your schools.

Some school psychologists are comfortable with the behavioral RtI piece, but not so much with the academic piece. I know this was true for me. I didn't have a deep understanding of the curriculum and assessments used by the teachers at my schools, particularly at the secondary level. I had to make a point of becoming more familiar with the curriculum and the teaching methods if I was going to be an educated member of the RtI team. A good place to start might be to seek outside resources for improving your knowledge of the reading and writing process and the most current research on interventions to support reading and writing. The National Reading Panel (http://national readingpanel.org/default.htm) and the National Center for Improving Student Learning and Achievement in Math and Science (http://ncisla.wceruw.org/) are both excellent resources.

## PULLING IT ALL TOGETHER

Response to Intervention (RtI) is a model that holds much promise. The move from a discrepancy model of eligibility for special education to a preventive and research-based approach makes intuitive sense to school psychologists and educators. By design, RtI brings both general education and special education staff to the same table to problem-solve on behalf of the students. Implementation of RtI is not without pitfalls. Because it is a relatively new model, there are many schools and districts that are struggling with the implementation phase of RtI. Likewise, the school psychologist's role is evolving from that of a gatekeeper to special education to one of being a keymaster of interventions and data-based decision making. The primary role of the school psychologist in the initial implementation of RtI is as a consultant and cheerleader for RtI's core principles. It is important for school psychologists to be active participants in RtI at all phases: exploration, early implementation, and ongoing improvement.

---

## Key Points

- RtI is a school reform that holds both promise and pitfalls. Like that of any educational reform, the quality of the reform is dependent on how successful each school staff member is in the implementation phase.
- RtI involves a mind shift for educators and parents: they need to see not a deficit from within the child but rather a mismatch between the child and the environment, supports, curriculum, and instruction.
- The core principles of RtI include high-quality, scientifically based classroom instruction; student assessment with a classroom focus; schoolwide screening of academics and behavior; implementation of appropriate research-based interventions; continuous progress monitoring of the effectiveness of interventions; and teaching behavior fidelity measures.
- Your roles in RtI vary, but the primary roles are as consultant and cheerleader for the core principles of RtI. Often you are best equipped to serve as an assessment and data consultant.
- In both academic and behavioral RtI, you can conduct assessment and intervention audits, and facilitate and train staff on data collection, tracking, and interpretation.
- Depending on your training and experience, you may find yourself more comfortable in academic or behavioral RtI. In order to be an effective consultant, you should seek additional training and knowledge about areas in which you have received less training (for example, reading development, math curriculum, bullying prevention programs).
- Tracking individual student progress at school sites involves some logistical challenges. For an RtI team to be effective, there needs to be a systematic and efficient way to track student progress for data-based decision making. One way is to hold a monthly RtI meeting to review all individual intervention plans with the RtI team and the students' teachers. A master binder, divided by month, is one way to keep track of when to follow up with particular students' progress.

## DISCUSSION QUESTIONS

1. In what phase of implementation of RtI are your schools (for example, exploration, early intervention, ongoing improvement)?

2. What is your current role in RtI at your schools? Do you see this role as evolving? What new skills have you had to acquire (or do you anticipate having to acquire) as your role changes?

3. Thinking in terms of the core principles of RtI, how might you adopt a leadership role in consulting or participating on your RtI team?

4. What core principle of RtI do you see as an area where you need more support or training? What resources are available to you to improve your knowledge in this area?

5. What are some of the pitfalls you have encountered in implementing RtI at your schools? What are some ideas for overcoming these challenges?

chapter | 6

# SPECIAL EDUCATION ASSESSMENT

A while back, I was walking in the streets of San Francisco, where I used to work as a school psychologist, and I saw a young man in his early twenties pointing at me and talking with his friends. I overheard him say, "Hey! That's the lady that put me in special ed!" For a moment, I panicked. Then he came up to me and gave me a hug and said, "Thanks, Dr. B; special ed was way easier than my other classes, and I graduated!" Phew. That could have gone either way. School psychologists are often seen as the gatekeepers or "deciders" of which students are eligible for special education. Even though the law states that eligibility is a multidisciplinary team decision, the reality is that everyone looks to you when it is time to make the eligibility decision. This chapter contains information about how to navigate what may be your most difficult role: special education assessor and "eligibility guru."

As Chapter Three taught you, half the battle of special education assessment is the case management. Figuring out a way to meet your legal timelines when you have a heavy caseload is one of the most challenging parts of being a school psychologist, even for "veterans." A whole new set of challenges arise once you have that assessment plan in your hand and you have to go forth with selecting measures appropriate to the referral question, efficiently writing a legally defensible yet parent-friendly report, and making eligibility recommendations that are grounded in special education law.

Although the nuts and bolts of assessment (for example, how to administer and score tests appropriately) and the details and history of special education law were, we hope, covered in your graduate school coursework, you may have a whole host of new challenges awaiting you in your new school district. These may include a lack of appropriate testing measures, less time than is needed to complete a thorough assessment, and specific district interpretations of special education law. This chapter contains information designed to help you streamline the assessment process for the purpose of maximizing the useful information you can provide to the IEP team during the special education eligibility determination process. An added bonus may be that you will make the right decisions, and a student on the street thanks you one day!

## THE ASSESSMENT PROCESS: FROM PARENTAL CONSENT TO REPORT WRITING

When you get an initial referral for a special education evaluation, where you start depends somewhat on how involved you are in the prereferral process. It may be that the first time you see the child's name is on the signed assessment plan. Alternatively, you may have been involved with the family, student, and teachers for several months or even years when the decision is made to move forward with testing. It is often easier to get started on assessing the student if you are not going into the situation without any prior information. Figure 6.1 is a flowchart showing the assessment process in cases where you have no prior information about the child. The process can be streamlined or adapted if you have been involved with the case before and already have portions of the background history available to you.

### Determining Timelines and Informing All Involved Parties of the Assessment

The first step in the assessment process depends on whether or not you are the case manager for the student. Typically, an assessment plan (an outline of what testing will be done and by whom) is generated by the case manager. If you are the case manager, the parent-signed assessment plan is returned to you, and your job is to alert the school staff who are involved in special education assessment. Typically, this is the special education teacher, who often serves as the case manager and conducts the academic achievement assessment. It should be noted that in some states, the academic achievement testing is done by the special education teacher, and in other states, achievement testing is conducted by educational diagnosticians, so you will need to determine whom to inform about achievement testing. School psychologists sometimes do the achievement testing; it varies. At times, you may also be informing speech pathologists or occupational therapists that they too need to assess the child. You will also need to calculate the legal timeline and determine the date by which the IEP meeting must be held in order to comply with special education law. As a side note, states and sometimes districts differ in the way they calculate legal timelines (for example, if they include weekends or vacations as days in the timeline), so you will need to check with your supervisor. I have found that to keep all parties on the same page with legal timelines and their obligations, a memo is better than a verbal reminder. Form 6.1 is an example of a memo that you can use to inform staff of the process.

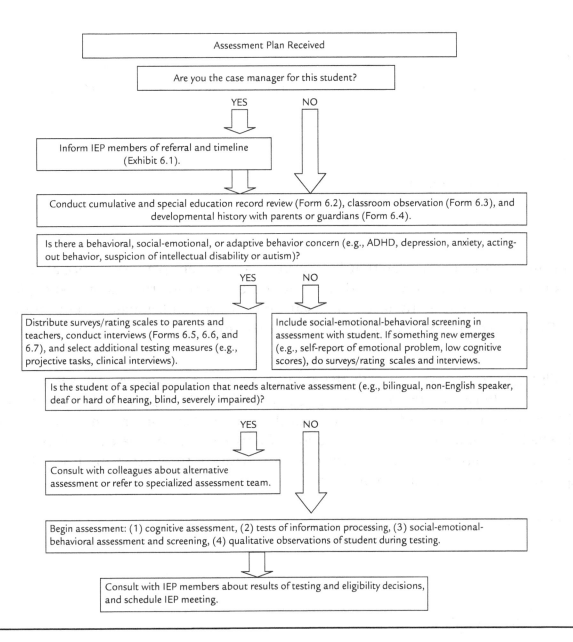

**FIGURE 6.1.** Assessment Flowchart: Initial Referral

# Psychological Services Memo: CONFIDENTIAL

**Date:** _____

**Re:** _____     _____     _____
       (Student Name)        (Date of Birth)    (Grade)

**To:** _____
      (IEP Member)

This memo is to inform you that I received an assessment plan for a special education evaluation for the above student. The parent signed the assessment plan on _____ (date). To meet the legal timeline, the Individualized Education Plan (IEP) meeting must be held by _____ (date).

I will begin my assessment with the student as soon as possible and will inform you when I am finished with the testing and am finalizing the report so that we can set an IEP date together with advance notice for the parent. Please let me know when you are finished with your portion of the testing (if applicable), and we can collaborate and discuss eligibility at that time. Please do not hesitate to contact me if you have any questions. My contact information is _____.

Thank you,

_____
School Psychologist

While we are on the topic of informing people about the assessment, it is also important to communicate with parents or guardians about the process. Some parents write a letter saying "I want an IEP," but they don't realize how much work goes into the process and can become frustrated if they are not given a time horizon or road map about what it takes to get to the IEP. I have found in particular that anxious parents become increasingly anxious with each passing day that they do not have the IEP meeting.

A wise school psychologist colleague of mine, who worked at a very affluent school with highly involved parents, once gave me a tip that I have found useful. It sounds so simple, but it works: call the parents at each step of the assessment process just to give them a "heads-up" about where you are. So, after you do a classroom observation, let them know you got started on the classroom observation. After you do your first testing session with the kid, make a quick call or send a brief e-mail to let them know you have started testing, and provide them with one positive part (for example, "The student was cooperative" or "We got through all the cognitive testing"). It can seem a bit much, but trust me—that quick contact here and there with an anxious or highly involved parent will prevent a longer phone call or a complaint that things are taking too long. Parents just want to know that their request is in the works. You know you are doing your best to get it done, but they don't. Sometimes you will have three cases to complete ahead of their request, but I wouldn't recommend telling them that. They don't care what your caseload is; they care about their kid. So just start on something and let them know you're doing it. You will also build a reputation with the parents for following through on your word, which builds trust for the IEP meeting.

## Reviewing the History and Gathering Environmental Data

Once you have informed team members (or have been informed) about the assessment plan's being signed for a student, you may be tempted to jump in with testing to get started. However, gathering a bit more data and doing the background history first have several advantages. First, knowing the student's school and special education history can inform your choice of test battery. Second, you may uncover another area of suspected disability that was not discussed in prereferral meetings. Third, you will have an opportunity to build rapport with the parents early on in the process and not be rushing around right before the IEP meeting to get needed background information.

I recommend starting with the school history. You can start by reviewing the cumulative records and special education records, in addition to interviewing or surveying the student's current teacher about the present level of performance in the classroom. Ideally, if you were involved in the prereferral process, you would already have this information and be able to write it up right away in your assessment report, but at times there is additional information in the cumulative folder, or the teacher has more information about the student that he or she was not comfortable sharing in a meeting with the parents. If you work at the secondary level, where there are many teachers to interview, you may want to send a brief survey about the child's strengths and areas of need for the teachers to complete, and then follow up with teachers who provided information that you need to have clarified (for example, "Seems withdrawn in class," "Acts out," "Not motivated").

With regard to the record review, I recommend writing the information into your report as you review it. You already have the files out, and the information is fresh in your mind, so get that part of your report done. That way, when you approach the end of the timeline, you will have a good portion of your background history already written. Trust me—you'll be happy you did!

If you weren't involved with the student during the prereferral process, you may need some structure in getting the key information from the records. Especially at the middle and high school levels, there can be a lot of information to sort through, and it is rarely in order—you'll find a kindergarten report card next to a standardized test from tenth grade. Form 6.2 is a template you can use to organize the school history and make sure you capture all the pertinent information.

# Cumulative and Special Education Review Checklist

**Student Name:** _____

**English proficiency:** _____          **Attendance history/issues:** _____

**Prior special education testing/outcome:** _____

**Vision/hearing/health issues:** _____

| Grade | Research-Based Interventions (Academic) | Other Interventions (Nonacademic) | Standardized or Curriculum-Based Test Scores | Teacher Comments and Areas of Strength and Need |
|---|---|---|---|---|
| Pre-K/K | | | | |
| 1 | | | | |
| 2 | | | | |
| 3 | | | | |
| 4 | | | | |
| 5 | | | | |
| 6 | | | | |
| 7 | | | | |
| 8 | | | | |
| 9 | | | | |
| 10 | | | | |
| 11 | | | | |
| 12 | | | | |
| Retention Year _____ | | | | |

When you review the record, it is worth noting if you then suspect another disability besides the initial referral question. For example, if the assessment plan was generated due to concerns about reading, but in reviewing the file you note a long-standing history of attention problems, you might want to consider assessing the student's attentional skills as well. Or if your referral was for a possible emotional disturbance, but you notice that the student has a history of ADHD and a seizure disorder, then you might be looking at assessment under another disability category as well, such as Other Health Impaired. By reviewing the records before you start testing, you will avoid opening the cumulative folder the week before the IEP meeting and realizing you should have done more testing.

It is also worth noting that depending on how your district and state interpret special education law, you may ultimately be determining eligibility through the RtI process. In this case, you will also have a section in your report that discusses the prior interventions in depth. Ask your supervisor and colleagues for templates and examples of the way your district documents RtI in eligibility reports. Chapter Five on RtI also provides resources describing the procedures for eligibility under RtI.

Another key source of information needed before testing the student is the classroom observation. In some states and districts, an observation is legally mandated; in others, it is optional. Whether or not this is a responsibility of the school psychologist in your district, I strongly believe that it is one of the most important parts of the assessment process. We all know that kids present very differently one-on-one in a quiet testing room than they do in a classroom of students. The classroom observation also gives you clues about the interaction dynamics between the student and the learning environment. For example, teachers can be so frustrated by a student's behavior problems that they start to think that the student is "always" off task. Your classroom observation may reveal that there are certain activities in which the child is off task and others in which he or she is engaged. This is important feedback that can be used to generate hypotheses and interventions.

Another benefit of the classroom observation is that you can generate recommendations for the student in the context of the classroom, rather than in the abstract. Teachers will respect your recommendations more if they are specific to the environment and you don't suggest activities and interventions already present in the classroom! Or you may discover that the majority of the students are off task, which suggests that the classroom environment may be playing a role in the individual student's difficulties. That is important information!

Further, you will be able to talk with the student about what you noticed in the classroom and probe further during the assessment (for example, "I noticed you were writing down the problems when you were doing math, but when it was time to write, you started moving around the room. Can you help me understand this?"). This can be helpful in clarifying the student's perspective on his or her learning. You can also give immediate feedback to the teacher about your observations so that the teacher does not have to wait until the IEP meeting to begin to implement changes in his or her teaching or interventions.

You may have your very own favorite classroom observation tool you use to gather information in a student's class. It could be a pad of paper, a checklist, or a structured time-sampling tool for measuring on- and off-task behaviors of your student versus a comparison peer. You may even be fancy and have one of those new smartphone or tablet applications in which you can track behavior electronically.

Form 6.3 is a template that I find useful for recording observations both of the student and of the teacher's behavior in relation to the student. It combines observations of the classroom environment with those of how the student reacts in the environment. If the student has more than one teacher, you'll find it interesting to see if there is consistency or differences in behavior and work production between classroom environments. Form 6.3 also has a section for noting behavior outside the classroom, which can be useful for referrals where there are social-emotional-behavioral problems. In these cases, the form allows you to gather information on the student's "hotspots" where he or she tends to get in trouble (for example, hallways or the cafeteria).

# Classroom Observation Form

**Student Name:** _____ **Grade:** _____

**Teacher Name/Class:** _____

**Number of Students in Class:** _____

**Seating Arrangement:** _____

**Lesson Topic:** _____

**Date of Observation:** _____

*Structure:*

_____ Rules posted     _____ Rules referred to verbally
_____ Rules stated in positive direction     _____ No more than five rules posted
_____ Schedule posted     _____ Schedule referred to verbally
_____ Attention directed to positive behavior     _____ Transitions are planned/articulated

*Interventions:*

_____ Token or point system     _____ Time-outs     _____ Punishment
_____ Contracts (individual)     _____ Praise     _____ Humor
_____ Contracts (group)     _____ Warnings     _____ Proximity control
_____ Verbal reprimands     _____ Physical restraint     _____ Cueing/Prompting
_____ Modeling     _____ Ignoring
_____ Opportunities for positive movement
_____ Other (list) _____

Narrative description of student in environment:




The following strategies/techniques appeared useful for student learning:




Observations of student interaction with others outside of classroom (e.g., hallway, lunch, recess, break time):

Copyright © 2012 by Rebecca Branstetter.

## Conducting a Developmental History with Parents or Guardians

Ideally you will already have gathered developmental information through your involvement in prereferral intervention teams. In other situations, a developmental history survey is sent home at the same time as the assessment plan (or during the prereferral meeting), and you will receive the information at the same time as the signed assessment plan. In still other cases, you will need to reach out to the parents and get a developmental history. I have found that doing the developmental history in person is best, but I totally understand that in a time crunch, you may just end up sending a survey home or calling the parent on the phone. For the "run of the mill" assessments where there is not a social-emotional-behavioral concern, sending home the survey or conducting a phone interview usually works just fine. If the referral reason is complex or the child has a complicated history, it is best to gather background information from the parents in person.

Your district may also have purchased a semistructured developmental history protocol to use to collect this information, or you may have to create your own. If you are not already using a developmental history form that you like, Form 6.4 is tool for you to experiment with; it is a two-page developmental survey that can be sent to the parents or used in an interview. I have found that this version captures all the key information, as well as critical items that, if endorsed, require further follow-up with the parent.

# Developmental History

Student's Name: _____  DOB: _____  Grade: _____

School: _____  Person Interviewed/Relationship: _____

## Household members living with child:

Name _____ Relationship _____ Age _____

_____  _____  _____

_____  _____  _____

_____  _____  _____

_____  _____  _____

## Family or significant people outside the household:

Name _____ Relationship _____ Age _____

_____  _____  _____

_____  _____  _____

_____  _____  _____

### *Developmental History*

Length of pregnancy: _____  Mother's and father's ages at child's birth: _____

Child's birth weight: _____  Type of delivery (Normal, C-section): _____

Mother's pre-/postnatal health: _____

Complications or unusual circumstances before/during/after birth? _____

_____

Baby's health (first year): _____

Age first walked: _____  Age first words spoken: _____  Age first sentences: _____

Date of last physical exam: _____  Any problems noted? _____

Doctor's name and contact information: _____

Date of last vision screening and results: _____

Date of last hearing screening and results: _____

Any ongoing medical problems or concerns? _____

Is the child taking any medication (prescription, over the counter, alternative medicines)?

_____

Any accidents/injuries/hospitalizations? _____

History of (check if applicable):

_____ Attention problems

_____ Hyperactivity/Impulsivity

_____ Neurological problems (e.g., seizures, loss of consciousness)

_____ Behavior problems (specify): _____

_____ Sleeping problems

_____ Eating problems (specify): _____

_____ Toileting problems (specify): _____

_____ Nervousness/anxiety

_____ Depression/sadness

_____ Gross motor problems (e.g., running, walking, throwing, catching, clumsiness)

_____ Fine motor problems (e.g., tying shoes, writing)

_____ Speaking (e.g., articulation, communication, understanding language)
_____ Difficulties relating to other children/peers
_____ Physical disabilities (specify): _____

## Current Speech and Language Development

Child's primary language: _____
Other languages spoken: _____  Language child prefers: _____
Understands and communicates _____ well _____ adequately _____ poorly
Do you and/or others have difficulty understanding your child's speech? _____
_____

Other speech problems? (e.g., stuttering, delayed speech) _____

## Current Social Development

Has many friends _____ Has some friends _____ Has almost no friends _____
Social strengths/areas of need:_____
_____

Activities at school/outside of school: _____
_____

Other hobbies/interests: _____
Has interest in hobbies/activities/friendships declined recently? _____

## Current Emotional-Behavioral Health

Does the family have any concerns about the child's behavior and/or emotional health?
_____
_____

Is the child able to take care of his or her daily life activities (e.g., personal care, safety, household tasks?) _____
_____

Describe how any experiences in the child's life, past or present, have affected him/her:
_____
_____

Any current or prior diagnosis of mental health problems? _____
_____

Any current or prior counseling/therapy? _____
Mental health provider or counselor's name/contact information: _____
_____

(If you wish to have the provider give information to help staff support your child at school, please provide us with a signed consent form.)
What support systems are available to the family? (e.g., extended family, neighbors, friends, community-based organizations, agencies) _____
_____

## Other

What are your child's strengths? What do you enjoy about your child? _____
_____

What do you think is the reason for any problems your child may be having at school?
_____

Is there anything else that would help school staff better understand your child? _____
_____

It is worth noting that in some school districts, English may not be the first language of some or many of the parents. If you do not speak the parents' language, you will need to find translators or support staff who can assist you with taking the developmental history. This is another reason it is preferable to do the developmental history early on in the assessment process. Trust me—you don't want to be scrambling for someone who speaks a subdialect of Tagalog the week before the IEP meeting!

## Deciding If You Need to Do a Full Social-Emotional-Behavioral Evaluation

Another key question you need to ask yourself before even beginning testing with a student is whether or not there is a suspected disability in the social-emotional or behavioral realm that will require standardized rating scales. After you have done your cumulative and special education review, classroom observation, and developmental history, you will likely have a sense of whether or not you need to do formal assessment or a screening in the social-emotional or behavioral areas. If there is any suspicion at all of ADHD, depression, anxiety, or acting-out behavior, or suspicion of an intellectual disability (for example, mental retardation or developmental delay) or autism, then you should administer a formal standardized rating scale. I hate to be redundant, but this is why gathering the background information before testing is key. You don't want to be conducting interviews or scrambling around trying to get a teacher or parent to fill out a rating scale a week before the IEP meeting.

You can use Form 6.5 to inform teachers that you will need their input before the IEP. Attach a survey to this form about the student's strengths and areas of need or a standardized rating scale and hand-deliver it. Form 6.5 is a teacher feedback form that I distribute to all of the student's teachers (core teachers as well as elective or special teachers, such as for art and PE). Acknowledge that you know they are very busy and that you very much appreciate their feedback; you can put it in their mailbox if you have a good rapport with the teacher already. A wise colleague of mine actually puts them in teachers' mailboxes with a little candy taped on the top. She says that teachers have a harder time ignoring it when there is a little treat attached. It's worth a try!

# Survey/Rating Scale Memo to Teacher(s)

# Psychological Services Memo: CONFIDENTIAL

**Date:** _____

**Re:** _____      _____      _____
          (Student Name)            (Date of Birth)      (Grade)

**To:** _____
         (Teacher)

This memo is to inform you that I received an assessment plan for a special education evaluation for the above student. In order to fully understand the child in his or her learning environment, I am interested in your input about classroom performance. As you know, working with a student one-on-one during testing does not provide the full picture of how he or she functions in the classroom. Teacher input is invaluable in the assessment process, and helps the Individualized Education Plan (IEP) team make eligibility decisions and appropriate recommendations for the student.

I am attaching a survey/rating scale for you to complete at your earliest convenience. In order for me to include your information in the assessment report by the legal timeline, I will need the survey/rating scale back by _____ (date). Please do not hesitate to contact me if you have any questions or concerns at: _____.

Thank you in advance for your time,


_____

School Psychologist

# Teacher Feedback Survey

**Student:** _____

**Teacher:** _____

**Grade/Subject:** _____

**Date:** _____

Please return to school psychologist by _____ (date). Thank you!

| | Excellent | Adequate | Needs Improvement | Unsatisfactory |
|---|---|---|---|---|
| Attendance/punctuality | | | | |
| Work completion | | | | |
| Group work | | | | |
| Ability to work independently | | | | |
| Following written instructions | | | | |
| Following verbal instructions | | | | |
| Organization | | | | |
| Homework | | | | |
| Note taking | | | | |
| Attitude toward learning | | | | |
| Attention/focus | | | | |
| Test taking | | | | |
| Peer interactions | | | | |

Areas of academic strength: _____

_____

_____

Areas of academic need: _____

_____

_____

Current grade (circle/underline, if appropriate): A B C D F

Positive behaviors and social interactions: _____

_____

Behaviors that impede learning: _____

_____

Recommendations for student: _____

_____

_____

Other comments: _____

_____

Thank you for your valuable input!

Form 6.7 is a form you can use if you elect to send home a survey or rating scale to the parents. If you have already established rapport with them, then it is probably fine to just send home the survey or scale and give them a call to let them know it is on the way. If it is a sensitive referral question, such as an assessment for emotional disturbance, autism, or an intellectual disability, then I recommend doing the survey with the parents in person, if possible. You also want to be sensitive if you work in populations where the parents' level of literacy or education is in question. If you suspect that they may not have the literacy skills to complete the survey, call them and ask them to come in for an interview and go through it with them item by item.

# Survey/Rating Scale Memo to Parent(s)

**Date:** _____

**From:** _____, School Psychologist

**Re:** _____  _____  _____
           (Student Name)                (Date of Birth)     (Grade)

**To:** _____
      (Parent/Guardian)

This letter is to inform you that I received the signed assessment plan for a special education evaluation for your child. In order to fully understand the student, I am interested in your input about the types of behaviors and feelings that help learning or get in the way of learning. Since you know your child best, parent input is invaluable in the assessment process, and helps the Individualized Education Plan (IEP) team make eligibility decisions and appropriate recommendations for the student.

I am attaching a survey/rating scale for you to complete at your earliest convenience. In order for me to include your information in the assessment report by the legal timeline, I will need the survey/rating scale back by _____ (date). Please do not hesitate to contact me if you have any questions or concerns at: _____.

Thank you in advance for your time,


_____

School Psychologist

Sometimes, despite your best efforts, you do not get the surveys or standardized rating scales back. In this case, write in your report that you attempted to get the surveys, and document your attempts (dates of attempts and types of attempts—by phone, in writing, home visit). Make sure you include a statement that you plan to solicit the teachers' or parents' feedback at the IEP meeting. You may not be able to make conclusive eligibility decisions without the information, or you may be able to get enough qualitative information at the meeting to make conclusions. At the very least you have documented that you attempted to assess the child in all areas of suspected disability.

## Selecting Appropriate Testing Instruments

Finally! You are ready to test the student. Or are you . . . ? Before you proceed with the testing, first ask yourself if the student is of a special population in which you need further training or assistance, or if you need to refer the student to a school psychologist or team that specializes in the population.

First, check to make sure that the student is proficient enough in English to proceed with testing in English, or that you are fluent in the child's native language. Often, there are English language development test scores in the child's cumulative folder to help you make this decision. Some districts have formal policies about whether these scores are used to determine which students must be assessed in their native language by bilingual psychologists; sometimes it is up to you to make the decision. Consult with your supervisor about how these decisions are made. In some districts, the case is referred out to a bilingual assessment team.

At times, there are no school psychologists who speak the language of the student. It is especially important to consult with your supervisor about how to proceed in these cases. The district may need to contract out or find a translator to work with you. The general rule of thumb is to do the best you can with the tools and resources you have in your district.

Second, ensure that there are no physical impairments that would invalidate your testing using a standard battery. For example, if you have a student who is deaf or hard of hearing or who has visual impairments and you are not trained to conduct alternative assessments, you may need to refer out to a psychologist who is trained in sign language or in assessing students with visual impairments. As you would for bilingual assessment, you will want to locate the best assessor and tools you have at your disposal for alternative assessments. If you are in a small district where you are the most trained, then seek outside consultation from your supervisor about how to conduct the best assessment possible.

Third, you may or may not be able to do an assessment for ADHD, depending on your training and, more likely, your district's policy. I have worked in districts where school psychologists were allowed to diagnose ADHD, and I have worked in districts where the diagnosis must come from a clinical professional, such as a psychiatrist or a physician. In the latter case, our role was to facilitate a referral to a medical professional by doing an "ADHD screening" in which we observed the child, gathered the rating scales, and consulted with the outside professional. School district policies vary, so ask your supervisor what your role is in ADHD assessment.

Finally, some school psychologists do not have much experience in assessing for autism or assessing students with severe impairments (for example, students with physical impairments or severe intellectual disabilities). If there is a psychologist (or a specialized team) trained in particular diagnostic evaluations, then consult, consult, consult! Your colleagues with more experience will definitely be able to guide you in selecting and administering assessment tools and may also be able to participate in a coevaluation with you for your first case or with complex cases.

## Selecting Your Testing Tools

Your testing battery may depend on the referral question and the prior assessments and interventions identified in the prereferral process. Your testing battery may also depend on the materials you have available in your district. I remember being surprised after graduate school at the limited testing kits that were at my disposal. In some districts, the same kits are shared by many psychologists, or they do not have your favorite test and have no plans to get it. It is even the case in some states that certain tests are banned for certain populations of students. Again, you do the best you can with the tools you have, and plan ahead if you need to borrow test kits from other psychologists.

In general, starting with the cognitive assessment is best, because results of the cognitive testing can guide your selection of other tests of information processing (for example, memory, visual processing, auditory processing, phonological processing, attention and executive functioning, visual-motor integration). Also, students are frequently the most attentive at the beginning of testing, and you want to get a good measure of their cognitive skills.

From there, the next step is to select tests of information processing to identify processing areas of strength and processing deficits. In some states, special education law is interpreted such that you must identify a processing "deficit" for eligibility for a specific learning disability; in others, you do not need to identify a processing deficit. Either way, information about how a student processes information can be one part of the puzzle for the IEP team to determine how to change the environment, curriculum, or interventions to support the student in areas of academic need.

It should also be noted that your job is to obtain not only quantitative information about cognition and processing but also qualitative information. For example, let's say two students both got a standard score of 80 (below average) on a processing-speed task. One could have gotten a low score because he or she was slow and accurate, and the other because he or she was quick and inaccurate. The interventions for these students will be different depending on the qualitative information you gather, even though they got the same test score. When assessing students, take notes about their test behavior: their approach to testing and qualitative information about what they do when items become difficult right away (Give up? Work harder? Make negative self-statements? Get angry at the test or at you?). And I recommend that you write down your observations or, better yet, type the information into the report *right away*. I know it's difficult to do, but trust me—if you don't, you will mix up one kid's test behavior with that of another kid you are testing around the same time. As when you write up the background history at the time you review it, you will thank yourself later!

## Beginning Your Testing with the Student

Okay, *now* you are really ready to do your one-on-one testing. How and when you take a student out of class for testing is generally one of those "learn-on-the-job" skills. Some things to keep in mind: in general, the older the student, the more aware and self-conscious he or she will be about being singled out. Little kids are easy; you just say, "We're going to go do some activities together about how you learn best!" or "We are going to do some work together today!" and they frequently skip right along next to you. Older kids will need some more finesse on your part. I usually go in during a natural break time or during independent seatwork. This reduces the chance that I will have to interrupt a group lesson, which results in the entire class's turning and staring at me or at the student I am there to retrieve. One time, early in my career, I entered a classroom and asked the teacher to excuse a student, and the student screamed, "No! I'm not special ed!" She refused to budge from her seat as the whole class looked on. Awkward.

Sometimes students will balk at coming with you. Those students who think you are there because they are in trouble, those who are self-conscious or anxious, and those who don't want their peers to see that they are working with the school psychologist are most likely to refuse to cooperate. In these cases, you can send a pass for them to come to meet you in the office, or call the classroom and have the student meet you in the hallway, or enter the class and whisper to the teacher to send the student out in a few minutes, so that no one knows that you were there for him or her. I also rapidly say, "You're not in trouble; don't worry!" before explaining the testing process. Especially with anxious or reluctant students, I lay out the agenda very specifically (for example, "We will do some activities to see if you are better at learning visually or verbally first") so that they know what to expect. I might even bring a checklist with the activities and rewards written down for them to see. With other students, the explanation that I am there because their parent wanted me to work with them to see how they learn best and whether there are any additional supports we can put in place at school for them tends to suffice.

In other cases, you will have to use your negotiating skills. Some students refuse to come for testing, but when you give them a choice (for example, "What class would you like to miss to come to testing?"), you can get them to join you. I don't fight it the first time by making them come. When I have done that, the test results are usually in question because of low motivation or effort. I try a few times with the choice technique. Then, if they still don't come, I use natural consequences to my advantage and say something like, "Okay, it's your choice not to come. The thing is, we have a meeting scheduled in two weeks where I am supposed to tell your parents and teachers how you learn best so that we can help school get easier and more fun for you. Would you like to call your [mom/dad/guardian] to let [him/her] know why I don't have any information about your learning, or shall I?" Then I usually whip out my cell phone and tell them it's totally up to them. So far, I have had only one kid who has flat-out refused, and I actually had to make the call. In that case, the mom then came in and sat in on testing with the kid and me, and we got it done. Most students won't present with that much resistance, but it is good to have some tools in your kit in case they do!

## Writing Quality Reports

In a recent poll on the Notes from the School Psychologist Blog Facebook page, school psychologists across the country had a unified complaint about report writing. It wasn't what I thought it would be (writing many, many reports in a short time period). It was that school psychologists felt that they worked very hard on writing quality reports, and *no one read them* except the psychologist a few years down the road when the children were up for reevaluation. They reported that most people at the IEP meeting just wanted to know if the child was eligible, and the report was not part of their concern. I have had that experience for sure, where I begin to explain the assessment results and how the student learns best, and someone interrupts and asks me if we can just skip ahead to whether or not the kid is eligible for special education. It's frustrating to say the least.

That being said, generating a quality report that meets legal guidelines is a huge part of our jobs as special education assessors. You don't want to skimp on the report because you think no one will read it and then, lo and behold, an attorney suing the district on behalf of the parent is going over it with a fine-tooth comb. Fear of litigation isn't the only reason to write a quality report, though! There are, in fact, parents, teachers, and special educators who do read the reports and take in the information to work with the student. You have a better chance of this happening if you supplement the technical information in your report with qualitative observations so that your reports "come alive" for readers. Use the technical language and scores, but then provide a reader-friendly sentence after them about what they mean for the student in learning situations. For example, instead of writing "Johnny earned an average score on a test of simultaneous processing," it might be better to describe the test: "On a test in which Johnny was asked to look at a puzzle with four different answer choices and select the piece that would fit a pattern, he performed in the average range." But then go on to describe his test behavior (for example, "When puzzles became more difficult, Johnny tended to speed up and did not carefully look at all answer choices"). Then write about what that might mean in the classroom and a possible intervention: "This suggests that in the classroom when performing complex visual tasks, Johnny may show an impulsive response style and make careless errors. He may require additional teacher support on visual problem-solving assignments and visually complex worksheets. He may also profit from verbalizing his thought processes to slow himself down when he encounters a difficult problem."

The IEP meeting is also your chance to make your report more accessible to key stakeholders who will be working with the student. Chapter Seven will provide you with information about how to be an excellent presenter and participant on the IEP team.

It is also worth noting that you will be more successful in getting people to value your reports if you generate high-quality, student-specific recommendations. Instead of creating these from scratch every time, you can start a master recommendations template. Create categories for relevant topics and organize recommendations according to those categories. A few topics you can start with are

- Classroom supports
- Home supports

- Attention, executive functioning
- Visual processing and memory
- Auditory processing and memory
- Visual-motor integration
- Reading
- Writing
- Math
- Oral language
- Study skills
- Test taking
- Social-emotional supports
- Oppositional behavior
- Friendship-building skills

Once you have your master list of recommendations, you can copy the whole list at the end of your report and go through them all, deleting the ones that do not apply to the student. Then tweak the ones you kept to make them student specific.

Speaking of templates, when you first start out as a school psychologist, you will likely spend a lot of time making and adjusting your templates. Even after ten years of practice, I am still adjusting my templates as I add new tests, think of new and better ways to describe results, and generate new recommendations. When I first started out, I had a great mentor who e-mailed me three different reports that met the criteria for district language and were a representative sample of the top three referrals—learning disability, emotional disturbance, and ADHD. Ask a colleague you respect for his or her templates or sample reports. Using the Find and Replace function in Word, you can change the kid's first name to "Xx" and the last to "Yy." You can have one master template for all referral questions, or a few that are tailored to specific referral questions—it's a matter of personal preference. I have templates for each category of special education. Other psychologists just pick a report about a similar kid they have tested before and alter it.

One thing I must mention though is to proofread your report carefully to make sure you have the child's name, birth date, and other demographic information written correctly throughout the report! I once read a report that had three different kids' names in it. It was a dead giveaway that the psychologist cut and pasted a few reports together. It looks very unprofessional, and you definitely want to avoid that embarrassment. Also, proofread for he-she and his-her errors, or make two sets of templates, one for girls and one for boys.

## A NOTE ABOUT OTHER TYPES OF EVALUATIONS

The majority of this chapter has looked at the assessment process for initial evaluations. You will also have reevaluations (triennials), and the work flow is a bit different, though the elements are mostly the same. The biggest difference between triennials and initials is that for triennials, the background information is already there for you, and you just have to update it. Another difference is that in some districts, you do not always have to do a full reevaluation, particularly at the high school level, when there have been several prior assessments already. You will have to consult with your supervisor about how the decision about whether to conduct a full evaluation or a review of records (or partial evaluation) is made in your district.

You may also be a part of a preschool diagnostic team, in which case you will be conducting both initial and transition evaluations. In the initial evaluation, you assess a student with a multidisciplinary team, and your role in the assessment and report writing is negotiated with the team. In the case of a transition evaluation, you will be participating on a team that assesses a student when he or she transitions from preschool services to school-age services (usually when the child is transitioning to kindergarten). The focus of this assessment is to determine the most appropriate level of service for the student to meet his or her needs.

## PULLING IT ALL TOGETHER

A big part of a traditional school psychologist's job is to conduct special education evaluations. Although the test administration, scoring, and interpretation elements of the process are typically covered in graduate school and during internships, the newly minted school psychologist is often left to his or her own devices regarding organizing the assessment process. Having an efficient work flow from the beginning of the referral process through the writing of the report is key for meeting your legal timelines and creating a quality assessment. This chapter provided one such assessment work-flow system that covers the key steps in the process. The next chapter will describe strategies for presenting your assessment information effectively in IEP meetings.

---

# Key Points

- If you are working in a more traditional school psychologist role, you will frequently be seen as the "gatekeeper" to special education and the "eligibility guru," in that the IEP team will often look at your testing results as the deciding factor.
- Organizing your testing caseload begins with developing a work flow that is efficient and guides you in selecting appropriate measures for the assessment.
- You may work in the role of case manager and be expected to alert other members of the assessment team when parents have provided consent to test for special education. It is recommended you do this in writing and provide the team with dates corresponding to the legal timeline.
- Quality assessments begin with a thorough review of background information, including cumulative records, prior interventions, special education history and developmental history, and input from current teacher(s).
- Classroom observation is an instrumental part of the assessment process that enables you to gain a full picture of the child in his or her environment. It also

*(continued)*

---

assists you in determining if you need to assess areas of suspected disability other than the one(s) listed in the referral.

- Background history and observations will guide your decisions about whether or not you should do a full social-emotional-behavioral evaluation including standardized rating scales.
- Consult with your colleagues and supervisors about assessment of special populations (for example, bilingual students, non-English speakers, students with physical impairments) or populations with which you have not yet had experience testing.
- Start your report-writing process at the beginning of your assessment. Write up background history, observations, developmental history, and testing observations as you go, when this information is fresh in your mind.
- A quality assessment report includes not only quantitative data but also qualitative descriptions in parent- and teacher-friendly language. This helps your readers understand what the results actually mean for the student in learning situations.
- Developing templates takes time, but it is an essential part of streamlining your report-writing process. At the beginning of your career, borrow templates from colleagues you respect. Developing your own templates is an ongoing process.
- Creating a master recommendations template can help you quickly tailor specific recommendations for students.

## DISCUSSION QUESTIONS

1. Do you agree that the traditional school psychologist is still seen as a gatekeeper to special education? What do you see as your current role in the assessment process? What is your ideal role?

2. Within the traditional role of special education assessor, what are some steps you can take to make your assessments and reports useful to parents, teachers, and the students you work with?

3. What is your current system or work flow for assessments? How might you adapt the assessment flowchart (Figure 6.1) to meet your needs at your particular district or school?

4. What tips or strategies do you have for streamlining your assessment process? What have you found to work well for remaining organized and increasing efficiency without sacrificing quality?

5. How do you generate quality reports that meet legal standards but are also reader friendly?

6. What obstacles in the assessment process do you find in your schools or districts? What have you done to overcome these obstacles?

# chapter 7

# THE INDIVIDUALIZED EDUCATION PLAN (IEP): FRIEND OR FOE?

I remember my first IEP meeting so clearly. I was presenting my findings from testing for the first time. I had never seen anyone present test results at an IEP meeting before, and I didn't know where to start. To make matters worse, it was a doubleheader—I was presenting on twins—and the only time the mom could come was seven in the evening. I kept that poor woman and my supervisor there until eight, trying to cover everything for both boys, as everyone's eyes glazed over. No one ever taught me how to present data quickly and efficiently. Now I can boil down my results into key points in about fifteen minutes. Also, no one taught me how to deliver difficult news well or how to deal with contentious IEP members, so I stumbled through countless IEP meetings for years before I got it down. There are still IEP meetings where I learn something new about how to present (also how *not* to present). This chapter will give you the highlights on being an effective presenter at IEP meetings. IEP meetings can be transitional and positive in the life of a child, or they can be perfunctory and useless. Their value depends largely on how the team works together and keeps the goal of improving student performance in mind (rather than eligibility alone), whether they use data to drive the decision-making process, and how well the team presents the information.

# BEFORE THE IEP MEETING

Preparation before the IEP meeting is key to having a successful experience. Preparation may involve gaining exposure to different presentation styles, learning your role in the IEP process, building consensus among school staff members, and being prepared for sensitive or tense IEP situations with parents and outside professionals.

## Learning About Your Role and Presentation Style in IEP Meetings

When you are first starting out in the field, perhaps in your internship or first year, observing other psychologists presenting at IEP meetings is a good way to begin developing your own presentation style. If you are assigned to a mentor or supervisor when you first join a school district, inquire if you can observe several different psychologists presenting at IEP meetings. I had the opportunity to do this, and I have integrated the points I picked up into my own presentation style. Also, I got to observe an IEP gone awry and how the psychologist skillfully brought everyone back into focus, which was invaluable. Even experienced school psychologists can benefit from observing their colleagues present at IEP meetings.

In addition to gaining exposure to presentation styles, you will also need to learn what other responsibilities will be assigned to you during the IEP meetings. Inquire ahead of time with the case manager and IEP team members about what forms you must complete and what portions of the process you are responsible for documenting. In many districts, your IEP document is online, and you have to write your part in draft form before the meeting. In less progressive or in under-resourced districts, the document is still handwritten, and it is especially important to draft it ahead of time, or the meeting will drag on forever as you write things out by hand. You may find that your only responsibility is to write up a summary page of your testing results and possibly an eligibility determination summary form. In these cases, you can copy the summary of your report and paste it right into the IEP document. In other cases, you may be responsible for writing or contributing to additional sections of the IEP, including academic goals and objectives, accommodations and modifications, behavior support plan and goals, and mental health goals. Consult with your supervisor or case manager ahead of time about what your role is in filling in written portions of the IEP. If you are new to IEP language and to writing IEP goals, objectives, and behavior support plans, ask your colleagues for samples so that you can use them as a model for your first IEP documents. Chapter Eight on consultation gives you some practical tools for ensuring that the IEP document accurately reflects the needs and strengths of the child and is positive, proactive, and practical for those who will be implementing it.

## Building Consensus on Your IEP Team

Another step you will want to take before the IEP meeting is to collaborate with all IEP members and build consensus about eligibility for special education and proposed intervention. At minimum, you will want to talk to the case manager or special education teacher about your findings so that, before the meeting, you two together can look at the student's data to see if they meet state and federal eligibility criteria. The law states that eligibility is a team decision, but let me tell you, if your school team is not on the same page about eligibility before the meeting, chaos can ensue. If you are not in agreement before the meeting, you look uncoordinated and unprofessional when you present results to the parent and say a child isn't eligible and a special education teacher (or general education teacher) says she thinks he is. This may get you stuck in a position of being the lone ranger "bad guy," defending your results. In my early years, I didn't do the groundwork in preparing the team when kids did not meet eligibility criteria, and it was not pleasant to have my own team disagreeing with me in front of a student's parent. I would also recommend that your consensus-building process include the administrator who will be at the IEP meeting. As a colleague of mine said, "Sometimes administrators go rogue at the meeting!" Consult with the administrator beforehand, or you might find yourself on the same page with your special education teacher only to have the principal throw a wrench in your plan by disagreeing with the eligibility decision.

Now let's say you've built consensus around eligibility and you are ready to have the IEP meeting with the parents. It should be noted that it is not good practice to inform the parents that your team has already come to a decision without them. Keep in mind that you are holding the meeting to present the team's recommendations to the parents and get their input, rather than to inform parents of an eligibility determination made in their absence. In essence, the law states that eligibility is a team decision, and parents are part of the team. I have been in some ugly IEP meetings that started out with someone on the team saying that we had looked at the data and that the kid was not eligible, even before we presented any data. It is much better to present the data, get the parents' input, lay out the criteria for eligibility, and then use the information presented at the meeting to say why the kid is or is not eligible. Then the decision is informed by data, and it doesn't appear as if the decisions were all made before even hearing from the parents. Sometimes parents present new information at the IEP meeting. (Surprise! Their doctor diagnosed the child with ADHD last week. Surprise! They have an outside independent evaluation that says the child has autism!) New data like that can change the eligibility picture. So you will want to save discussions of eligibility for special education for the end of the meeting.

Now let's consider a different scenario. If after consulting with all IEP team members you cannot come to an agreement about eligibility, what do you do? In some schools, my word about eligibility is taken as the authority, and in other schools, I am fought every step of the way. Usually, the IEP team members are technically fighting with the way the law is written, not with me. A classic case is in a school where the discrepancy model of SLD is still being used, and the kid has average or above-average intelligence and a processing disorder, but no statistically significant discrepancy between ability and achievement scores, and is therefore not eligible. Yet the kid is struggling in class and not meeting his or her potential. IEP team members will try to fight your decision if you say the student doesn't meet eligibility criteria, because they just want help for the kid (and may see special education as the only avenue for help). You may have to hold the line, even if you see the logic in the argument, because of the law or district policy. If someone on the team is vehemently fighting you on eligibility for a particular student, it is worth presenting the case to your supervisor or an experienced colleague for advice. Whenever I run into a sticky case where eligibility is not clear-cut and I can't get my team to agree,

I seek outside consultation. In rare cases, I have brought district-level administrators or my supervisor with me to IEP meetings to support my eligibility decision, or have written a dissenting statement in the IEP document.

## When to Share Results with Parents Before the IEP Meeting

There are times when I will share the results of my testing with the parents before the meeting. The first instance is when parents request the written report before the meeting. I usually accommodate the request when possible. There are other times when the report is ready only the night before or the day of the IEP, so this isn't practically possible. In those instances, I tell the parents that I will do my best to get the report to them before the meeting and keep them posted on my progress. Or, in lieu of giving them a written report before the meeting, I will do a phone or in-person meeting to share key findings. Some parents who are more ardent in their advocacy for their children will state that it's their legal right to have the report before the meeting. Check with your supervisor about the state regulations and district policy on this. In general, parents are entitled to "school records" when requested in writing, but if the record doesn't exist yet because you haven't written the report, you may not have to comply with the request, legally speaking. For the purposes of building rapport and mutual cooperation, I usually try my best to comply with these requests to provide parents with the written report before the meeting.

How you deliver a report to parents in advance is also important. There are cases where it is perfectly appropriate to e-mail the report or provide a written copy of the report to the parents without meeting with them. For example, if it is a relatively straightforward triennial report and the parent is not learning for the first time of a disability, sending on the report without being available to interpret it for them is fine. If eligibility or continuing eligibility is in question, and this is written in your report, it could be problematic to have parents learn that information for the first time without explanation. In cases like these, and others, I insist on meeting with the parents to share the results as I give them the report.

In general, there are two other situations in which I meet with parents before the IEP meeting. First, if the parents are anxious about the testing results or eligibility or were hesitant to grant consent to test in the first place, I tend to offer a pre-IEP meeting with me to go over "preliminary results." This will give the parents the chance to digest the new information about their child and have any emotional reactions with you there to educate, guide, and comfort them in private. It is often much easier for the parents to hear results one-on-one than in a larger group. The other benefit is that by the time the meeting comes, the parents will have had time to think about the results and do some research on the disability so that they feel more a part of the IEP process. The other situation in which it is advisable to meet with the parents before the IEP meeting to share results is when you are letting them know of a sensitive diagnosis or a diagnosis you think will blindside the parents. I remember a case where the parents referred their child for testing because they suspected ADHD, and the child actually met criteria for an autism spectrum disorder. I knew that autism was not anywhere on their radar, so I met with them beforehand. I typically meet parents in advance if their child is being diagnosed with an intellectual disability (sometimes referred to as mental retardation or a developmental disability), ADHD, autism, or an emotional disturbance. These diagnoses are more likely to be met with an emotional reaction, such as disbelief, anger, sadness, denial, or blaming, than if a parent is learning of a learning disability. You will have to gauge each parent. There are certain parents who will also have a strong reaction to a learning disability diagnosis. It goes a long way to having a successful IEP meeting if you can prepare the parents for the discussion that will take place at the meeting by giving them some time to have an initial reaction with you there to support them. Some practical suggestions for delivering difficult news well are presented in the next section about strategies to use during the IEP meeting.

## Collaborating with Outside Team Members in the IEP

I wish someone had warned me about the possibility of a surprise "guest" at an IEP meeting. In my first year as a school psychologist, I was frequently blindsided by outside participants—advocates, attorneys, and private psychologists, for example—showing up to the meeting, armed and ready to be contentious. The first way to prepare is to collaborate with the case manager setting up the IEP meeting and check to see if the parents plan to bring someone with them. Often parents will let the case manager know they are bringing someone else, and then you will have a heads-up. At other times, you may already be aware of an outside professional who is involved in the case, and you might want to ask the parent point blank if that person will be attending the IEP meeting. If you already know that this person they plan to bring is a contentious person and has an agenda that is incompatible with the school's agenda, then it is good to consult with your supervisor in advance. In some cases, it has been necessary for the district to bring legal representation to the meeting if a parent is bringing a lawyer. At these meetings, the parent may audio-record the meeting, and the district will also want to audio-record it. You want to make sure you are not putting yourself in a lion's den of possible future litigation without proper support! Seek consultation and, when possible, get district support.

In some cases, the parents will bring their surprise guest, and that guest will have a surprise report with him or her that contradicts your findings. Parents are of course entitled to get independent evaluations, but there may be cases where the meeting needs to be rescheduled in order to review the evaluations if they are presented on the spot. Or you can use the meeting time to share out district findings and then set a second IEP meeting to review the outside report and make final eligibility decisions at that time. It's not necessarily all doom and gloom when an outside professional comes to your IEP meeting. For example, a parole officer from the juvenile justice system who comes to a meeting where truancy is an issue can give you some more leverage on the intervention side of the meeting. At times, an outside professional can advocate for a child in a way that you cannot because of your ties to your district and your district's policies. An independent evaluation may be exactly what you need to make a case for eligibility or ineligibility when that evaluation corroborates your data. I have had IEP meetings where the outside professional and I are on the same page about the student's diagnosis, which extends the validity of my results for the parent. Often I have gotten consent to collaborate with outside professionals in advance of the IEP meeting and have coordinated efforts in the best interest of the child. There have been specific situations that may arise for you as well in which the child is having a concurrent assessment by an outside professional, and it is necessary to collaborate so that your test batteries do not overlap and invalidate results. Use caution and seek consultation, however, when there is an attorney or advocate involved in an independent evaluation. Everything you say can be used against the district, as you are representative of the district. Nothing is "off the record"!

# DURING THE IEP MEETING

If you have ever been to an IEP meeting that lacks an agenda or "road map" for how information will be presented, you know it can be a very long and possibly unproductive meeting. For parents, not knowing what will be discussed at the meeting can also be an anxiety-provoking experience. That is why I recommend that at the outset of the meeting, you give parents an overview of what you will be presenting. If you just launch into findings, the parents and support staff will not know where you are going or what the findings mean for them or the child.

## Laying the Groundwork for Presenting Results

I usually start with a brief introduction to special education eligibility and the role of the school psychologist, using my "thirteen doors" speech. The speech goes something like this:

> Thank you for coming today. I am eager to present the results of how your child learns best and to develop a plan together to support your child. While our school has supports in the general education environment, it is our job to see if your child is eligible for additional special education supports. In order to be eligible, a child must have both a documented disability and evidence that his or her needs cannot be met in general education with supports.
>
> There are thirteen "doors" into special education. Each door represents a disability category. Once a child is in through that door, the team decides what the most appropriate plan is for the student. The door he or she goes through does not always dictate which services or placement a child will get. Special education is not a place, but rather a tailored program for each child based on his or her learning profile and which door or eligibility category best fits the student. [Speech changes based on referral question.] Given the information from the team's initial meeting, we were particularly interested to see if your child has [list areas of suspected disability]. Those are [number] possible doors into special education services. There were other doors I did not look into, but I can say that some students also have [list areas of disability that do not apply] that result in special education eligibility. Our speech therapist looked into the door of speech and language impairment and will present later [if there was a speech and language area of suspected disability]. I focused on your child's areas of suspected disability. First, I will address the question of [insert first suspected disability].

At this point, you would briefly explain the criteria for each area of suspected disability to lay out the road map for what your findings mean. It gives parents and teachers a mental "file" for the information you are about to present. I also bring along with me a copy of the normal curve (see Figures 7.1 and 7.2, in English and Spanish, respectively) and point to the areas as I talk about the descriptors. I give a very brief overview of the difference between standard scores, scaled scores, T-scores, and percentiles. I usually liken standard scores to a chapter or end-of-course test because it is a composite score, and liken scaled scores to quizzes or parts of a test. I also make sure to give a concrete example of a percentile score so it is not confused with a percentage (for example, if your child were in the 45th percentile, that would mean that if you lined up 100 kids his age, he would do better than 45 of them).

Once you have oriented the parents to what the scores mean about their child in relation to same-age peers, you will want to explain eligibility criteria. The following are some sample explanations of the most commonly assessed areas of suspected disability; you can use and adapt them as you explain each "door" you looked into for eligibility:

1. Specific learning disability (using the traditional discrepancy model, in which IQ tests are given to make discrepancy determinations):

> In order to meet criteria as a student with a specific learning disability, there are three main criteria. [If average IQ is required by your state/district] First, the child must have average to above-average intellectual or cognitive abilities [point to average/above-average range on normal curve]. [If average IQ is not required by your state/district] First, we look at where the child falls in terms of his or her cognitive score compared to other students his or her age.
>
> Second, the child has to have below-grade-level academic scores in reading, writing, or math that are statistically significantly lower than his or her cognitive score [point to cutoff score on normal curve]. This means the child is not doing as well in academics as we would expect of a child with his or her intelligence. This difference is also sometimes determined by other tests and classroom data.
>
> Last, the reason for this difference between the child's potential and his or her academic performance has to be due to a processing problem [if applicable by your state's interpretation of the law], and not other factors like poor attendance, lack of instruction, emotional challenges, learning a second language, low intelligence, and so on. A processing deficit means that there is one way that the child has difficulty learning—for example, on looking tasks, listening tasks, phonics tasks, or hands-on tasks—but the other ways are intact. This is why it is called a "specific" learning disability—it is one specific way that the child has trouble processing information, or it is one area of academic achievement that is difficult for him or her.

2. Specific learning disability (using the RtI model):

> In order to meet criteria as a student with a specific learning disability, there are four criteria. [List same three criteria as above, as applicable.] In addition, it must be demonstrated that the child's needs cannot be met within the general education environment with supports. We must demonstrate that the

| Score Type | Far Below Average | Below Average | Low Average | Broad Average Range | High Average | Above Average | Far Above Average |
|---|---|---|---|---|---|---|---|
| Standard Scores (SS) | 55 | 70 | 85 | 90 100 110 | 115 | 130 | 145 |
| Scaled Scores (ScS) | 1 | 4 | 7 | 8 10 12 | 13 | 16 | 19 |
| T-Scores (T) | 20 | 30 | 40 | 42 50 57 | 60 | 70 | 80 |
| Percentiles (%ile) | ≤1-2 | 3-15 | 16-24 | 25-74 | 75-84 | 85-97 | ≥98 |

**FIGURE 7.1** Normal Curve: English

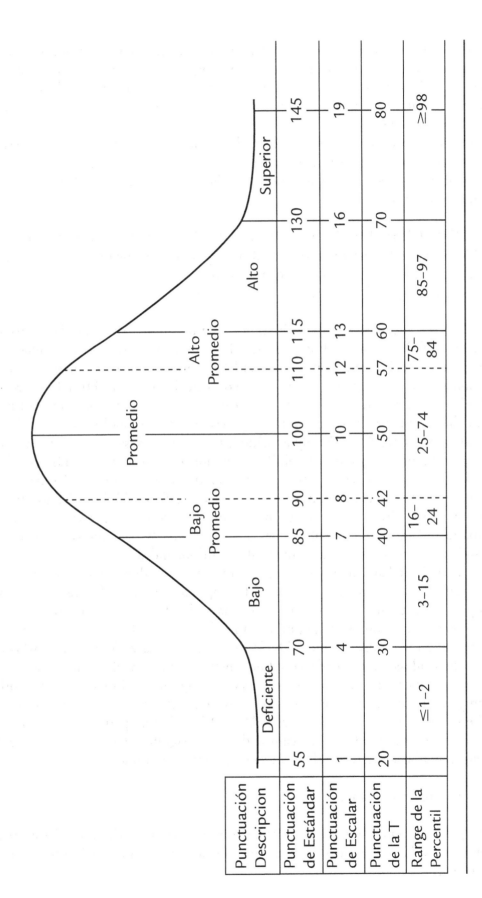

| Punctuación Descripcion | Deficiente | Bajo | | Bajo Promedio | Promedio | Alto Promedio | | Alto | | Superior |
|---|---|---|---|---|---|---|---|---|---|---|
| Punctuación de Estándar | 55 | 70 | | 85 | 90 | 100 | 110 | 115 | 130 | | 145 |
| Punctuación de Escalar | 1 | 4 | | 7 | 8 | 10 | 12 | 13 | 16 | | 19 |
| Punctuación de la T | 20 | 30 | | 40 | 42 | 50 | 57 | 60 | 70 | | 80 |
| Range de la Percentil | ≦1-2 | 3-15 | 16–24 | | | 25-74 | 75–84 | | 85-97 | 70 | ≥98 |

**FIGURE 7.2** Normal Curve: Spanish

academic problem cannot be remediated with targeted intervention. The way we do this is by providing intervention, taking data, and continually monitoring the child's progress and tweaking the intervention to the child's need. If after a certain amount of time the child is not responding to a research-based intervention, or if the rate of improvement is such that we can see that a short-term intervention is not going to help the student catch up to his or her classmates, we seek to better understand the strengths and weaknesses of the child through assessment and then consider additional supports—in this case, special education services.

3. ADHD (Other Health Impairment). Whether or not you are able to diagnose ADHD in the school district will vary by district policy. In some districts, you must have a doctor's verification for eligibility; in others, you can make the call. Your description will vary depending on the policy.

ADHD is considered a medical disability, so it falls under the special education category of Other Health Impairment. There are two main criteria for eligibility. [If a doctor's verification is required] First, we must have a doctor's verification that your child has ADHD. [If you can diagnose ADHD] First, your child must show attention/hyperactivity/impulsivity in more than one setting, and the symptoms must be severe and present before school entry. That is, a child cannot have ADHD only at school, in a certain class, or have developed it when he or she got to school. There is not a single test for ADHD. The data gathered from testing, surveys, observations, and rating scales have to form a constellation of symptoms that fit the profile of ADHD. In addition, the inattentive/hyperactive symptoms cannot be due to other factors, such as situational factors; emotional problems, such as anxiety or depression; learning problems; poor sleep; a general medical condition; and so on.

Second, we have to demonstrate that the child's needs cannot be met within the general education environment with supports. The second criterion is very important, because there are many students with ADHD who can function in the general classroom with supports and modifications. There must be a significant educational impact from ADHD in order to qualify. So a student who is meeting grade-level standards would not show an educational impact. A student who is not meeting grade-level standards or has significant difficulties with work completion despite supports might be showing a significant educational impact. The mere presence of a diagnosis of ADHD is only one part of the equation. We have to ask ourselves as a team if there is a significant educational impact that cannot be addressed in the general education environment.

4. Emotional disturbance:

My job is to figure out the main thing that is getting in the way of learning for your child. Sometimes a child's feelings and behavior can interfere with learning.

[If average or above-average cognition] After evaluating the child's cognitive abilities, we can see that he or she has the potential for learning and does well one-on-one with clear structure and support. We don't always see this potential in the classroom because of the emotional and behavioral challenges [give examples].

[If below-average cognition, but due to test behavior] After evaluating the child's cognitive abilities, we can see that his or her behavior is interfering with his or her learning, even in a quiet testing environment. These difficulties are even greater in the classroom, due to emotional and behavioral challenges [give examples].

[If below-average cognition, but you are unsure of how test behavior and emotions affected scores] After evaluating the child's cognitive abilities, he or she earned below-average scores, though it is difficult to tell how much his or her scores were impacted by emotions and test behavior [give examples].

[For all students] Think of emotions and behavior as a cloud that covers your child's true potential. [You can draw a cloud over the cognitive or academic test scores on the normal curve at this point.] Our main goal is to help your child manage his or her feelings and actions in the learning environment, or to "move" this cloud. For students whose main challenge is managing emotions and behavior, the disability category or "door" that best captures their challenge is called "emotional disturbance." Sometimes the label makes parents uncomfortable, but it is a way to gain access to additional services to support your child. We know from the history that he or she has had these challenges for a long period of time, and in several different areas, not just at school. Our goal is to support your child at school so that we can move the cloud that is masking his or her learning potential.

5. Intellectual disability, mental retardation, developmental delays:

There are three main criteria for a student to be considered as having an intellectual disability. First, the student must show significantly below-average scores on standardized cognitive tests [point to below 70 on the normal curve]. As you know, cognitive tests are tests of solving brand-new problems without any help. So a low score doesn't mean a child can't learn; it means that he or she will continue to need adult support to learn new things and will require repetition and practice.

The second criterion is that the student must show adaptive behavior challenges. This means that the child must show that he or she has difficulties functioning in an age-appropriate manner and being self-sufficient in the community, whether it has to do with personal safety, personal care, communication, getting around the community, or socialization. You and your child's teacher completed surveys about what your child can do independently in the school and larger community. Your child's strengths are in the areas of [list adaptive behavior strengths]. He or she still needs assistance in [list adaptive behavior weaknesses].

Last, the child must have had these difficulties across his or her lifespan. You reported that your child had difficulties as a toddler with learning new things independently. [List developmental challenges prior to school entry.] Now that he or she is in school, your child needs continued support from his or her teachers in learning new things and applying skills to new situations. Although the label "intellectual disability" is uncomfortable for many parents, it is important to remember that this label will enable you to gain access to more support for you and your child. This is a lifelong challenge, and the more early intervention and support we can get for your child, the better.

6. Autism:

One of the "doors" into special education that we looked into was under the category of autism. It is important to note that the educational criteria for autism are not exactly the same as the criteria used by clinicians in the community. The educational diagnosis of autism is better thought of as "autistic-like" in that if a student shows symptoms that are like autism and there is an educational impact, he or she may be eligible for services. In the community, the criteria are often more stringent to receive the diagnosis. Receiving the diagnosis alone is not enough to qualify a student for special education, as we also need to show that there is an impact on the child's educational performance. What is most important is not the label but that we identify the symptoms that interfere with learning and target those symptoms.

The first group of symptoms is in the area of socialization. Part of school is learning to get along with, and relate to, one's peers and adults. [Discuss observations of child's impairments and strengths in social interaction.] The second group of symptoms is in the area of communication. In order to function in school, children need to be able to have to-and-fro conversations with others either verbally or nonverbally. [Discuss observations of child's impairments and strengths in communication.] Finally, there are some symptoms that prevent students from participating in the classroom community, such as repetitive or ritualized patterns of behavior, and restricted interests. [Discuss observations of child's impairments in terms of repetitive and stereotyped behaviors.]

Taken together, we see a constellation of symptoms that cluster together to meet criteria as a student who has an educational diagnosis of autism, or "autistic-like." Autistic-like symptoms are like tin foil on top of a bowl of learning potential. We must address the symptoms of poor communication, socialization, and restricted behaviors to "peel off" the tin foil to allow access to learning. We cannot know how deep the bowl for learning is until we work on the symptoms that are getting in the way. The IEP team is here to develop interventions and supports to get access to your child's learning potential. I understand that the label may be difficult to hear, but it is helpful if it gives us access to more support for your child.

## Other Helpful Tips When Presenting at an IEP Meeting

There are a number of other tricks of the trade in presenting at an IEP meeting that you might want to try:

- Bring visuals to illustrate data. Show, don't tell! In addition to bringing a normal curve to show where test results fall, you can also bring samples of your actual testing materials to show what kinds of tasks you asked the child to perform. It is better to show a sample item from the actual test than to try to explain the test verbally. This gives parents and teachers a chance to make a connection between the child's performance and the learning tasks he or she may have in class or during homework.

- Use the parents' concerns to guide your focus in your presentation. Ask them at the beginning of the meeting, "Do you want an overview of findings, or are there specific questions you want answered by the time I'm done presenting?" That way, you know in advance if they just want the punch line (for example, eligible or not? SLD or ADHD?) or if they want the details too. They may even present a concern that was not on your radar at all, and you can address it for them.

- Condense your findings into a fifteen-minute presentation if possible. Do this by picking key information to focus on and by giving a brief example of items from each in the following areas: cognitive and processing strengths and areas of need, what the results mean in relation to the classroom and to the student's learning, and the student's social-emotional-behavioral functioning. Trust me—an overview is fine, because your report has the details.

- After each section (cognitive, processing, social-behavioral) stop and ask the parents, "Does that sound like your child?" so that you can involve them in the process. They may provide a good example of what you are talking about as reflected in the test scores, which helps the team better understand the child. Or if they say that your findings are different from their experiences, you can better understand what they are observing and make connections about why your results were different (for example, your tests are more structured or more novel; you built in rewards and breaks). This question can also be directed at the student's teacher, to see if there is consistency or inconsistency between your findings and his or her observations in the classroom.

- Be sure to include the student's strengths in your presentation whenever possible. As school psychologists we are used to talking about deficits and disabilities, but we cannot lose sight of the fact that we are talking about deficits in someone's child. Imagine that every child you test is someone's precious baby and be empathic about what it would be like to sit in a room for an hour or so and hear what your child cannot do.

- When the child is not eligible for special education services, frame it as a positive. Sometimes people get shortsighted and think that if a child is not eligible for services, this is a negative thing. In fact, it can be positive, because that means either the child is not disabled or the child's disability can be managed in a less restrictive environment. Also include information about how the child's needs will be supported in the general education setting.

- At times, parents (and teachers!) can have strong emotional reactions to news about a child's disability or eligibility, including anger, sadness, denial, and guilt. Good counseling and consultation skills are also good IEP skills. Use such techniques as reflective listening (for example, "What you're saying is . . ."); normalizing reactions (for example, "It is perfectly normal to have mixed feelings about what we've learned about your child's learning today . . ."); reframing (for example, "From your raised voice, I can see you are very passionate about us understanding your child"); and noticing and exploring reactions (for example, "If those tears could talk, what would they say?").

- If your team "goes rogue" and publicly disagrees with your eligibility findings, argue your points using data. If the team *really* goes rogue and makes a student eligible when you disagree, simply document your dissent on a continuing notes page of the IEP. After the meeting, talk to your supervisor about what went down so that he or she is aware of the situation.

- There may be times when people are rude to you in the meeting. I have had advocates and outside professionals insult me, interrupt me, and roll their eyes at me. Dealing with nasty people is a challenge, but school psychologists have the skill set to model calmness and professional decorum! For example, if you are habitually interrupted, use such statements as "I listened quietly while you spoke, and I would like to have the same professional courtesy extended to me when I am speaking. I will certainly allow you to respond when I am finished." As a last resort, if you or your team members are being verbally abused to the point that the meeting is no longer productive, consider adjourning the meeting and rescheduling, perhaps with district representation and a highly structured agenda.

- You will be working with parents who vary widely in terms of their levels of education and experience. Some will be nearly as educated as you are on child development, and some will not understand your findings. You have to tailor your presentation style so that you are explaining things in a way that all parents can understand. If you have involved the parents in the assessment process along the way, you should have a good understanding of their level of functioning and how to best communicate your results.

- If you are working with parents who do not speak English and you are not fluent in their language, seek out an interpreter who understands special education, when possible. There are some specialized terms they need to know, and you do not want sensitive results to be presented incorrectly because the interpreter doesn't have the specialized vocabulary to relay the information to the parent accurately.

- Some parents will also present with their own mental health issues and can make irrational demands at IEP meetings. I had a parent once demand that we write into the IEP that the special education room had to be kept at exactly 68 degrees or she would sue the district. I usually advise the case manager to simply document the parent's request in the continuing notes page and then document why the district can or cannot comply with the request. I don't fight it in the meeting. Sometimes just writing down the parent's complaint is all that is needed. If it goes further into a formal complaint, there are compliance officers in the district who are able to handle these types of requests should they advance to litigation. Pick your battles.

## AFTER THE IEP MEETING

It is tempting to cross the IEP off your to-do list the second the meeting ends and bolt out of there, as you probably have many more testing appointments and meetings in your future to get to! However, it is good for rapport to walk the parents out of the meeting and do a quick debrief of the experience. I often walk parents to the main office to sign out and ask them how they thought it went. To end on a positive note, I also leave them with a few points on the child's strengths and the action plan we set.

Sometimes it is necessary to also debrief with the IEP team. It should go without saying, but do make sure that the parents are out of earshot before you start debriefing! Sometimes among IEP team members, we make comments that we wouldn't make in front of the parents, and it is not a good scene if the parents hear you talking about them right after they leave. When debriefing the IEP meeting with your team, make sure that if there were any action items listed, each team member knows who is responsible for the item and what the timeline is. Write down in the follow-up plan any obligations you have.

## PULLING IT ALL TOGETHER

The IEP process is designed to be one of mutual collaboration and problem solving in order to help a struggling child succeed in school. The degree to which the IEP is a meaningful process or a perfunctory paperwork hour depends on how well your team works together, how information is presented, and the extent to which the data obtained are used to guide the decision-making process about the best way to serve the student. New school psychologists and veterans alike have room to improve in their presentation of test findings. Much of the groundwork for an effective IEP meeting is done before the meeting, in building rapport with the parents, building consensus among team members, preparing for outside participants, and relaying information to parents in advance of the meeting in certain situations. During the IEP meeting, providing a road map of what you will be presenting in the larger context of special education eligibility can prepare team members for findings. Using visual aids, such as the normal curve, and demonstrations of testing materials can bring your findings to life as well. Throughout the process, modeling empathy, professionalism, and calmness will also help you manage emotional reactions to findings. You can use your counseling tools to handle uncomfortable or contentious situations. When appropriate, you may require additional district-level supports for particularly challenging cases. Finally, debriefing the IEP process with the parents and the team is a good way to identify what worked and what didn't in the presentation style in order to make improvements for subsequent IEP meetings.

---

### Key Points

- Preparation for IEP meetings is key to their success. Observe other psychologists presenting their results to get an idea of the different styles and approaches you can integrate into your own style.

---

*(continued)*

- Building consensus about special educational eligibility is key for a smooth meeting. You will want to consult with the case manager or special education teacher, general education teacher(s), and the administrator in advance of the meeting. If you cannot build consensus, seek consultation from your supervisor or an experienced colleague.

- Parents may request your report before the IEP meeting. To the degree possible, accommodate this request. In general, it is better to give them the report in person or offer interpretation over the phone instead of just e-mailing them or sending the report home. This is true especially in cases where the parents are learning of a disability for the first time or if it is a sensitive disability, such as autism, emotional disturbance, or an intellectual disability. You may also want to meet in person if a parent is highly anxious about the IEP meeting and findings, or was reluctant to grant consent to test in the first place.

- Be prepared for outside participants in the IEP meeting, such as independent evaluators, attorneys, advocates, private psychologists, parole officers, and other support professionals. Try to find out in advance if parents are bringing an outside professional and collaborate with him or her. Use caution, however, if the person is an attorney or advocate, as everything you say can be used against the district in court. Nothing is "off the record."

- During the IEP, it is useful to provide the team with a road map of how your findings fit into the larger picture of eligibility for special education. The "thirteen doors" speech is one way to set the stage for the meeting and explain your role in the process.

- Explaining the disability criteria in parent- and teacher-friendly language goes a long way toward helping the meeting participants understand the child's learning and educating them on disabilities and eligibility. The disabilities that school psychologists most frequently have to explain are SLD, ADHD, emotional disturbance, intellectual disability, and autism.

- Use visual aids when presenting data. Show examples of the testing materials so that the team can make connections between your testing and the activities in the classroom that are similar to your testing.

- It is good practice to debrief with parents and the team members after the IEP meeting is adjourned. This way, you can talk about what went well in the presentation and what to improve on in subsequent IEP meetings.

# DISCUSSION QUESTIONS

1. If you are a new school psychologist, what has your experience been in presenting at IEP meetings? What do you think has gone well, and what do you need to improve on? What tips or strategies from this chapter do you think you can use right away at your next IEP meeting?
2. For new and experienced school psychologists, what is your biggest challenge in presenting at IEP meetings? What tools do you have to overcome these challenges? Are there any specific tips or strategies from this chapter that you think will be useful for addressing your challenges?
3. Managing emotional reactions in IEP meetings can be challenging. Discuss an IEP in which a parent or staff member became emotional and how you handled it. In retrospect, what would you have done differently or in addition to what you did?
4. How are final eligibility decisions made among your IEP team members? Is it easy or difficult for you and your team to come to a consensus about eligibility? What supports are in place at your district when there is disagreement on the team?
5. The chapter presented several ways to explain eligibility to parents in an easily understandable way. What other effective ways have you found to explain eligibility? Do you have other analogies to help parents understand their child's disability?

# chapter 8

# DO YOU HAVE A MINUTE?

## How to Be an Effective Consultant

I know I am going to have a busy day at work when I am approached immediately upon entering the school building for a "hallway consultation" before I even get a chance to put down my giant bags of testing materials. I know it will be a *really* busy day if the principal pops her head out of her office and intercepts me to consult before I can put down my purse. For a school psychologist, there are so many daily "on the fly" consultations that you could spend all day consulting and never get to any of your other tasks. Equally challenging, if not more so, is when you have to consult with a staff member about a student and he or she does not welcome your consultation. As mentioned in Chapter Two, one of the biggest challenges in working within a school system is dealing with the multitude of personalities of parents, school staff, coworkers, and community-based professionals. You need to be a skillful consultant with both the "voluntary" and "involuntary" consultee in order to help school staff and parents understand and support children's development.

All school psychologists, but especially new ones, have the additional challenge of feeling pressure to have the "right" answer when they are approached about a difficulty with a child. They may be expected to give a quick-fix answer to a complex problem, or the school staff member may want them to solve the problem for him or her by working with the student directly. Believe me—there were many instances in my first few years when teachers and administrators would come to me for advice about students, and I would have no idea how to help. I had instincts and hunches, some knowledge of the research on the topic of concern, but really no practical advice. The good news is that you don't need all the right answers to be an effective consultant. You need to be able to ask the right questions and know how to collaborate with the consultee to find the answer together.

There are many different philosophies, theories, and techniques to guide you when consulting in the schools. Some school psychology training programs explicitly teach consultation skills, and some do not. The benefit of having a research-based framework for consultation is that you know that the techniques have been tried and tested over time. This often comforts me when I am deep in the process of trying to help a teacher better understand a student, and we are getting nowhere fast! I trust the process and stay the course instead of giving up. The framework for this chapter draws on Caplan and Caplan's consultee-centered consultation model (1999). The basic idea is that working with support staff (primarily teachers, called the "consultees") about a student's mental health or academic issues can help the child, even without your directly working with the child. The added bonus is that you have actually helped the teacher develop a new skill set, new strategies, or a different framework, allowing him or her also to be more effective with future incoming students with similar challenges. This kind of consultation is primary prevention at its best.

## WHERE THEORY MEETS REAL LIFE

Like any good theory, the consultee-centered consultation theory is great . . . in theory! The reality of working in a school system with a multitude of personalities and ever-evolving challenges is that you need to be flexible in applying the theory in your day-to-day life. This section highlights common consultation situations a school psychologist encounters in his or her daily work, and gives tips for effective consultation as well as strategies for avoiding common consultation pitfalls.

### Behavioral Consultation

*"You* have *to do something about Johnny; he is out of control!"*

These consultations often take the form of the hallway grab—some desperate teacher stops you in the hall and pleads for help because she is at her wits' end with a behaviorally challenged student. Whether the student is presenting severe acting-out behaviors (physical aggression or extreme oppositionality) or more "mild" behavioral challenges (getting out of his or her chair, making rude comments, or not starting on his or her work), the important thing is that the teacher sees the behavior as a huge problem and is seeking help.

First, congratulate yourself that the teacher has a relationship with you that permitted this help-seeking behavior in the first place! Some teachers are highly anxious or fearful that you will be judgmental about their teaching or classroom management skills if they seek help. The only problem is that in this scenario, you are on your way to do something else and don't have time to do any deep problem solving in that moment, and the teacher's comment indicates that she wants *you* to take care of the problem. The following steps are recommended in this situation.

### 1. Evaluate If the Child Is a Danger to Himself or Others in That Moment

If you rush off and tell the teacher that you'll talk with him later, you may be leaving him with a dangerous situation. Say something like, "Is there an emergency situation right now that I can help with, or can we talk during your prep period or lunch or after school today?" If there is an emergency related to safety, then assist the teacher right away. (See Chapter Eleven for strategies for assisting in a crisis situation.) If there is not an emergency, agree on a time to talk later. It is also important to note that the school should have a schoolwide plan for emergency situations (for example, when a child is being violent in the classroom). If there is not, this is a point about which to consult with your administration at a schoolwide support team meeting.

### 2. Meet with the Teacher to Get a Better Sense of the Problem

Help the teacher transition from the global ("He's out of control all the time!") to the specific by asking When, Where, and What questions. I avoid Why questions because they elicit the teacher's conjecture rather than information about the specific behavior exhibited by the student. Examples of useful questions include "What does 'out of control' look like in the classroom?" "When are you most likely to see this behavior?" "What happens right before the behavior?" "Where in the classroom are you most likely to see this?" "How do you respond to the behavior?" and "When you do X [insert positive behavioral strategy, such as praising positive behavior], how does he respond?" It should be noted with that last example that the teacher may not be implementing any positive behavioral strategies, but I ask the question to plant the seed anyway. Even if she is being proactive and positive in responding to the student's behavior, she may not be aware that it is working, because she is so focused on when it is *not* working. If she's not using such strategies, she might consider doing so because you brought them to the forefront of her mind.

### 3. Identify What the Teacher Has Already Done

After you have homed in on the behavioral problem such that you can picture it in your mind clearly, ask the teacher what he has already tried in the classroom, or what other teachers who have the student have tried. You can also ask him what he has tried that has *not* worked. A big no-no in consultation is jumping in with your fabulous ideas before asking what has already been tried. If you tell a teacher what he should be doing with a nice quick fix (Have you tried positive reinforcement? Moving his seat? Calling his parents?), he might get annoyed because he already tried those things, and you appear patronizing or unhelpful. Find out what the teacher has done already, because chances are, he wouldn't be grabbing you in the hall in desperation if the quick fixes worked. The purpose of this initial meeting should be to identify the problem and the strategies that have proven ineffective, not to provide advice. The biggest gift you can give a teacher is to help him conceptualize the problem in a new way. For example, maybe Johnny doesn't "refuse to work all the time," but he refuses when the teacher gives him a writing prompt, when he is seated next to Jill, when the teacher gives him a warning by putting his name on the board, and typically on Mondays after visiting his dad. That makes the problem more "bite size" for the teacher to manage.

### 4. Build Empathy for the Child by Keeping the Focus on the Child's Perspective

It is tempting in consultation to focus either on what the child is doing to misbehave or what the teacher is doing (in your mind) that is contributing to the problem. Often, by the time a teacher is meeting with you, she may be superannoyed or fed up with a kid's behavior. Maybe this particular kid reminds her of a kid with whom she was unsuccessful in the past, and the similarity is triggering an emotional reaction. Building empathy for the child who is misbehaving can go a long way toward helping the teacher expand her view of the current situation in her classroom. One technique I frequently use is the "wondering out loud" technique. After the teacher presents the litany of complaints about the kid, I might wonder out loud, "Wow. He sounds really out of control. I wonder what it is like for him to feel out of control all the time . . ." or "I wonder what goes through this kid's mind when he is the only one whose name is on the board . . ." Sometimes this can shift a teacher's focus from all the misbehavior and think about the child's perspective. Even if the teacher doesn't have that "aha!" moment in the consultation session about how hard it is for a kid to be out of control, the seed is planted for her to look at the child in a new way.

### 5. Offer to Visit the Classroom Before Offering Suggestions

After you have homed in on the problem, made it bite-size, and tried to build empathy for the child, the teacher may want practical suggestions for what he should do today or tomorrow with the child. It is very tempting to jump into the solution phase at this point. However, I find it extraordinarily helpful to lay eyes on the kid before doing so. As an observer, you might be able to identify other factors in the equation that the teacher isn't seeing because he is so busy teaching. You may also find that the kid's behavior is either more or less extreme than the teacher's presentation of the behavior. The observation may also help you build empathy for the teacher, when you get to see how difficult it is to have students with behavioral challenges in the classroom. You can use the behavioral observation tool from Chapter Six (Form 6.3) during the observation, or do a formal time sampling of the target behavior for the child and a comparison peer (or both). This will allow you to bring data back to the teacher about the "when and where" of the behavior, as well as about classroom factors that might be contributing to the problem.

### 6. Schedule a Follow-up Meeting to Share Observations

It is extraordinarily important to be as nonjudgmental and positive as possible in sharing your observations. Teachers may be anxious about your seeing them in the classroom during a time when they are not successful working with a student. They may also externalize the blame by placing the problem entirely within the child and seeking you to validate how bad the behavior is. Expressing empathy for the teacher is a good place to start. Tell her that you can see why she sought support for this child, and, regardless of how severe the behavioral difficulties appear to you, thank her for giving you the opportunity to see them "live" in the classroom.

From there, share your observations by focusing on the child's reaction to the environment, not the teacher's behavior. I usually start with the hard data (for example, "During whole group time, he was on task 70 percent of the time, but when the class transitioned to independent work, he was on task 30 percent of the time, whereas a comparison peer was on task during independent work 50 percent of the time" or "I observed him to curse at other students six times during the fifteen-minute observation period"). Then ask the teacher what she makes of the data, and whether your observation period was a "typical" sample of his behavior. Frequently, the teacher will note that it was a "good day" when you observed. I see this as a positive thing. Sometimes when you are observing, teachers put extra effort into supporting that child. It is a great segue into the positive teacher behaviors that you observed. Like the students we work with, teachers also benefit from *at least* a 3:1 ratio of positive to negative feedback! I usually say something like, "When you did X [insert behavioral intervention technique], I noticed that Johnny responded by starting on his work," or "When you did Y [insert good classroom management technique], Johnny did not curse at you." Then, when you have given a few positives, throw in constructive feedback, such as, "However, I noticed that Johnny cursed after you put his name on the board as a warning. Is this a typical reaction for him?" This can help the teacher identify ineffective behavioral strategies in her practice.

## 7. Develop an "Appetizer" Action Plan

Based on the observation and the positive teacher behaviors that supported positive student behaviors, the next step is to develop an action plan with the teacher. A common pitfall of consultation (as well as when developing any classroom or individual behavior plan) is to start too big and set unrealistic goals. Frame for the teacher that we need to teach the child the skills to behave, and as when teaching any skill, we may need to "undo" bad habits first and start small. I usually use an analogy of biting off more than you can chew—instead of putting all the behavioral problems on the plate for intervention, I suggest we start with an "appetizer" for us to try out first. I have the teacher pick the behavior that he thinks is interfering the most with learning (usually, it's the one that bugs him the most too), and we target that behavior first. You could also start with a behavior that is more easily changed, so that you begin with a success before tackling the "big" behavior. Here is where you can tap into a teacher's knowledge base and help him feel empowered. Ask him, "What have you done in the past with similar students with [targeted behavior] that worked for you?" or "Given the observations I shared, what are one or two things we could try during [specific work period] to see if they are effective in curbing [target behavior]?" or "What is one skill we can teach Johnny to do instead of [target behavior]?" Bite size is key! You want to give the teacher and student a "taste" of success first. Then the teacher can work on generalizing the effective strategies to other work periods and indeed other students.

## 8. Follow Up!

Sometimes after a really good consultation session, I feel like chalking up a victory and moving on to my list of other students. A common pitfall in consultation is not following up. Imagine you went to a personal fitness trainer one time and learned some great exercises, and then the trainer never followed up to see how you were doing. The odds of your continuing to follow the plan you agreed on for the long term diminishes without the check-in. Set a time with the teacher to follow up with the plan. I usually follow up within the first week, as the plan is fresh in the teacher's mind and she is, I hope, still energized to make changes. Sometimes you only have time for the before-school "stop and chat" with the teacher, but it is ideal if you can set up at least a twenty- to thirty-minute follow-up time. Some follow-up is better than none, though, so make sure you do at least a five-minute check-in, and then set up a longer chunk of time later.

To avoid putting myself in the role of a supervisor instead of that of a consultant, I usually ask the teacher about the child's reaction to the plan, not if he is following the plan. So I might ask, "What was the child's reaction when you did [agreed-on teacher strategy]?" instead of "Did you do the behavior chart this week?" If the teacher responds that he hasn't tried the strategy yet, you can then problem-solve about what part of the plan didn't work. It may be appropriate to reset the goal to be an even smaller bite, or the strategies may need to be examined for better ease of implementation.

### 9. Be Available for Future Consultations

It goes without saying that consultation takes time and that classroom challenges are ever evolving. Don't give up on the process. Rarely do consultations result in nice and tidy behavioral changes in teachers and students. Think of each consultation as a way to plant this seed with a teacher: if you want a child's behavior to change, you will likely have to change how you interact with the child. Each time a teacher consults with you, you are encouraging the process of reflection on the teaching practice itself as well as the expansion of the tools and strategies available for working with behavioral challenges in the classroom.

## Social-Emotional and Crisis Consultation

*"You have to see Johnny right away for counseling!"*

School psychologists are commonly seen as people who can work with a student, fix her up, and ship her back to class to learn. True, we often possess a skill set that allows us to do "psychological first aid" and help students in need of de-escalation or those with adjustment issues and such mental health challenges as depression and anxiety. Chapters Nine, Ten, and Eleven contain information about counseling techniques for individual students, groups, and crisis situations. It may also be the case that counseling is not part of your role. However, consultation offers an opportunity for you to expand teachers', parents', and administrators' understanding of child and adolescent mental health issues so that they can work more effectively with all students, regardless of whether you work directly with the student in a counseling role or not. Effective consultation about the social and emotional needs of a student can help expand the skill set of the teacher so that his or her future interactions with students are more well informed. The following steps are recommended when a teacher, parent, or administrator ("consultee") comes to you with a concern about a student's immediate mental or emotional health functioning.

## *1. Listen and Reflect Back the Concern*

The first step is to gather more information about what the consultee is observing that brought her to you in the first place. Similar to the approach in behavioral consultation, you need to understand the intensity, duration, and severity of the problem before generating appropriate responses. After allowing the consultee to share her observations about the child, ask pointed questions about how long she has had the concern, and if the concern is present at both home and school. For example, there is a big difference between situational depression (for example, the student recently lost a family member and is in the normal grieving process) and pervasive depression (for example, the student lost a family member three years ago and is showing a protracted depression). Reflecting back the concern is also a good way to make sure you understand the consultee's concern accurately. I also ask if she thinks the social-emotional concern is having an impact on learning and if so, how she sees it affecting classroom performance. This gives you a sense of whether or not there is a functional impairment for the child as well.

## *2. Offer to "Check In" with the Student to Get the Student's Perspective*

This visit with the student is another information-gathering technique, not counseling. Collaborate with the parents and ensure they are comfortable with you checking in with the student. In some emergency cases, you do not need parent permission to check in one time with a student, and you will need to be prepared if a student reports being a danger to himself or herself or others (see Chapter Eleven on crisis counseling). Doing the "check-in" is a skill that is built over time. If you are a new school psychologist, you may feel uncomfortable or unprepared for pulling a child out of class to do a social-emotional screening, especially if the concern is a new one for you (for example, cyberbullying, cutting, suspicion of sexual abuse, presence of psychotic symptoms). In these situations, call your supervisor or an experienced colleague and consult with him or her before you do the check-in to get a "road map" of how to do the check-in and ask questions that will guide intervention.

In general, the main purpose of the check-in is to identify the child's take on the problem reported by the consultee rather than to complete a diagnostic evaluation. Before doing the check-in with the child, give her information about the limits of confidentiality during the meeting—in other words, tell her that you will not share anything without her permission, unless she reports a dangerous situation (harm to self, harm to others). In some cases, the child endorses symptoms that are interfering with her emotional and school functioning, and in some cases, she denies any problem whatsoever. Your job is to get your finger on the pulse of the situation by gathering the child's subjective experience so that you can consult with others about how to support the student.

At the end of your check-in, ask the child if she is comfortable with your sharing what you've discussed with her teacher or parent. In my experience, most kids are surprisingly okay with your sharing their experience with others. For those who are not, you can explore the resistance and come to an agreement about "themes" you can share with others to help the situation (for example, "Johnny talked about sadness and bullying") versus specifics ("Harold is bullying Johnny, and Johnny cries every day after school"). Depending on the age of the child, you can also come up with a few ideas for intervention or supports she might need or want.

### *3. Follow Up with the Consultee About the Check-in*

Now you are ready to clarify the social-emotional concern for the consultee as well as develop an action plan for supporting the student. Share what the student allowed you to share, and together you can determine what level of intervention is needed (for example, continued check-ins, counseling with you, counseling with a school-based mental health professional, in-class support, linking parents and family to outside supports, and so on). In addition to providing a support plan for the particular student you are consulting about, you can also use this as an opportunity to expand the teacher's knowledge about the student's particular social-emotional difficulty. The National Association of School Psychologists Web site (www.nasponline.org) offers some great reproducible one- to two-page descriptions, research, and tips for working with students with a particular social-emotional challenge. You can explain the handout and highlight a few key points that are appropriate for the particular student. If you are not an expert in the specific social-emotional concern, do not be afraid to say so, and offer to connect the student with someone in the community who is an expert.

### *4. Follow Up!*

If you end up working with the student directly, you can continue consulting with parents and teachers about progress and the intervention plan. If your role was purely consultation, you should definitely follow up to find out if the intervention plan was implemented. I also find it useful to consult with the teacher about his or her ongoing observations of the student in class and to answer questions about how to support a student with an emotional challenge in the classroom. This is done much in the same way as the behavioral consultation process detailed earlier in this chapter: identify the concern, observe the student, provide feedback, and follow up. You might develop your own "consultation binder" that contains your notes and the student plan, as well as flags for when your follow-up meetings with the teacher are scheduled. This way, you can remember to provide the important ongoing consultation teachers need to support students with challenges.

## Academic Consultation

*"Johnny is failing, and I don't know what to do!"*

School psychologists are often called on to be experts in learning and behavior. Although many of us feel right at home with our training in behavioral and social-emotional intervention, we can sometimes feel a little out of our league when it comes to instructional techniques, especially if we have never been a teacher or have not had training in curriculum. What we do have to offer is a developmental perspective on learning. We are taught about typical and atypical development of reading, writing, and math, and can identify early warning signs of disabilities in these areas. We can also consult about the interplay among emotions, behaviors, the classroom environment, and learning. When a teacher or parent comes to you about an academic concern, either individually or in a problem-solving team situation, you can utilize your consultation skills to help guide the intervention, even if you are not an expert in the academic area. Chapter Four discussed ways to facilitate academic interventions, such as by familiarizing yourself with the curriculum and intervention supports at your school. Chapter Five on Response to Intervention also highlighted how to be involved in prevention of academic problems, in early intervention, and in consulting on a data team. This section gives a few practical tips on how to consult with teachers about academic difficulties in sticky situations.

### 1. During an Academic Consultation, a Teacher Says, "You've Never Been a Teacher Before, So You Wouldn't Understand"

There is some validity to this statement if you indeed have never been a teacher before. It is usually advisable to enter the consultation relationship by putting this out there right away. The school psychology consultant brings her unique expertise and skill set to the table, and the teacher brings his. I typically start the consultation with something like, "My expertise is in the interplay between student learning, emotions, and behavior. I typically work with students one-on-one or in a small group, so I'm going to rely on you and your expertise as a classroom teacher to help me understand how things work in your class. I want you to think of my suggestions as a 'menu' of general options you can choose from, but please let me know if the suggestions do not apply to your classroom or the student, and we can find a way to tweak them so they work for you." This way, you have set the stage for a collaborative process of problem solving, rather than positioning yourself as the "expert." You and the teacher both bring something to the problem-solving table.

### 2. During an Academic Consultation, You Feel Unequipped to Provide Any Suggestions Because You Don't Know Enough About the Curriculum

I will be the first to admit that my training in graduate school left some gaps in my knowledge about certain academic areas. I focused most of my energy on learning about reading and writing development in the early grades, so when I found myself in a consultation about a high school student struggling in algebra, my suggestion bank was empty. Instead of faking my way through the consultation, I instead admitted that I wasn't an expert on algebra intervention, and asked the teacher to share her expertise on what had worked in the past with similar students. It turned out that she had a whole host of interventions; she just needed someone to bounce ideas off of to realize the breadth of her knowledge as well as to sort through the multitude of ideas to find the ones that best fit her student. She left the consultation feeling great because she had taught me something, and I left feeling great because I had a few new ideas for supporting students in algebra. In the consultation process, we can even model for teachers that it is okay not to know the answer, which can be comforting for them. Sometimes we both agree to look for further resources and information together and reconvene to build both our knowledge bases. When consultation is well done, the benefits are bidirectional; I learn as much from my teachers as they learn from me.

## Consultation During the IEP-Writing Process

You can also apply consultation skills when the team is constructing, writing, and editing the IEP document. In particular, you will want to be equipped with consultation tools for crafting meaningful behavior support plans and goals. I have been in so many IEP meetings and have seen so many IEP documents where the behavior support plan is either unrealistic or too generic. I have cringed when I've seen that the "plan" is really just to tell the child what he should be doing (for example, "Johnny will do his homework"). Let me tell you, if just informing the kid what he should be doing was going to work, it would have worked way before a behavior plan was needed! Again, you can use your consultation skills to get across the point that if we want the child's behavior to change, the adults need to change as well, because whatever it is we are doing isn't working. You can make this point by asking questions like "How is telling Johnny to do his homework different from what we are doing now?" and "What supports that we are not already using can we put in place to assist him with his homework completion?"

We want to be careful that the team isn't using the wrong lens for the student as well. Sometimes behavior support plans are heavily focused on rewards and punishments, operating from the assumption that the behavior comes from a lack of motivation. Often the behavior actually comes from a skill deficit. Perhaps Johnny isn't doing his homework because he doesn't know how to do it or because he has a low tolerance for frustration when he doesn't get it right away. Your intervention may be different if you can uncover the root of the behavioral challenge. I sometimes use an analogy that the team can relate to: "If you put calculus in front of me and you promised to reward me if I finished it, but I didn't know how to do it, you wouldn't see a change in my behavior, because it isn't a motivation issue; it's a skill deficit issue." An excellent resource that illustrates this concept in detail, along with offering practical suggestions for consulting with school staff about kids with challenging behavior, is the work of Ross Greene, psychologist and developer of the Collaborative Problem Solving approach, www.livesinthebalance.org.

You can also make sure that the team is targeting the behavior in a positive way. We don't want any behavioral goals that are worded in the negative ("Johnny will not curse at his teacher when he's frustrated"). Sure, we want to see a reduction in the negative behavior, but we also want to build Johnny's skills. So you could rewrite that goal as "Johnny will use appropriate language and seek help when he is frustrated." You can also guide people in making positively worded goals by applying the "sleeping person" rule: don't make any rules that a sleeping person can do (for example, stay in seat, be quiet, not call out in class). Positively worded goals encourage positive behaviors (for example, ask for permission to leave seat, speak about school topics at appropriate times, raise hand to participate). Goals should also be realistic and doable. As I've mentioned elsewhere, I use the "SMART" test: is the goal **S**pecific, **M**easurable, **A**ttainable, **R**ealistic, and **T**ime bound? A good example of such a goal would be "Johnny will increase his homework completion rate by next report card period from 50 percent to 75 percent," rather than "Johnny will do all his homework." I sometimes use an example of setting a fitness goal. If I write "Get in shape" as my goal, that doesn't give me any information about what I should be doing. I also don't want to be unrealistic and say, "I will go to the gym seven days a week"; if I go six days a week (sounds pretty good to me!), then I end up falling short of my goal. We want to train our IEP team members to measure small steps in the right direction. If I go to the gym two days a week and people tell me I should have gone seven days, that's pretty discouraging to me. We must build into our behavior support plan ways to acknowledge or reward successive approximations to the goal.

I know this is preaching to the choir here, but you would be surprised how often I come across IEP goals that are generic, negative, or unrealistic, and the only "intervention" is to tell the student to do the expected behavior. The good news is that badly written goals are an opportunity to consult with the team in a way that helps them understand the importance of setting specific, doable goals. If we are vague, we won't know what we expect the kid to do, whether we're making progress or not, or whether our strategies are working or not. Trust me—the kid won't either!

## Dealing with Negative Nancy and Naysayer Ned: Working with "Involuntary" Consultees

There are times when you are called on to consult with teachers who are not exactly open to consultation. Sometimes principals ask school psychologists to work with particular teachers who are struggling with classroom management or having ongoing problems with a student. At other times, you might be in a student support meeting, and the teacher is not very open to taking suggestions or looking at the problem in a new way. He or she may shoot down all advice in advance of trying an intervention because "it's not going to work" or "we are just enabling the student, and it's not fair to the other students to give him special treatment." There are many reasons why teachers can be closed to consultation. If you can identify the source of the resistance, you may be able to break through and form a collaboration.

First, you may be experiencing resistance because you have not adequately built rapport with the teacher. Some teachers take to consultation right away, and others have to trust that you are there to be a support to them. You may be facing the ghosts of your predecessors—teachers may have had bad experiences with school psychologists. In these situations, it helps to have social interaction with the teacher (for example, meet for lunch, chat her up on the playground, stop and chat after school) without an agenda. Chances are, if you can build a collegial relationship with her, she is more likely to be open to consultation in the future. Also, be patient and provide empathy and support, even if you are met with closed door after closed door when you consult. Each time you provide nonjudgmental support, you are building rapport that may lead to that door being open for consultation in the future.

Teachers may also be resistant to consultation out of fear of being judged, or they have anxiety around your observing them and their teaching. Again, building rapport is key to getting the teacher on board. Take care that with each interaction, you are keeping the focus on the child, making neutral observations about the child in the environment (as opposed to what the teacher is doing), and keeping your comments about the teacher's behavior positive at first. It also may help to downplay your role as an "expert" until the teacher's anxiety is lower. If the teacher's challenges with dealing with classroom management or with a particular student are due to lack of knowledge, it may be appropriate to provide some strategies he can "experiment" with, and then to follow up to see how those worked. If the teacher's challenges are caused by a lack of confidence, then reinforcing strategies that he is already using by making neutral observations is the way to go.

Sometimes a teacher is just plain burned out or is having a strong emotional reaction to certain students. She may be emotionally charged, and having one more persons in her class trying to "help" is only further confirmation for her that she can't handle it on her own. Here is where empathy for the teacher comes in. Imagine going to your job every day and not feeling successful, then on top of it, having all these "experts" coming in to tell you what you're doing wrong. It is not a fun place to be. In these situations, you may be initially acting more in a counseling support role for the teacher. Sometimes the best thing you can do for the kids in the class is to support the teacher or connect her to supports. It is not advisable, however, to "play therapist" with the teacher, but you can lend an empathic ear, acknowledge and validate her challenges, and continue to make yourself available if she needs support.

It is also true that there are some teachers who, despite your best efforts, remain highly resistant to consultation. In my first few years, I was relentless in trying to "convert" them into appreciating my consultation efforts, but to no avail. It is worth noting that you need to balance your efforts for the sake of your own sanity! Focus first on the teachers who are willing to work with you, and keep chipping away at the resistant teachers by identifying their resistance and continuing to build rapport. Don't expend all your emotional energy on highly resistant or emotionally unstable teachers; you will burn yourself out! (See Chapter Twelve for more tips on preventing burnout.)

## The Uncomfortable Teachers' Lounge Consultation

Teachers' lounges have a culture all their own. In some, the culture is one of venting and toxicity, full of cringe-worthy comments about children. In others, there is a social vibe, and the topics are not about kids at all. In some, there is collegial bouncing off of ideas in between bites. You have to navigate the teacher's lunchroom very carefully in order to maintain confidentiality. I have had the experience of walking into the teachers' lounge and having a teacher say, "So, what did you find out about Johnny in your testing?" or "Wasn't Johnny's parent outrageous at the IEP meeting?" If you answer or engage, you risk the whole teachers' lounge knowing all of Johnny's information, and the scene could turn into a discussion among other teachers about when they had Johnny in their class. I usually say something neutral that redirects the teacher, such as "I have been meaning to talk with you about Johnny [or the IEP]. Do you have time after lunch [next period, after school] to chat?" This sends a subtle message that I want to talk about Johnny, but not in that moment in front of everyone.

## PULLING IT ALL TOGETHER

School psychologists are frequently called on to consult, but consultation skills are not always explicitly taught. Even if you have learned these skills in graduate school, the on-the-job experience of consulting can be fraught with challenges, such as resistance to consultation, finding the time to consult, and confidentiality concerns. Consultation is a great tool, however, for helping students indirectly. By problem solving with a teacher about a particular student, you are also helping the teacher build his skill set for working with the next student with a similar issue who comes through his classroom door. Consultee-centered consultation (Caplan & Caplan, 1999) is an effective model you can use to expand the repertoire of teachers, support staff, administrators, and parents on a variety of academic, behavioral, and social-emotional student concerns.

## Key Points

- Consultation is an important tool for school psychologists. Whether it is "on the fly" or in a structured meeting setting, effective consultation can help problem-solve for one student and, in doing so, expand the consultee's repertoire of strategies for other students with similar challenges.
- You may be seen as an "expert," but you do not need to have the "right answers" to be a good consultant. Having a process, good questions, and good listening skills facilitates problem solving with the consultee.
- You may find the Caplan and Caplan (1999) model of consultee-centered consultation useful when consulting in the schools.
- School psychologists are typically called in to consult about students' behavioral, social-emotional, and academic challenges. The consultation process is similar for all types of consultations in that you first need to establish rapport with the teacher and take time to identify the problem before jumping into solutions.
- The behavioral consultation process involves shifting the global to the specific, identifying what the teacher has already tried, building empathy for the child, collecting and sharing observational data, generating an "appetizer" or a "bite-size" intervention for one target behavior, and following up on progress.
- In social-emotional consultation, you may also be involving the parent in the information-gathering phase, conducting a check-in with the student to get his or her own perspective, and educating those who work with the child about strategies to support him or her.
- In academic consultation, your level of expertise and the number of practical solutions you have to offer will depend on your training and experience. You may serve as a consultant about typical academic development and early warning signs for learning disabilities, and may serve on a data team or RtI team in tracking interventions. If you are not well versed in the curriculum or research on a certain academic area, you need to admit this to the teacher and either tap into the teacher's knowledge base or make a plan with the teacher to seek solutions together and reconvene.
- Consultation in the IEP meeting is another way you can indirectly help students. By helping team members create meaningful behavior support plans and goals, you can reframe difficult behaviors, develop a plan that is more likely to work, and ensure accountability. Using the SMART test for goals (**S**pecific, **M**easurable, **A**ttainable, **R**ealistic, and **T**ime bound), you can guide the team to a plan that is more likely to work than if the goal is general or negatively worded, or doesn't teach the child a replacement behavior.

*(continued)*

- Working with consultees who are resistant to consultation can pose a big challenge. Identifying the source of the resistance can help you break through it. Resistance may be due to a lack of trust or rapport, lack of knowledge or confidence, anxiety or defensiveness, being emotionally charged, or burnout.

## DISCUSSION QUESTIONS

1. What are the key messages about being an effective consultant that were brought up in this chapter? What makes a good consultant?

2. What have your experiences been in consulting in the schools thus far? What tips or strategies would you offer a new school psychologist for being an effective consultant?

3. Which type of consultation are you most comfortable with? Behavioral? Social-emotional? Academic? Which are you least comfortable with? What resources are available to improve your consultation skills in the area you are least comfortable with?

4. How do you handle consultee resistance? What tips or strategies have you found to be effective for breaking through resistance? Was there anything from this chapter you could try right away for working with "involuntary consultees"?

5. Do you agree or disagree that you do not have to work directly with a child to make a difference (Caplan & Caplan, 1999)? What do you see as the main role of the consultant in the schools?

# chapter 9

# INDIVIDUAL COUNSELING

School psychologists are often called on to do individual counseling with students. However, school psychology preparation programs vary in the level of training in this area. I remember when I first started out in the schools, I was often sent the most challenging students for counseling, and I was probably the least experienced mental health professional on-site. I also remember that I had way more referrals for individual counseling than I could possibly take on, especially with my testing caseload. I constantly found myself ill-prepared for the crisis situations that would arise in counseling, especially when it came to reporting suspected child abuse and when students reported dangerous situations. Not only that, but I was busy creating consent forms, gathering therapeutic materials, finding a confidential space, learning about limits of confidentiality and mandated reporting, managing the practical aspects of which students to see and when, and trying to find supervision from a more experienced clinician.

Even after many years in the profession, I am still constantly challenged in my role of counseling students. In some schools, I have had to learn how to help students cope with serious community violence and threats of safety. In other schools, I have had to learn how to help students not freak out when they get an A–, while their anxious parents hover over the process, demanding to know what their child has said in sessions and e-mailing their concerns to me at three in the morning. Each counseling case presents its own unique challenge! This chapter will highlight the types of counseling roles you may be faced with, describe the primary theories that inform school-based counseling, and provide you with practical tools to use for individual counseling. It will also cover the "sticky situations" you are most likely to encounter in your role as counselor.

## COUNSELING ROLES

Mental health and counseling delivery systems in the schools are ambiguous at best. There are often several staff members who might fit the bill as someone who can do counseling—school counselors, school social workers, marriage and family therapists, clinical psychologists (rarely, but it happens), and school psychologists. Within each of these professions, there are often interns performing counseling duties as well. Part of your first challenge in taking on the role of counselor is to figure out which mental health professionals are on-site, what their roles are, how they get referrals, and what types of students they see. I remember one year at a rather large (and chaotic) middle school, we held a coordinated services team meeting and discovered that one child was receiving counseling from three different providers! Yikes! Not only is that a triplication of services, but from a therapeutic standpoint, it must have been hard for the kid to talk about her problems with three different people. This is why participating on a school intervention team is important. You can get a sense of the referral process so that you don't duplicate services or end up letting students who are in need of counseling fall through the cracks.

After you figure out who provides mental health services at the school site and what their referral processes are, it is important to consult with these providers so that you know which students each of you will be seeing for counseling. The type and number of referrals for counseling you receive are contingent on many factors, including your state and district regulations, your caseload and available time, and your school's service delivery model. Some school psychologists are forbidden by state regulations to do any individual counseling. In some districts, school psychology counseling services are written into the IEP as a service needed to address the disability (sometimes called a Designated Instruction and Service, or DIS). It is written into the IEP the same way speech services or occupational therapy services would be written in. In other districts and schools, counseling services by the school psychologist are provided at the discretion of the school psychologist, depending on whether he or she has time in between completing other necessary activities. There are also special situations where schools have set aside money for school psychologists to spend more time at the school site doing counseling ("buying" psychologist time).

One thing that I have found to be consistent across all these situations is that there are often more referrals for counseling than there are openings for the school psychologist. Deciding on which students to see first is often a challenge, and one to be negotiated with your support staff and administration, perhaps at a coordinated services intervention team meeting. In some schools, I have been assigned only students who do not have health insurance, as we had a counselor on-site who could bill health insurance for counseling services. I have also been given cases in which I have rapport with the parent from testing the child for special education, or in cases where the parent is unlikely to have the resources (emotional or financial) to access community-based services.

In general, when you have a high referral rate, you want to refer out to community-based services when you can, and reserve your time for students who wouldn't normally have access to mental health services. A student also will be pushed higher on your counseling priority list when there is an immediate safety concern or emergency situation, and referring a family out to services would take too long.

Finally, you may use your own discretion regarding which cases you accept, depending on your comfort level with the referral question. When you are first starting out, you might want to begin with less complex cases to get your feet wet in the counseling role, instead of putting yourself in a position where you are dealing with issues beyond your expertise and comfort level. You can, however, elect to take more complex cases if you have a great supervisor with whom you can consult on an ongoing basis.

## TYPES OF SCHOOL-BASED INDIVIDUAL COUNSELING

There are many theoretical orientations and approaches to counseling. Your training program and subsequent professional development will likely guide your approach and methods. In some training programs, there is a heavy emphasis on counseling, and in others, it is not a focus at all. In general, there are four main theories of counseling that I have had experience with in the schools: psychodynamic therapy, play and art therapy, cognitive-behavioral therapy (CBT), and solution-focused brief therapy. As a school psychologist, you may pull from all of these models in an eclectic approach, or wed yourself to one particular model. I find that most people initially work with the model they were trained in, but then expand their counseling techniques to incorporate other models that are appropriate for the situation. Each model is described in the next sections, and a resource list is presented in Exhibit 9.1 if you want to further explore a model or improve your tools and skills in a particular orientation.

### Psychodynamic ("Insight-Oriented") Therapy

I know what you're thinking. You are trying to imagine where the little couch is going to fit in your tiny school psychologist office to practice psychodynamic therapy. Well, I have news for you—there's definitely no room for couches and no time for full-blown psychoanalysis in the schools! Psychodynamic therapy does not necessarily mean traditional psychoanalysis, in which the process is completely nondirective, the focus is on the past to explain the present, and the goal is to reveal unconscious conflicts. What school-based therapy incorporates from psychodynamic therapy is that the relationship is the most important part of the therapy process. The student may experience transference—a reaction to you based on who you remind them of. I have had children relate to me as though I were a mom, and have had teens relate to me as though I were a peer. I have had angry children relate to me as they do with their teachers. You may in turn experience countertransference (treating the child as a mom, peer, or teacher would). Your job in this role is to notice and explore the relationship the student is having with you and others. You may or may not explicitly interpret it for the child, but you are aware of it. Your role may also include helping, in a nonjudgmental way, the child develop insight about his or her feelings, actions, and thoughts. For example, when working with a student who is having anger issues, you could say, "I notice that when I brought up your teacher, you stopped talking and balled your fists up. Can you tell me about that?" Or if a student says something like, "I wish you were my mom!" you could explore by asking, "What things do I say or do that you wish a mom would say or do?" or "Are you comfortable telling me a little bit about your mom?"

Psychodynamic therapy is not a quick fix. The relationship and insights in therapy often take time to develop, and the nondirective nature of the therapy means that you may not be immediately addressing the referral question. There are some students who are more likely than others to benefit from a psychodynamic approach. First, the student with higher cognition will have a higher capacity for insight and would be a better candidate for the approach. Second, the student who is disconnected from school or frequently truant may benefit from the approach, as it is nondirective, nonjudgmental, and focused on developing a therapeutic relationship and attachment within the school context. Last, a student who is not in crisis or in a dangerous situation would be a better candidate for psychodynamic therapy than a student who needs more directive therapeutic assistance to remain safe.

## Play and Art Therapy

Play is a natural medium for children to express themselves, especially at the elementary school level. That being said, I have used play therapy and more specifically art and narrative therapy techniques with middle and high school students as well. Play gives children and adolescents the chance to express themselves indirectly or to play out issues that may be too difficult to put into words, whether because they are too emotionally challenging or there are language development issues. Schaefer and Drewes (2009) identify several therapeutic benefits of play: it provides opportunities for self-expression, access to the unconscious, creative problem solving, and behavioral rehearsal; facilitates relationship bonds and rapport; and gives the child power, control, competence, and self-control. Not to mention that it is an easy sell job as a school psychologist to say to a child, "Would you like to come visit my playroom?"

Play-based therapy can also incorporate techniques and ideas from other schools of thought, such as psychodynamic therapy or CBT. Gary Landreth (2002), a prominent researcher on play therapy, states it best: "In play therapy, toys are a child's words and play is the child's language" (p. 149). Play is the developmentally appropriate medium, but how directive or nondirective you are in the play and whether or not you incorporate other techniques can vary. When I was first starting out, I had been trained in only a few play therapy techniques (for example, sand tray, art activities), but as I've gotten more experience and training, I can pull from both psychodynamic theory and CBT principles in the play therapy room.

The first order of business is to set up your playroom. As we went over in Chapter Two, finding space can be a challenge. If you are lucky enough to have your own space, setting up a playroom is easy. Landreth (1991) offers a detailed list of all the "ideal" toys and games to have in your room, stating that toys should be "selected not collected" (p. 117). You must remember this when you are at Target, or you will go broke! I have a few favorite play therapy materials that are easy to obtain and to store at the school site, and I recommend a few essentials:

- **Sand tray with figures.** You don't have to go out and get a fancy-schmancy sand tray. Just get a large plastic box. I fill mine with Moon Sand, which is a combination of sand and play dough. It is a bit more expensive than actual sand, but it really is fun because the kids can mold it and shape it. (You can find a recipe for a homemade version online if you're interested.) I have some figurines of key people of many ethnicities in the sand tray as well—family members, people representing occupations (especially police, firefighters, teachers, soldiers, and yes, even lawyers), popular cartoon characters, and fantasy figures (princesses, wizards, and so on). Throw in a "magic wand" while you're at it. You'll hear all kinds of wishes revealed. I have also been turned into a frog or put under a no-talking spell when I have asked questions that were difficult for the child. I also have many animals and dinosaurs. You have no idea how many times that dinosaur morphed into a teacher or a principal and put kids in detention! For this reason, the "aggressive" figures are important to have in your tray; however, I avoid toy guns and knives. Although traditional play therapists will have these latter materials, it is better to avoid keeping these at school, given the current zero-tolerance policies at schools regarding guns and weapons of all types (even fake weapons). Don't worry—kids will turn that toy vacuum or their fingers into a gun anyway.
- **House(s).** If you have room, it is good to have a little house (or two for working with kids in divorced families). I got my houses from the PTA at one of my more affluent schools. I simply advertised in the PTA bulletin for some dollhouses that families no longer wanted. I actually ended up with a small village that way, and was able to put a dollhouse at each of my three schools.
- **Schoolhouse.** If you don't have room for a dollhouse, you must at least make room for a schoolhouse! My schoolhouse has enabled me to get a really strong sense of kids' take on their school experience. You can find inexpensive old Fisher-Price schoolhouses with the figures and desks and such on eBay or Craigslist. (Garage sales are another place to build up your play therapy materials.)
- **Interactive turn-taking games.** Plan on purchasing or soliciting donations for games aimed at a range of ages. You would be surprised, however, by the number of adolescents who end up playing the games for younger kids too, so keep them all out as options. Classic games like UNO, checkers, chess, mancala, Candyland, and other simple board games are good for teaching students about taking turns, playing fair, and reining in impulsivity. You can also get therapeutic board games (such as the Ungame), anger management games, friendship games, and so on. I find the Creative Therapy Store (www.creativetherapystore.com) to be a good resource for these types of games.
- **Art supplies.** At a minimum, keep the following materials in your space for art therapy activities: crayons, markers, paints, scissors, glue, stickers, and various types of paper. I often make "books" with students on certain themes (for example, memory books for grief and loss), have them draw themselves at school or at home, or just give them a blank piece of paper and see what they draw.

- **Puppets.** In general, I try to limit the stuffed animal collection because they are hard to keep clean, but a few puppets are good for role plays. I usually have one puppet of the more aggressive variety (crocodile, dinosaur, or the like) so that I can see how kids react to aggressive stimuli.
- **Optional if you have some extra funding.** The Emotes are fun tools for building feeling vocabulary and coping skills. They are little figurines that can go in your sand tray or be used separately with storytelling books (available in English and Spanish). Each Emote represents a different emotion. They are kind of like Japanese anime figures, so the boys tend to gravitate toward them. I have had boys ranging from kindergarten through middle school enjoy these little guys. There is also a Web site (www.emotes.com) where you can download free games and materials.

If you are a school psychologist nomad, you may be setting up your "play therapy bag" to bring with you to different rooms. In this scenario, you will need to be very selective about which toys or games to bring with you, or you will end up having yet another cumbersome bag to drag around with you all day. You might just sample from the list here, and of course, skip the sand tray in favor of a lunchbox full of figures and toys. I have sometimes rotated toys in the bag, and it is fun for kids to see what I've brought on any particular day. Students will readily inform you if you are missing their favorite toys, and you can pack more strategically as you get to know each individual student.

## Cognitive-Behavioral Therapy (CBT)

The basic premise of CBT is that if you change your thoughts, you can change your feelings and behaviors. It was originally developed with adults, but has been extended to children and adolescents, often using art and play activities. CBT is generally more structured and directive than play therapy. It is most commonly used with students experiencing depression and anxiety, although it can be applied to other specific problems (for example, anger management, difficulties making friends, family relationships). The basic process is to help the student understand the connection between her thoughts, feelings, body sensations produced by feelings, and actions. As the child's counselor, you take on the roles of coach, educator, and facilitator of the process. In particular, you can help the child understand which thoughts lead to negative feelings, and help her change those thoughts. For example, if a child feels anxious every time she has the thought, "This sentence isn't good enough" or a child feels sad every time she has the thought, "I am terrible at math," you can gently help her test the evidence that her thought is true or not true and help her come up with a more positive replacement thought. For example, saying, "This sentence may have errors, but that's how I learn," or "I am good at some math problems, and I am still learning how to do other math problems," might help with black-and-white or negative thinking.

Fortunately, there are many resources now for implementing CBT with children and adolescents. Some are scripted step-by-step programs; some are resources with a variety of techniques you can integrate into your counseling tool kit. I have found a few resources that move beyond describing the theory of CBT and give actual practical techniques to try with students. These resources are listed in Exhibit 9.1. As for structured programs, the Coping Cat program is a good place to start for working with students with anxiety, and the PANDY program (Preventing Anxiety and Depression in Youth) has fun art activities as well as educational material on both depression and anxiety. Both programs introduce the child to a cartoon figure who teaches him how to manage his depressive or anxious thoughts. As for techniques to integrate into psychodynamic or play therapy, I recommend looking at Robert Friedberg's books. They are practical and give you a series of activities to try out. The books are also broken down by age group and presenting problem. In many ways, CBT is a good match for school-based treatment, as it is typically brief and solution focused, and it teaches students new skills to better manage their emotions.

## Solution-Focused Brief Therapy

Another popular model of treatment in school settings is the solution-focused brief therapy model. As the name suggests, it is a model that focuses on solutions, not problems. It is present oriented and helps the child or adolescent learn from times when the problem was less severe or absent, or helps him think of realistic solutions to specific problems. For example, there may have been a time in the student's life when he wasn't bullied or when he had less anxiety about school, and by focusing in on what was happening during that time, he may be able to come up with some solutions or positive responses to his current situation. In doing so, he becomes more hopeful and confident that he can solve his current challenge.

Your role as counselor is similar to that in CBT in that you guide, coach, and ask questions that help the student become aware of what she wants to do differently to achieve her goals. You help the student tap into resources, both internal and external (family, teachers, friends) who can support her. You might ask the student to imagine a situation where the problem was not there, as if a magic genie granted her a wish and she was no longer bullied, anxious, or without friends. What would things look like? How would things be different? In this way, you can get at some of the changes the child could actually make and problem-solve with that new information. It is a strength-based model that aims to target a specific situation and give students tools to cope with specific difficulties. It is a good match in the schools, where you are often brought in to work with a child with a situational problem.

EXHIBIT 9.1. RESOURCES FOR COUNSELING

*Psychodynamic Therapy*
- Siskind, D. (1999). *A primer for child psychotherapists.* New York: Aronson.

*Play and Art Therapy*
- Creative Therapy Store: www.creativetherapystore.com
- Drewes, A. A. (Ed.) (2009). *Blending play therapy with cognitive behavioral therapy: Evidence-based and other effective treatments and techniques.* Hoboken, NJ: Wiley.
- Drewes, A. A., & Schaefer, C. E. (Eds.). (2010). *School-based play therapy* (2nd ed.). Hoboken, NJ: Wiley.
- Emotes: www.emotes.com.
- Landreth, G. L. (2002). *Play therapy: The art of the relationship* (2nd ed.). Muncie, IN: Accelerated Development.

*Cognitive-Behavioral Therapy*
- Coping Cat program:
  ○ Kendall, P. C., Choudhury, M., Hudson, J., & Webb, A. (2002). *The C.A.T. project workbook for the cognitive behavioral treatment of anxious adolescents.* Ardmore, PA: Workbook Publishing.
  ○ Kendall, P. C., & Hedtke, K. A. (2006). *Cognitive behavioral therapy for anxious children: Therapist manual* (3rd ed.). Ardmore, PA: Workbook Publishing.
  ○ Kendall, P. C., & Hedtke, K. A. (2006). *Coping Cat workbook* (2nd ed.). Ardmore, PA: Workbook Publishing.
- Friedberg, R. D., & Crosby, L. E. (2001). *Therapeutic exercises for children: Professional guide.* Sarasota, FL: Professional Resource Exchange.
- Friedberg, R. D., Friedberg, B. A., & Friedberg, R. J. (2001). *Therapeutic exercises for children.* Sarasota, FL: Professional Resource Exchange.
- Friedberg, R. D., & McClure, J. M. (2002). *Clinical practice of cognitive therapy with children and adolescents: The nuts and bolts.* New York: Guilford Press.
- Friedberg, R. D., McClure, J. M., & Garcia, J. H. (2009). *Cognitive therapy techniques for children and adolescents: Tools for enhancing practice.* New York: Guilford Press.

*Solution-Focused Brief Therapy*
- Murphy, J. (2008). *Solution-focused counseling in schools* (2nd ed.). Alexandria, VA: American Counseling Association.

## BEGINNING COUNSELING

Once you have identified who is referred to you for counseling through the school's referral process, you will then need to manage some logistics. First, you need to get the parents' permission and the student's buy-in. When I first started out in school psychology, I was amazed that there wasn't a standard district consent form for counseling. I had to create my own. Check with your supervisor to see whether there is a district-wide counseling consent form or whether you should create your own. To save you time, Forms 9.1 and 9.2 are sample consent forms (one in English, one in Spanish) you can use as a guide to write your own. They include the introduction of the school psychologist, a description of the type of counseling you will do, and the limits of confidentiality. I would also recommend running a draft by your supervisor to make sure it covers everything.

# *CONSENT FOR INDIVIDUAL COUNSELING*

[Name of School]
[School Year]

I, _____ [Parent/Guardian Name], agree to allow _____ [Student Name] to receive individual counseling services from [Your Name], School Psychologist, at [Name of School] for the academic school year [20xx–20xx]. I understand that [Your Name] has a legal obligation to protect the safety of my child. I will be informed if my child reports being in a dangerous or abusive situation. I understand that I may revoke this consent at any time by signing and dating a written notice to that effect.

Parent/Guardian

Print Name _____

Parent/Guardian
Signature _____ Date _____

# PARENT/GUARDIAN INFORMATION

Home Address:
City, State, Zip:
Home Phone:                OK to leave messages?    YES    NO
Work Phone:                 OK to leave messages?    YES    NO
Cell Phone:                  OK to leave messages?    YES    NO

Emergency Contact:_____

Please indicate how you prefer to be contacted:_____

Please indicate a good time to reach you:_____

Please indicate anything that will be helpful to know regarding working with your child: _____
_____

## *CONSENTIMIENTO PARA CONSEJERÍA INDIVIDUAL*

[Name of school]
[School year]

Yo, _____[Nombre de los Padres/guardiáns], consiento que _____[Nombre del Estudiante/Nombre de la Estudiante] reciba servicios de consejería individualizada de [Your Name], Psicóloga de la [School Name] por el año escolar [school year]. Comprendo que [Your Name] tiene la obligación legal de ver por la seguridad de mi hijo(a). Así mismo, serán informados si el niño(a) da informes de estar en peligro o en una situación de abuso. Comprendo que puedo suspender este consentimiento en cualquier momento.

Padre o guardián
Nombre _____
Padre o guardián
Firma _____ Fecha _____

## INFORMACIÓN DEL PADRE/DE LA MADRE O GUARDIÁN

Dirección:
Ciudad, Código postal:
Teléfono (casa):               ¿permiso para dejar un mensaje?   SÍ   NO
Teléfono (trabajo):            ¿permiso para dejar un mensaje?   SÍ   NO
Celular:                       ¿permiso para dejar un mensaje?   SÍ   NO

Contacto de emergencia: _____

Por favor indique como prefiere ser contactado(a):_____
Por favor indique la major hora para contactarle: _____
Por favor indique cualquier cosa o detalle que sea importante o que puede ayudarnos a trabajar con su niño(a): _____
_____

As a general rule of thumb, I make an appointment with the parent to talk about the form instead of just sending it home. It helps you explain the process, clarify confidentiality, and sometimes even alleviate fears about your calling Child Protective Services (CPS). If the form is sent home without phone or in-person contact, parents might read the part about reporting if their child is in a dangerous or abusive situation and decide that they don't want their child in counseling. I do encourage you to keep that part of the consent form in your version, though, so that you can set out from the beginning that you are a legally mandated reporter. If you discuss this with the parents in person, you can answer questions about this so that they may feel more comfortable with giving permission. I should also note that I usually have these consent forms on hand when I go to IEP meetings, student-focused team meetings, and disciplinary meetings. At these meetings, parents are often open to counseling, and you can get consent right then and there instead of tracking them down later.

After getting parent permission, I meet with the principal to find out about an appropriate time to pull the student for counseling. Some principals are strict in that they don't want kids pulled out of academic time, so you are limited to seeing the student during electives or special classes (art, PE, music, and so on). If it is okay to pull them during academic time, you will want to negotiate with the teacher about when the least disruptive time would be (beginning of class, end of class, independent work time, and so on). I also check with the parents after the school staff find a good time, to make sure that they understand which part of the school day the student will be missing.

In your initial meeting with the student, you should also check to make sure you aren't pulling him out of his favorite part of the day! The student's participation level is much higher if he isn't missing out on something fun for him. When possible, you can give him a choice of two times so that he feels he is a part of the process. The initial meeting with the student can be challenging. It is usually easier if you have already established an ongoing relationship with the student, whether through being in meetings with him or being in the classroom. It can be trickier if you are meeting a student for the first time to tell him his parent agreed to put him in counseling. The age of the child is also a factor. In general, younger kids are more open to leaving class without knowing much about what they will be doing. Older students can go either way; some are so excited to get out of class that they go with you right away, and some are embarrassed when someone comes to the class to get them. No matter the age, anxious students may need some preparation from their teacher or parent that you will be coming to talk with them, and assurance that they are not in trouble.

I usually try to get the student during a natural break, such as a passing period for older students or during a transition time for younger students. In some cases, I will approach the student at the beginning of class while everyone is settling in. For students who I anticipate will be embarrassed or hesitant to come with me in front of their friends (usually adolescents), I sometimes send a pass to them to meet me in the main office, or call the class and ask the teacher to send the student to the office.

Once I meet the student, I usually say something like, "Can we check in for a moment?" and I swiftly follow it with "You're not in trouble" so that she doesn't get nervous that she's done something wrong. I usually begin my counseling speech on the way to the room, so that there isn't an awkward silence as we walk together. I engage in small talk and introduce myself as "someone who works with students to help them do better in school and problem-solve any troubling situations that might be happening in their lives." I normalize the process right away, saying, "I work with a lot of students of all ages for a variety of reasons."

Once you get to your office, you can explain what counseling is to the student, and why she was chosen to participate. Usually I start with the reason for referral in kid-friendly language. I say something like, "Your mom/dad/teacher thought it would be good for us to check in every week about [referral concern]." I then explain some of the activities or the process we will using (play therapy, CBT, solution-focused brief therapy, or psychodynamic therapy). I usually segue quickly into the confidentiality speech, which is something like, "Everything you say or do during our time together is confidential, which means that I won't tell your parent or teacher what you say. The only time I would need to let someone know what you say is if you tell me something that makes me think you or someone else is in danger. Then I would need to get help." I allow for questions and then usually proceed with a getting-to-know-you activity or allow the student to pick an activity. For very anxious children, I sometimes offer a menu of activities they can pick from to start.

It should also be noted that you may experience some anxiety about your role as a counselor when you are first starting out. If this is true for you, remember that the relationship alone is therapeutic. You don't have to say or do everything just right in your sessions. Years from now, kids aren't going to remember much of the details of what you said in sessions, but they will remember how they felt in your office. You already know from your role as an assessor how to build rapport with kids. This is an extension of that role. If you end up just playing a card game in the first couple of sessions, that is perfectly okay. You will hone your skills with each child you work with. It would also behoove both new and experienced school psychologists to have some sort of ongoing consultation with a more experienced colleague. It is invaluable to bounce ideas off of another professional about treatment goals, the therapeutic process, and, of course, those sticky situations that arise during counseling. You might also seek out continuing education or workshops to get more information about ethical and legal situations that arise, as well as enhanced techniques for counseling.

## DURING COUNSELING: DOCUMENTATION AND STICKY SITUATIONS

Once you begin counseling with students, you will likely encounter some challenges that you were not explicitly taught how to handle. Even after many years of counseling, you will still have moments when you are left wondering how to deal with a sticky situation. In these circumstances, you will need to ensure that you are properly documenting your sessions and considering all the factors when it comes to reporting abuse, protecting the safety of the students you are counseling, and warning others who may be in danger.

### Documentation

As we learned in Chapter Three on taming the Bureaucracy Monster, documentation is very important. We need to document our counseling sessions with students. There are a number of ways this can be done, but I find the simplest method to be the "SOAP notes" method. I also suggest that you write up your case notes right after each session, even if you are superbusy and off to see the next child. It takes but a moment, and the details are fresh in your mind. At a minimum, do all your counseling notes at the end of the day. If you try to remember the session a day or two later, your notes won't be as helpful or accurate.

The elements of SOAP notes are:

**S**ubjective. This is a description of your subjective experience of the session, how things went, and how the child was in the room with you.

**O**bjective. This is an objective description of what the child said or did.

**A**ssessment. This is your take on the child's reaction to the session activities and on progress toward treatment goals.

**P**lan. On the basis of your assessment, set a plan for the next session and write in anything else you plan to do, such as consult with parents or teachers.

Exhibit 9.2 is a sample of SOAP notes that you might write for a child with whom you are doing a combination of CBT and play therapy.

SOAP notes can be useful for keeping the student's goals in mind, as well as refreshing your memory from week to week about the progress toward goals and possible related activities. They are also helpful in the rare cases where you may be subpoenaed to testify about your work with a student. Remember that you are the holder of privileged information and thus are also responsible for keeping the case notes in a confidential space and keeping them for the legal time requirement (typically seven years after

EXHIBIT 9.2.  SAMPLE SOAP NOTES

Date: 9/12/12
**Student:** Johnny

**S**—Johnny came willingly to the counseling room, but appeared somewhat preoccupied with something. He was quiet and shy and didn't initially engage in the check-in game of "feeling thermometers." He seemed sullen. Toward the middle of the session, he seemed to warm up to being in the counseling room, and engaged more in activities and discussion.

**O**—Johnny reported that he was feeling 2 out of 10 on the happy feeling thermometer and 10 out of 10 on the anger feeling thermometer. He said that he was teased at lunch by a boy in his class. He shrugged his shoulders when asked what thoughts popped in his head during this interaction. Using puppets, we played out the interaction and rehearsed some "bully busting" things to say next time.

**A**—Johnny is making progress on his "feeling/strength of feeling identification goal." He is still working on identifying the thoughts that he has when feeling angry. He seemed better able to express thoughts and do behavioral rehearsal with the puppets as the medium.

**P**—Continue to do check-ins with feeling thermometers and work on thought identification, perhaps through cartooning activity. Consult with Johnny's teacher about her observations of teasing at lunch and other times.

the child turns eighteen, but check your state regulations). You can keep them on your school site in a locked cabinet while you are working there, but if you change schools or leave the district, you will need to take and store all your counseling notes at home. They are your responsibility until you can legally destroy them.

## When You Need to Call Child Protective Services (CPS)

As school psychologists, we are mandated reporters of child abuse. I remember my first call to CPS so vividly. A fourteen-year-old student had just reported that his dad hit him when the dad came home from the bar at night, and sometimes made the child drive the dad to the next bar. The child left my office, and I sat there paralyzed for about ten minutes. Whom do I call? What do I say? Do I tell the child I'm calling? Will the parent find out it was I who called? These are all natural questions to ask, and the answers sometimes are clear-cut and sometimes not. My general rule of thumb for deciding on "to call or not to call" is that if you're even wondering about calling, you should call, because you have reasonable suspicion at that point. There can also be legal repercussions for not reporting, so err on the side of caution. Sometimes I call just to consult about whether what the child said is reportable, and document my call. About half the time, I tell the CPS worker the situation, and he or she says it's not an incident that requires a mandated report. The other half of the time, the worker takes the report, but what happens after that could be absolutely nothing, or it could end up with the child removed from the home that night. Remember, it's not your job to decide if the child is telling the truth or if there really is child abuse occurring. It is also not your job to investigate. If a CPS worker asks you to go back and further interview the child, let him or her know that you are not trained in this type of investigation. It is your job to report what you see and hear when you suspect the child is being exposed to harm or neglect, not conduct a full investigation.

One of the hardest things about making a CPS report can be the impact it has on your therapeutic relationship with the student or the family. Although the call is "anonymous," it usually doesn't take kids or parents a detective's license to figure out it was you. Sometimes, with older students, I tell them that I have to make the report and remind them of what we talked about in their first session. That way, I can provide them with anticipatory guidance about the range of events—from nothing, to someone coming to interview them further—that could happen. Then I am able to help the student process the emotional reaction (fear, anger, sadness, relief) then and there. Some school psychologists inform the parents that they made the report, but I rarely do so unless I have a really good rapport with them. In some cases, the parents never come back to me asking if I was the reporter. In other cases, parents have called to see if I had made the call. If parents call demanding to know if it was me, I typically say that I am indeed a mandated reporter, but anyone can call CPS at any time. I tell them that the CPS process is anonymous and confidential and that I can't give any information about reporting to them. I quickly pivot off the "who made the call" conversation and ask them what is going on for the family right now and if I can be of assistance. In most cases, once the dust settles from the initial reaction, I have been able to continue working with the student and rebuild rapport with the parents. These situations are often uncomfortable and complex, though. It is worth calling your supervisor or an experienced colleague and consulting with him or her throughout the process.

In terms of practical advice for making the actual CPS call, be sure to have a print-out of the student's demographic data, such as parents' names and addresses, and the names and ages of siblings in the house. CPS will ask for that information. Be sure to get the name of the CPS worker you reported to and put his or her name in your case notes along with a note that you reported your suspicion. You will then likely have to send copies of the report to CPS, and in some schools, the principal keeps a copy. I also keep a copy and put it in the child's confidential counseling file for my records.

It is also worth noting that sometimes teachers and administrators will learn of information that is CPS-reportable and try to get you to report it for them. Telling you about the suspicion is not sufficient, and it is not your responsibility to call on their behalf (though it is very common, in my experience, for principals to try to "palm off" reporting on you). Usually, in these situations, I remind them that the person with the firsthand knowledge must make the report, because CPS may ask questions about how the child reported the situation, which I will be unable to answer. I then offer to make the report together with him. I sit with the teacher or administrator with CPS on speakerphone and "walk" him through the call and the paperwork. That way, he is trained in the future if he needs to make a call. Like school psychologists, teachers and administrators are also mandated reporters, and need to learn how to make reports. It goes a long way, however, to have the school psychologist by their side for making the report. Chapter Eleven will also address CPS reporting.

## When a Child Is a Danger to Himself or Others

We are also responsible when a child presents a danger to himself or herself or others. There will likely be times in individual counseling sessions when you have to do a threat or suicide assessment. Having a few key questions at your disposal will help you through the process. More will be addressed on this topic in Chapter Eleven, but it is important to note that most counties have a "child crisis" number you can call to consult with a mobile response team if you have reached the level of concern that the child is in imminent danger or is in danger of hurting someone else. Find out this number from your supervisor or colleagues. You may also want to identify colleagues experienced in counseling and in assessment of danger to self or others early on, before a crisis occurs, so that if one arises unexpectedly one day in a session, you will have your go-to person to call for a consultation.

## Sticky Confidentiality Issues

It is always difficult when teachers and parents want to know about how therapy is going for the child, what she is saying, and how she is doing. You may even have information that might be helpful for teachers and parents to know, but can't share it. One of the ways I provide needed feedback to adults working with the child is to share generalities and "themes" that have come up in counseling (for example, "We are working on anger management," or "The theme of peer relationships/bullying/low academic self-esteem is coming up"). The other way I collaborate is to ask the parents or teachers for their observations of the student recently, and guide them toward the theme (for example, "What types of situations have you seen that make Johnny angry? What does he typically do when he is angry?" or "What have you observed about Johnny's friendships?"). That way, I can check in on progress outside the counseling sessions without telling the teacher specifically what Johnny has been reporting about his anger or his friendships.

Another tip for collaborating with adults without violating confidentiality is asking the student's permission to share the theme with the other adults in her life who are trying to help her. If there is something that I think might be helpful for the parent or teacher to know, I ask the student if she would be willing for me to share her point of view on the topic. I have been surprised at how many students are okay with this. If it is framed in a positive way of trying to get outside support or better understanding from the adults in their lives, they are usually fine with your sharing, if you tell them exactly what you will say. If a student is older, sometimes I ask if she'd be willing to have a joint session with the parent or teacher to share her thoughts as well. We role-play what it would be like to share her thoughts and feelings, and it can be a good exercise in self-advocacy.

## Terminating Counseling

One of the interesting differences between school-based and community-based counseling is that there is often a "natural" termination time at the end of the school year, rather than termination based on the student's having met his treatment goals. Of course, there are times when your student will have met the treatment goals before the end of the school year. There are other times when goals have not been met, but you must terminate because of summer break. The process is similar in that you want to leave time for the termination and talk about it up to a month before actual termination.

If you are working with a student long term over the school year (as opposed to doing brief therapy), I recommend that you casually bring up termination about a month before ("So, we only have four more times we get to meet before summer break") and see what the student's reaction is. Sometimes there is no reaction at all in the moment, but in the coming weeks, you may see some regression and a return to the original symptoms that brought the student to counseling in the first place. It is important to allow the process to unfold, and to notice and explore it with the student. She may be behaviorally demonstrating that she still feels that she needs you. There are other reactions to termination as well. Sometimes students begin showing hostility toward you, a reaction I like to call, "You can't break up with me; I break up with you!" Yet others will pull back and refuse to come to final sessions. There are some kids who have trouble with good-byes and transitions. And of course, some kids are just fine with ending counseling and want to plan a little party to celebrate. All of these reactions are normal and frequently occur.

You may also have a reaction to ending with a student as well! Sometimes we want to tie up a bow on our therapy box and have a happy ending, but many times, endings are messy. I remember one case where the student and I had planned our "end of counseling celebration" activity of making a cake together in the school kitchen, and I got all the supplies and was all ready, only to find out that the mom pulled the student out a day early to move out of town. So much for my plan to tie a bow on the pretty therapy box and eat cake in celebration! Knowing in advance that endings can be messy and feel incomplete makes it a bit easier for us as school psychologists to be okay with the process.

## PULLING IT ALL TOGETHER

Providing counseling in the school is an invaluable service, because you are connected to the life of the child at school, can easily consult with adults about their observations outside the counseling room, and can serve students who may not otherwise receive services. Counseling in the schools presents the dual challenge for school psychologists of being comfortable doing counseling with students as well as navigating the logistical difficulties (for example, getting referrals, finding space, making the student feel comfortable coming to you in a semipublic setting, and dealing with issues of mandated reporting and confidentiality). School psychologists vary in their training experiences and their level of comfort with doing counseling.

Four main orientations in school-based counseling were discussed in this chapter—psychodynamic therapy, play and art therapy, cognitive-behavioral therapy, and solution-focused brief therapy. Many school psychologists start out using the orientation in which they were trained and then blend treatment modalities as they become more experienced and have further training. Ongoing consultation and preparation for "sticky situations" is needed for new school psychologists and seasoned veteran school psychologists alike.

## Key Points

- School psychologists' counseling role varies by the school, district, and state in which they work. Some are not allowed to do counseling or do not have interest in counseling, some have their counseling services written into IEP documents, and others do counseling in their "free time" when they are not doing assessments.
- How you will get referrals for counseling also varies. To avoid duplication of services and ensure that your school is effectively servicing the students with mental health needs, it is worth participating in a coordinated services team meeting to discuss the service delivery model at your school with other mental health providers. In some cases, you may be facilitating a referral to a community-based agency because of a high number of referrals at your site and few school-based resources.

- Four main counseling orientations in the schools are psychodynamic therapy, play and art therapy, cognitive-behavioral therapy (CBT), and solution-focused brief therapy. Each modality has a different theoretical framework and techniques. School psychologists often begin counseling in the modality in which they were initially trained and then expand their tools and training over time. Resources for each modality are presented in Exhibit 9.1.

- Beginning counseling with a student requires some logistical planning. You must get parental permission, consult with school staff about when and where to do counseling, be strategic about how you pull kids out for counseling, and explain counseling in a way students understand. You should also discuss the limits of confidentiality with all involved parties—teachers, parents, administrators, and the student—before beginning counseling.

- Documenting the work you do in counseling with the student is essential. Taking SOAP notes is one way to quickly and efficiently document the work you are doing in your sessions.

- During counseling, many sticky situations can arise (for example, having to report to Child Protective Services, doing threat and suicide assessments). It is a good idea to identify a few experienced or trusted colleagues who can make themselves available for consultation before the situation occurs. You can also call CPS or a Child Crisis hotline for consultation. More on this topic is covered in Chapter Eleven.

## DISCUSSION QUESTIONS

1. What counseling services are available at your school(s)? How are referrals made? What is the service delivery model for counseling?

2. What background and training experience do you have with regard to school-based counseling? Were you trained using techniques from one particular theoretical orientation? Do you feel that this training and orientation is a good match for your schools' needs?

3. Is there an orientation with which you would like more training or experience? What resources and training opportunities are available to further explore other treatment modalities?

4. Have you experienced any logistical problems in seeing students for counseling? What are possible ways to overcome these problems?

5. What is your preferred way of documenting counseling services?

6. What sticky situations have you come across in your role as counselor? What did you do? What would you do differently next time?

# chapter 10

# GROUP COUNSELING

Grouping students in need of counseling services sounds like such a simple and great idea—you see more students in need, consolidate your time, and get to observe group dynamics and teach interpersonal skills. In reality, simply putting a bunch of kids with issues together in one group can be a recipe for disaster! I remember in my first year, the middle school where I was assigned really wanted me to work with the kids with anger management issues, so I dutifully put together a group of eight boys exhibiting acting-out behavior. Within ten minutes of starting the group, I realized this was a huge mistake. Kids were doing WWE wrestling moves on each other and cursing each other out, and I had no control over the group. I managed to get them under control for eight of the longest weeks of my life, but then they all banded together and went on a stealing and vandalism spree together. It wasn't the type of "group cohesion" I was hoping for. I basically inadvertently formed a gang. Even though I was taught group process and theory in graduate school, I didn't know how to apply that information to running a successful group in the school system.

## STARTING A GROUP: FACTORS TO CONSIDER

In order to have a successful counseling group, you must spend a good amount of time preparing. Counseling groups must be well thought out in terms of group composition, level of structure, focus, and logistics. When you are first starting out, the whole process can be a bit overwhelming, but once you get your groups going, you will start to establish a rhythm and learn what works and what doesn't. Each time you conduct a group, you will be more comfortable, and the process will be more streamlined. Each group you run gives you more tools for the next one. This chapter will help you with some of the preparation phase of creating a counseling group at your school.

## Conduct a Needs Assessment at Your School

First, you will want to determine what the school's most pressing need is for group counseling services. This can be done informally by talking to the principal and teachers about what kinds of problems they are having with students. It can also be done more formally through the use of a schoolwide intervention team. The needs for counseling are so varied by school site: when I ask what types of groups might be beneficial for the students at the school, the issues the staff want addressed range from grief, loss, divorce, and having parents in jail, to social skills training for students on the autism spectrum, combating perfectionism, and fostering cultural pride among certain ethnic groups. Many times, there are requests for working with students with oppositional and defiant behaviors. Conducting the needs assessment does not commit you to leading any certain type of group, but if the school staff identify a group focus that is pressing for them, you will build goodwill by listening to them and developing a group to target that need.

## Deciding What Type of Group to Run

In general, I put groups into three different categories: problem-based groups, resilience-based groups, and combination groups. In general, in a problem-based group, you are working with students around a certain problem—lack of friends, acting-out behavior, or internalizing problems, such as depression, anxiety, grief, and so on. Students in the group can range from showing extreme difficulties with the problem to being a positive peer role model who does not experience the problem. In general though, the students are mostly homogenous in that they share a particular challenge. It doesn't mean that you focus on the problem per se; it just means you have grouped the students by a common challenge they experience.

In the resilience-based group, the focus is on building strengths, regardless of the problem—teaching friendship and social skills, developing talents, or learning a new skill. The students are more heterogeneous in that they do not share one main area of difficulty. Whether you select a problem-based group or a resilience-based group with a range of kids who are "at risk" for a variety of reasons is up to you. You may have materials available for a scripted group program for a certain population, or you may have been trained in a more open-ended group counseling process. Both types of groups can be helpful to students.

One piece of advice I was given early on from a supervisor is to bring your own strengths and interests to the group. If you are artistic, you might want art to be a big part of your group. I have conducted groups that involve dance, as this is an area of interest for me. I have even held a knitting club with middle school students (boys and girls!) where they learned to knit while we talked about issues in middle school. A counselor I know loved cooking and gardening, and she brought that theme and related activities into her girls' group. You can bring in all kinds of activities and interests to the group, and the students often profit from your enthusiasm as a result.

Your focus for the group will depend on your training and the materials you have available to you. In general, a scripted or curriculum-based package of materials is an easier way to begin your group counseling experience than trying to start with an open-ended group. There are many such programs that you can draw from. Some examples of curriculum packages you can purchase to structure your groups include Lego-based play groups for children on the autism spectrum, trauma-focused group play therapy, group sand-play therapy, group play therapy for anger management, and group play for students with ADHD. (See *School-Based Play Therapy*, 2010, edited by Athena A. Drewes and Charles E. Schaefer, for further information about these specific groups.) You can also adapt individual counseling techniques to the group setting. For example, you might use a social skills curriculum such as Darlene Mannix's *Social Skills Activities for Special Children* (2008), which includes lessons covering a range of skills, from making and keeping friends to accepting rules. For a more cognitive-behavioral approach, *What Works When with Children and Adolescents: A Handbook of Individual Counseling Techniques*, by Ann Vernox (2002), offers such activities as role plays, songs, and games to address certain social-emotional challenges. Finally, you also might consult with a school-based counselor if you have one at your school, as he or she may have some off-the-shelf counseling curricula to share.

You can also develop your own group and create your own agenda and focus. I tend toward the blended approach, in which the referrals are for a certain risk group (problem-based group), but the process is more open ended and strengths based (resilience-based group). At my schools, I have developed a boys' group and a girls' group that I run every year, and my schools have come to know what the group is about and who might be a good candidate for the group. The advantage of having an ongoing resilience-based group is that I can tailor it toward any population of students. The group I run is called the Talent Group; it began as a group targeting students with oppositional behaviors (a need identified at my middle school). Instead of teaching the students how to comply with rules through a series of lessons, the group focuses on building their strengths or "talents" and developing group collaboration skills. We have a group project, so they must learn how to cooperate, negotiate, disagree without being disagreeable, and talk to each other respectfully. The value of the group process is that they learn these skills in a real context of coming together to achieve a common goal, rather than through isolated lessons. I learned from my early mistakes, of course, and I think carefully about group composition before putting a bunch of students who are argumentative and oppositional in a group together!

## Deciding Who Is in Your Group

I really can't say it too many times: careful consideration of group composition is key to a successful group. To illustrate the concepts behind forming a group at your school, I will use my Talent Group as an example. To put together the initial referral list for my group, I solicit the expertise of the teachers and support staff who know the students best. If you participate on a schoolwide intervention team, you can ask the team members to nominate candidates for the group. It is important to tell them that you want a range of students, from those who are high functioning to those ranging from low-risk to high risk for the targeted problem. In my case, the "problem" is oppositional behavior. It can be very difficult for staff to think of the range of kids. Typically they will give you a referral list of all the high-risk kids. In order to cast a wider net in terms of referrals, I usually take staff through a process of explaining my group and soliciting referrals using a rubric for sorting students into "low," "medium," and "high" risk for the target problem. Exhibit 10.1 is an example of a form I use to get my referrals for groups composed of students with oppositional and defiant behaviors.

EXHIBIT 10.1. SAMPLE GROUP REFERRAL FORM

Dear School Support Staff Team,

I will be beginning two **HMS Talent Groups** beginning in a few weeks (one for girls and one for boys). The focus of the groups is to help students develop an area of talent in a confidential, supportive, and fun setting. Though the group's focus will be on building strengths, the referred students can be at-risk for or currently presenting disruptive behavior disorders (for example, Oppositional Defiant Disorder, Conduct Disorder).

The focus will be on **sixth-grade students,** as a *preventive* intervention for students, instead of providing intensive treatment with a child with a behavior problem later on in middle school. One or two model sixth-grade student leaders may be appropriate for the group as well.

The total number for the two groups will be 5–6 boys and 5–6 girls. I am looking for referrals for **low-risk** (none of the symptoms listed), **medium-risk** (1–2 symptoms), and **high-risk** (3 or more symptoms) students:

- Often loses temper
- Often argues with adults
- Often actively defies or refuses to comply with adults' requests or rules
- Often deliberately annoys people
- Often blames others for his or her mistakes or misbehavior
- Often is touchy or easily annoyed by others
- Often is angry and resentful
- Often is spiteful or vindictive

In general, a mixed group with one high-risk student, a few medium-risk students, and a few low-risk or "model" students is the best makeup for a group. **Cast a wide net with your referrals,** and I will interview each student to determine his or her interest level and appropriateness for a group. Some students can roll over into individual counseling if they are not a good match for a group.

Thanks!

*Rebecca Branstetter,*

School Psychologist

# Initial Referral List for HMS Talent Groups

Check if referred student is low, medium, or high risk

| Student Name/ Grade | Low | Medium | High | Name of Support Team Member (who has a connection with the student or family and can help facilitate getting buy-in from student or parental consent) | Talent or Interests of Student |
|---|---|---|---|---|---|
| **BOYS' GROUP** | | | | | |
| | | | | | |
| | | | | | |
| | | | | | |
| | | | | | |
| | | | | | |
| | | | | | |
| | | | | | |
| | | | | | |
| | | | | | |
| | | | | | |
| **GIRLS' GROUP** | | | | | |
| | | | | | |
| | | | | | |
| | | | | | |
| | | | | | |
| | | | | | |
| | | | | | |
| | | | | | |
| | | | | | |
| | | | | | |
| | | | | | |

I typically put the group referral form in the team members' mailboxes before the meeting, and then during the meeting, we can all discuss who might be good in the group. Sometimes, because of a past history of which you might not be aware, there are bad combinations of students. This does not necessarily mean that the students cannot be in a group together; at times, the group can be the vehicle for repairing a relationship between two students. Teachers and support staff often have a good sense of who would work well in a group together, so solicit their advice. You can also identify support staff team members who have a connection with the student or family and may be helpful in generating the student's interest or getting parental consent for participation (or both).

After assembling your list of possible candidates, the next step is to decide on the size of your group. If I am conducting the group alone, I find that five or six students usually works well. If you have a cofacilitator, you might be able to put seven or eight in a group together. In either case, I suggest picking only *one* high-risk student for the group and having mostly low- and medium-risk students in the group. Definitely aim to include at least one or two positive role models if you can. You can even explain to the parents of the role models that their son or daughter was selected to be a leader in the group, so they aren't perplexed as to why the student was referred for counseling. This can sometimes be a tough sell for parents of the role model. You will want to assure them that no harm will come to their child by being a leader in a group, and that you will check in with the child about his or her experience after the first one or two sessions. If the child is uncomfortable with participating at that time, then she or he can withdraw from the group.

Once you have put together your initial list, the next step is to see if the students are interested in the group. The beauty of calling your group the Talent Group or something positively worded (Friendship Group, Leadership Group, and so on) is that it is a much easier sell than the Anger Management Group or the like. I usually present to the student that he has been "nominated" to participate in the group by his teacher (counselor, principal) because he has been identified as having a special talent. You can reference the hobby, interest, or talent that the team put on your referral form. Then you can explain what membership in the group will entail. If the student is unsure, you can tell him that he can think about it and decide later. Some students want to know who else will be in the group before they decide. This is why you cast a wide net for referrals—you may have reluctant students who are not going to just jump on board right away, but if you get one of their friends in the group, they are often more comfortable with joining.

Once you have the student's interest, you can then tell her that you will be contacting her parent or guardian for permission. If she is older, in middle or high school, you can send the permission slip with her, and call the parent or guardian to explain the group and let him or her know to expect it. Exhibit 10.2 is a sample explanation of the group and permission form in English; Exhibit 10.3 is the same form in Spanish. It is important to call the parents or guardians in advance of receiving the permission slip, so that they are not blindsided by a request for their child to be seen in group counseling. In addition, you can explain the benefits of the group and answer any questions they may have. This is particularly important if your group is focused on something that has to do with the parent dynamic, such as divorce or grief. Parents may have additional questions about what you will be doing in sessions.

EXHIBIT 10.2. SAMPLE GROUP COUNSELING PERMISSION SLIP (ENGLISH)

Happy Middle School
Dr. Rebecca Branstetter, School Psychologist
Phone: (XXX) XXX-XXXX
E-mail: rbranstetter@happyschooldistrict.edu

Dear Parent/Guardian,

Your child has expressed interest in participating in the **HMS Talent Group**. Research has shown that when students feel successful in at least one area, they tend to have more success in school. Therefore, this group was designed to help students develop an area of talent in a confidential, supportive, and fun setting.

The group will consist of three parts:

1.  Students will identify an area of talent that they want to enhance or develop (such as a career interest, hobby, sport, or personal interest).
2.  Students will help each other develop an action plan to explore their talent.
3.  Students will plan and host a small celebration to showcase their talents to members of their families and/or family friends.

Attached is a permission form for participation in the Talent Group. The group will meet once a week for 10 weeks during lunch or PE. The celebration and talent showcase will take place at the end of the group. Details will follow, and parent assistance with the celebration will be appreciated!

Please do not hesitate to contact me with any questions about the Talent Group. I can be reached at HMS on Tuesdays all day and Thursday afternoons at (XXX) XXX-XXXX. I look forward to your child's participation!

Sincerely,

Dr. Rebecca Branstetter

School Psychologist

# CONSENT FOR SMALL GROUP COUNSELING

## Happy Middle School

I, _____, agree to allow _____
           (Parent/Guardian name)                                (Student's Name)

to receive small group counseling services from Dr. Branstetter, School Psychologist at HMS, for one individual session/orientation to the Talent Group (which may include a pregroup survey) and a 10-week session during the academic school year 2012–2013. I understand that Dr. Branstetter has a legal obligation to protect the safety of all the students in the group. For this reason, I will be informed if my child reports being in a dangerous or abusive situation. I understand that I may revoke this consent at any time by signing and dating a written notice to that effect.

Parent/Guardian

Print Name _____

Parent/Guardian

Signature _____ Date _____

### *PARENT/GUARDIAN INFORMATION*

Home Address:

City, State, Zip:

Home Phone:                          OK to leave messages?        YES        NO

Work Phone:                          OK to leave messages?        YES        NO

Cell Phone:                          OK to leave messages?        YES        NO

Emergency Contact: _____

Please indicate how you prefer to be contacted:

_____

Please indicate a good time to reach you:

_____

Please indicate anything that will be helpful to know regarding working with your child:

_____

EXHIBIT 10.3. SAMPLE GROUP COUNSELING PERMISSION FORM (SPANISH)

Happy Middle School
Dra. Rebecca Branstetter, Psicóloga Escolar
Phone: (XXX) XXX-XXXX
E-mail: rbranstetter@happyschooldistrict.edu

Querido Padres/Guardíans,

Gracias por su interés en el Grupo de Niños con Talento. Las investigaciones han demostrado que cuando los estudiantes se sienten existosos en por lo menos un area, suelen tener más éxito en la escuela. Así que este grupo fue disenado para ayudarles a desarrollar algún area de talento en un ambiente divertido y con apoyo.

El grupo consistirá de tres partes:

1. Los estudiantes se identificarán algun area de talento que quieren avanzar/ desarrollar (por ejemplo, una futura carrera, deporte, pasatiempo, o un interes personal).
2. Los estudiantes se ayudarán en disenar un plan de acción para explorar el talento.
3. Los estudiantes planearán una celebración para compartir con sus familiares y amigos sus talentos.

Adjunto hay una forma de permiso para la participación en el Grupo de Talento. Este grupo se juntará cada jueves por 10 semanas durante la hora del lonche o PE. La celebración se tomará lugar en un jueves despues de las horas de clases. Les enviaré los detalles. ¡Cualquier ayuda que usted ofrezca será muy agradecida!

Por favor, si Ud. tiene preguntas, comuniquese conmigo los Martes todo el dia y los Jueves por la tarde a (XXX) XXX-XXXX. Me emociona mucho la participación de su hijo/hija.

Muchas Gracias,

Rebecca Branstetter

# PERMISO PARA PARTICIPAR EN EL
# GRUPO DE ACONSEJERIA

Happy Middle School

Yo, _____, doy mi permiso
(Nombre de los Padres/Guardíans)

para _____
(Nombre del Estudiante/Nombre de la Estudiante)

participar en el grupo de aconsejería con Dra. Branstetter, Psicóloga Escolar de Happy Middle School, que consiste en una sesión individual/orientation al Grupo de Talento (que puede incluir un cuestionario), y una sesión de 10 semanas durante el ano escolar 2012-2013. Yo entiendo que Dra. Branstetter esta obligada por la ley proteger la seguridad de todos los estudiantes en el grupo. Asi, como los padres serán informados si su hijo/a está en una situacion peligrosa o abusiva. Yo entiendo que tengo el derecho de quitar este permiso en cualquier momento por escribir y firmar una nota a la escuela.

Nombre de los Padres/Guardíans _____

Firma de los Padres/Guardíans: _____

Fecha: _____

## INFORMACIÓN DEL PADRE/DE LA MADRE O GUARDIÁN

Dirección:

Ciudad, Código postal:

Teléfono (casa):                    ¿permiso para dejar un mensaje?   SÍ   NO

Teléfono (trabajo):                 ¿permiso para dejar un mensaje?   SÍ   NO

Celular:                            ¿permiso para dejar un mensaje?   SÍ   NO

Contacto de emergencia: _____

Hay algo que será importante saber antes de trabajar con su hijo/a?

_____

_____

## Choosing a Cofacilitator

If you are lucky enough to have another support staff member who can cofacilitate the group with you, go for it! A cofacilitator is nice to have in groups for a number of reasons. First, you can split the duties and legwork in the planning phase and in getting consent. Second, a cofacilitator may have an area of expertise that you can learn from. You can also "debrief" together after the session, and the cofacilitator may have a perspective on the group dynamics that you missed because you were focusing on a different element in the group. Third, you can play "good cop–bad cop" during the actual sessions when it comes to rule enforcement, so that you are not the only one in the bad-cop role in the session. Finally, if you have days when you are sick or have to deal with an emergency, an IEP meeting, or a crisis, you can call on the cofacilitator to run the group without you.

There are a number of school staff members who would make excellent cofacilitators. For groups focusing on social skills or social pragmatics, a speech and language therapist often makes a great cofacilitator. They often have expertise in social communication with students on the autism spectrum as well. For social-emotional concerns, the school counselor or a school social worker is often a nice match for cofacilitation. If you are lucky enough to have these supports at your site, utilize them!

## Deciding on When and Where to Hold Your Group

Similar to the issues raised in Chapter Nine with regard to individual counseling, finding a time in the school day to conduct a group can be tricky. In general, if you keep your group members in the same grade, it works better for logistics because they have the same schedules. You may find that you can pull the group members during an elective time. I also find that having groups during lunch works well. If you can get funding from your school or are willing to pay out of pocket a bit, you can also periodically order pizza for the group. Pizza is the number-one predictor of group attendance! The downside to holding a lunch group is that you give up your lunchtime. But if you are like many school psychologists I know, you don't take a full lunch anyway! (Do stop by Chapter Twelve, which talks about preventing burnout, for a mixed message about the importance of taking lunch for yourself!)

Once you decide on the time for your group and get approval from the teacher(s) and principal, you will want to streamline the reminder process for your students. If the students are not all in the same class, it can be challenging to gather up all the students for group. If the group is made up of middle or high school students, they may be in several different classes, and you will spend half of your group time trying to wrangle up all the group members. In these situations, I tend to deliver group reminders and passes to the students in the morning, and they can show them to their teacher after attendance, or to hall monitors if they have to leave the lunch area. Exhibit 10.4 shows a sample group reminder you can pass out. I tend to leave the date blank so that I can just photocopy and cut up a whole bunch of passes at the beginning of the group to save time each week.

EXHIBIT 10.4.  SAMPLE GROUP REMINDER

---

# *REMINDER!*

# *Today is Girls' Talent Group!*
*This pass authorizes you to leave after attendance is taken
for Elective (1:15 -2:10)*

*Meet the group in the Music Room*

*VALID DATE:* _____

---

## Deciding on the Level of Structure in the Group

School-based counseling groups tend to have more structure than groups run in clinic-based settings. They tend to be more short term and focused. I remember when I first started out, I was trained in a more open-ended psychodynamic group process, and it wasn't a great match for the needs of the school and the students. The students I was working with needed more structure (hence the WWE wrestling problem I mentioned at the beginning of this chapter). There may be situations where you do not need a high level of structure—for example, if you are running a play-based group. Similar to individual counseling, your group can have different theoretical orientations—psychodynamic, play based, cognitive-behavioral, or solution focused. The framework will guide you in how much structure your group will have, as will the personalities of the group participants (for example, students with oppositional or impulsive behaviors need more structure). In general, though, you might want to create some general guidelines or structure for the group, usually in terms of both a week-by-week format and a routine agenda for each session. You can deviate from the structure if the group's needs call for it, but it is nice to have at least an outline or sketch of how you will spend your time. I typically try to balance content (what we are going to do) with process (what happens in the course of the group that day). Within the first or second session, I typically engage the group in deciding on a few simple rules, generated by the kids and edited through the group process. The group can make a poster listing the rules, and you can post it and have the group review it at the beginning of each session.

I always start each session with the daily agenda (for example, the agenda item for the day may be deciding on what the group wants to do for their end-of-group celebration). If the group deviates from the plan, then we talk about the process (for example, talking about how when the group started trying to make a decision together, we heard disrespectful language). Groups are unique in that you can still have a successful group even if you don't get to the agenda items, because you can notice and explore the group process. As a general guideline for the content part of the group, Exhibit 10.5 shows a sample ten-week outline for the Talent Group, and Exhibit 10.6 is an example of a daily agenda for one session.

EXHIBIT 10.5. SAMPLE TEN-WEEK AGENDA FOR TALENT GROUP

| Week Number | Focus of Group | Activities |
|---|---|---|
| 1 | Orientation | · Explain purpose of group<br>· Discuss confidentiality<br>· Conduct icebreaker to get to know other group members |
| 2 | Group norms | · Conduct icebreaker/team-building activity<br>· Create group norms and write them on large poster<br>· Discuss reward system for following group norms ("Talent Group dollars") |
| 3 | Introduction to individual talents | · Review norms and rewards system<br>· Conduct team-building activity<br>· Discuss differences and similarities between hobbies, interests, and talents<br>· Create visual of overlapping and unique talents of group members<br>· Provide Talent Group dollars for following group norms |
| 4 | Introduction to talent showcase | · Review norms and rewards system<br>· Conduct team-building activity<br>· Introduce idea of holding a talent showcase at the end of group (provide examples)<br>· Brainstorm ideas for talent showcase<br>· Provide Talent Group dollars for following group norms |
| 5 | Assigning group roles; continue talent showcase brainstorming | · Review norms and rewards system<br>· Discuss roles in group and decide who gets each role (e.g., "banker" for Talent Group dollars, beginning-of-session norm reviewer, activity cofacilitator, etc.)<br>· Conduct team-building activity<br>· Discuss how Talent Group dollars can "pay" for snacks and special activities for talent showcase<br>· Continue to brainstorm group plan for talent showcase<br>· Provide Talent Group dollars for following group norms |
| 6 | Planning for talent showcase | · Review norms, rewards system, and roles<br>· Provide visual for key decisions to be made in planning talent showcase (e.g., who, what, when, where, how)<br>· Begin discussing "what" the showcase will be (e.g., art project, dance, video, photographs, special activity)<br>· Provide Talent Group dollars for following group norms |
| 7 | Planning for talent showcase | · Review norms, rewards system, and roles<br>· Provide visual for key decisions to be made in planning talent showcase (e.g., who, what, when, where, how)<br>· Discuss "who, when and where" of showcase (e.g., Invite others? Just the group? Hold it during regular group time or after school? In group room or auditorium?)<br>· Provide Talent Group dollars for following group norms |

| 8 | Planning and rehearsing talent showcase | · Review norms, rewards system, and roles<br>· Provide visual for key decisions to be made in planning talent showcase (e.g., who, what, when, where, how)<br>· Discuss the "how" of the showcase (How will we get snacks? How many Talent Group dollars are needed to "buy" snacks?)<br>· Allow for practice of showcase<br>· Provide Talent Group dollars for following group norms |
|---|---|---|
| 9 | Rehearsing talent showcase | · Review norms, rewards system, and roles<br>· Review plan for showcase<br>· Rehearse showcase<br>· Provide Talent Group dollars for following group norms |
| 10 | Talent showcase | · Hold showcase/celebration<br>· Reflect on group and on group process |

EXHIBIT 10.6. SAMPLE DAILY AGENDA FOR TALENT GROUP

# Session 4: Introduction to Talent Showcase

11:00–11:05: Post agenda and review group norms.

11:05–11:20: Conduct team-building activity: "Creative Coloring Project" from *104 Activities That Build* (Jones, 1998).

11:20–11:30: Reflect on and process team-building activity.

11:30–11:45: Introduce idea of talent showcase and provide examples of previous showcases. Discuss how to brainstorm and be a positive group member (e.g., using active listening, not criticizing others' ideas). Brainstorm ideas with group for their talent showcase and write down on poster paper. Discuss how groups come to decisions when there are a lot of good ideas. Provide Talent Group dollars for following group norms.

11:45–11:50: Count Talent Group dollars and discuss which behaviors earned the group rewards. Do "checkout" of things group liked about today's session and things they want to change for next week.

# WHAT TO DO WHEN THINGS GET MESSY

Groups are messy! Things often don't go according to plan, and group dynamics can throw all kinds of curve balls your way. It's part of what makes a group fun and engaging to conduct! Rarely do groups follow the exact trajectory you planned. In general, you will see some initial anxiety about being in a group; some group norming, as members start to follow the group norms; then group "storming," as they deviate from the norms or break into subgroups; and then, if you are lucky, some group cohesion. But as in individual counseling, you will come across exceptions to the rules, and problem situations. Here are a few problems situations I've encountered in running groups at schools and some possible ways to deal with them.

## A Student Wants to Drop Out of Group

This can happen at any phase of the group process. A student may want to drop out after the first day, when things don't go her way, or before the official end of the group. Or she may want to skip a session or two and come back. The best way to deal with this is by setting an expectation up front about group participation. Typically, I do this as part of developing norms with the group by posing these questions: Do you have to come to all the group sessions? What do we want to do if someone is absent or doesn't want to come to group? What if someone wants to drop out of the group? The students will often come up with their own rules that are acceptable for the group. I have seen it trend a few ways: either the group is very lax about group attendance (you can come and go) or superstrict (if you miss one time, you are out!). You will want to guide them toward socially appropriate life skills: for example, when you miss a session, let other group members know; if you no longer want to be in the group, come and tell the group why you are making the decision (rather than just disappearing from the group); even if you want to quit, you stick out a group until the end because you made a commitment. Establishing the attendance rules in advance allows you something to fall back on if a group member tries to drop out. It should also be noted that there are some groups where attendance is mandatory (for example, when you are serving a student as a part of his or her IEP). In these situations, you want to point out early on that attendance is mandatory unless the student is absent from school, and identify consequences for missed sessions (for example, a call to parents).

## Group Members "Gang Up" on Another Group Member or Members

Often called "subgrouping" in the group therapy literature, this is a highly uncomfortable situation in which you bear witness either to one person being singled out or to seeing your group break into cliques within the group. When this happens in session, I usually practice the "notice and explore" technique. For example, I once had three girls gang up on the fourth girl and tell her they didn't like her ideas and didn't want her in the group anymore. The girl started crying. I commented on the process using my "wondering out loud" technique: "I wonder what it is like for Sally to sit here and have everyone say these things to her." Or I might reference the group norms of using respectful language or problem solving together, and ask the group how we can practice positive group norms together. Usually this is enough to get the group members to shift their focus to problem solving and expressing their thoughts and feelings without ganging up. If it continues, however, I will put a stop to it with more firm expectations of group behavior. I will also later check in with the person who was being ganged up on and process the experience with him or her.

## The Group Is Out of Control

When you plan out the group dynamic and are strategic about not putting a bunch of high-risk students together in a room, you reduce the chances of the group members getting out of control. However, it is always good to have a few tricks up your sleeve if things get a little wild. First, in running a group, you need to evaluate your own tolerance for energy levels. I have a moderate level of tolerance for things getting a little wild, but some people have a lower or higher level. If you're getting that feeling that something unsafe could happen if you let things go, it's time to rein things in a bit and take more control of the group.

One way to be prepared is to have a structured positive behavior plan in place for your group, particularly if you are working with a population prone to acting out. You might create a token economy with Stop and Think dollars or Talent Group dollars, and you can distribute them to the group for appropriate behavior. Later, they can redeem or spend the dollars on prizes or earn group privileges with them. I typically never take away the dollars unless things are really getting out of hand. I might say something like, "I will have to start taking some of the group dollars away unless I see everyone return to his seat." The key is, the moment the first group member sits down (or does the expected behavior you asked him to), then you give dollars and point out the positive behavior. Then they tend to start to positively pressure each other to sit down or follow the rule.

If that doesn't work, then your last response should be to terminate the group for the day. I would say something like, "It seems as if the group cannot be safe and follow the group rules today, so we will have to end group now and try again next week." This is when a cofacilitator is really helpful, because he or she can help walk the group members back to class. If you don't have a cofacilitator, you might call the secretary in the main office or a teacher you know who is on break and ask him or her to assist you in making sure the students get back to class. Having to end the group for safety reasons rarely occurs, but it is good to have a plan in mind if you do have to.

## A Student Leaves the Group Without Permission

Again, prevention is key to keeping group members in the room with you throughout the group. During the phase when you establish group norms, bring up the idea of the group's making a rule about staying in the group the entire time, and what to do if someone has to leave. Similar to the process for a student who wants to drop out of the group, teach the social skill: if you have to leave early, then you let the group know why.

## A Group Member Does Not Participate

This is not an uncommon situation. You might have a shy group member, and you might have really dominant group members who overshadow the quieter ones. You can comment on the process by saying things like, "I haven't heard from Sally in a while. I would like to hear her thoughts." She may or may not have anything to say, but you've given her space to do so. If she doesn't respond or says that she has nothing to say, then you can just say something like, "In group, it's okay not to have something to say, but if you do think of something, let us know, because your opinion is valuable." I also try to weave in team-building and cooperation games into sessions, which allows room for everyone to participate. As noted earlier, you might check out the book *104 Activities That Build: Self-Esteem, Teamwork, Communication, Anger Management, Self-Discovery, and Coping Skills* (Jones, 1998) for some ideas.

## PULLING IT ALL TOGETHER

Group counseling is one role that school psychologists may take on in order to serve more students, meet an unfulfilled counseling need at the school, or build relationship skills among students. As with individual counseling, there are several theoretical orientations that can guide your group. Your group may be a problem-based group, in which the group members all share a similar challenge; or your group may be a resilience-based group, in which the members have different challenges. Both types of groups can be positive and solution focused; the difference lies in how homogeneous or heterogeneous your group members are. Your group may be more scripted and structured or more process oriented. In reality, much of the group work done in school systems is more structured, focused, and short term than in clinical settings.

Group work also poses some unique logistical challenges. The planning phase of a group is often the lengthiest and most important one. You can begin with a needs assessment at your school in order to determine the focus of the group. Selecting group members who are appropriate for the group and finding the right group composition are the next challenges. In general, a balanced group of low-, medium-, and high-risk students (only one or two of the latter) is preferred over a group of all medium- and high-risk students. After you put together your referral list, you need to talk to the student to see if he or she is interested, obtain parent permission, and find a good time and place for your group. You may also want to recruit a cofacilitator.

Once you have your group members, a number of challenges can emerge during the actual group. You should have a general outline and week-by-week agenda for the group, but allow for flexibility if the group's needs change. Learning to balance content (today we are doing X) with process (I notice that Y is happening) is an ongoing skill to develop.

## Key Points

- Conducting groups in the school is both rewarding and challenging. There are many factors to consider before starting your group—the composition, level of structure, focus, and logistics.
- In general, there are problem-focused groups and resilience-focused groups in the schools. Problem-focused groups tend to group kids by similar problem, and resilience-focused groups tend to group a mix of kids with varying problems. Both groups can aim to teach positive skills.
- In the schools, structured or scripted curriculum groups are typically used rather than open-ended process-oriented groups. Especially when you are first starting out with your group, you might want to select a packaged curriculum rather than develop your own. As you get more comfortable with group facilitation and process, you can develop your own group materials or integrate new ideas into the scripted group as a modification.
- The first step in starting a group in the schools is to conduct a needs assessment with the support staff and teachers at your site. This will allow you to get some ideas about what type of group is needed. You do not have to do whatever group the school staff recommends, but by asking for input, you will be seen as a school psychologist who responds to the staff's specific requests.
- Second, you need to decide on what type of group you want to run. As in individual counseling, you may have a particular theoretical orientation (for example, play based, solution focused) that will guide your group. You may have access to certain group counseling curricula that you want to try out. You may also want to develop your own curriculum for a group. Decide in advance on the level of structure you want in your group. However, be flexible in balancing content (today we are doing X) with process (I notice that when we tried to do X, Y happened).
- Third, use care in deciding on your group composition. Solicit referrals from the school staff at either a school-based intervention team meeting or informally. Cast a wide net for referrals, from "role model" students to high-risk students. You will want a balanced group, with mostly medium-risk students and a few students on either end of the continuum.
- Next, work out final logistics. When possible, enlist a cofacilitator. Speech pathologists, school social workers, and counselors make great cofacilitators. Decide when and where to hold your group and get permission from the teacher(s) of the students and your principal.
- Finally, ask the students if they are interested in participating, and get parent permission. Be sure to call the parents and explain the group instead of just sending home a permission slip.

*(continued)*

- During the actual group, you may encounter some messy situations—students leaving the group, behavioral challenges, and so on. Avert some of these situations by bringing up group attendance policies at the beginning when the group is creating its norms and expectations. For groups at risk of acting-out behavior, consider having a structured positive behavior support system and a back-up plan if safety issues arise.

## DISCUSSION QUESTIONS

1. Have you ever run a group before? What was your experience?
2. What tools do you have available for running groups? Do you have any scripted curriculum-based group materials? How might you locate additional resources and training for running groups?
3. What are some pros and cons of running a scripted curriculum-based group in the school? An open-ended process-based group?
4. What are some pros and cons of having a problem-focused group? A resilience-focused group?
5. Is there anyone on your school site who might be a good cofacilitator? What steps might you take to enlist and work with this person?
6. If you have already run groups, what level of structure do you prefer to have? Do you have an agenda and outline for your groups? Is each group run in a similar way, or does it vary week by week? After reading this chapter, what new ideas do you have for modifying the next group you run?
7. What is the "ideal" group composition for you? How might you solicit appropriate referrals for this composition of students?

# chapter 11

# THE DREADED LATE-NIGHT PHONE CALL

## How to Deal with a Crisis at Your School

There is nothing worse than getting a call in the evening from the principal at one of your schools saying that there has been a crisis. I have received that phone call for a wide range of crises: suicide, homicide, a teacher having inappropriate relations with a student, weapons or violence on or near campus, death of a teacher or student, and an influx of student refugees from natural disasters. Part of your role as a school psychologist is to be prepared to deal with whatever type of crisis comes your way. The problem is, even if you had some training in graduate school on theories of crisis management, you are never quite prepared for the unique circumstances that present themselves during a time of crisis. The good news is that there are some general principles of crisis management that will get you through crises and prepare you for the unknown.

Although there are many different approaches to crisis management, this chapter focuses on the approach known as Psychological First Aid (National Child Traumatic Stress Network & National Center for PTSD, 2006). This technique is often used for natural disasters or crisis events in order to prevent or lessen symptoms of posttraumatic stress disorder (PTSD) and to foster short- and long-term coping skills. It is also useful in school- or community-based crises. In this approach, the goal is to contain the crisis by establishing contact and support, triage the affected parties to an appropriate level of intervention, provide skills for coping, and follow up after the crisis. A complete field guide is available for free on the National Child Traumatic Stress Network Web site (www.nctsn.org/content/psychological-first-aid).

## PREPARATION FOR A CRISIS

The first step in preparation is to identify the supports currently in place, before the crisis occurs. You may be in a school district where there is already an established crisis intervention team, and you will follow the directions of this team. You may also be in a school district where the psychologists are the crisis team, and if the crisis happens at your school, you call your supervisor or lead psychologist to deploy the team. If you are in a small school district, you may not have an official crisis team, and you and your school staff tend to your own crises. Investigate who is on your crisis team and what resources are available in the event of a crisis. Your supervisor or the school principal may be the best person to whom you would address these questions.

Once you have identified who is on the crisis team, the next step is to investigate procedures already in place for responding to crises. Schools are typically required to have crisis response plans in print and available at each site. It is good to get a look at this document, as staff are oftentimes unfamiliar with the plan, and then they have to locate, dust off, and frantically read through the plan when something happens. Investigating the school's procedures before the crisis is important because crises sometimes produce a "too many cooks in the kitchen" problem—disjointed efforts with different procedures going on—that makes the crisis more stressful. I remember one crisis at a local high school where a student was killed in a drive-by shooting, and the high school was full of district psychologists as well as three different counseling agencies. The district psychologists were trying to contain the crisis and triage those who needed the most support, and the counseling agency staff were holding full-on counseling sessions that actually opened up more psychological wounds. They were assuming that everyone was traumatized, and they went around to all the classes to ask who needed counseling. They ended up with a list of 150 students who wanted counseling, and there was no capacity for that. Further, the outside agencies didn't document whom they saw, and there was no way to follow up with the students once the agency staff left. Coordination is key, and the principal is the main person you will want to consult with to make sure there is a streamlined effort.

Once you have identified who is on the crisis team and what steps are currently involved in the school's crisis response plan, you will want to consult with the principal about logistics. Some questions to ask:

- How has the school handled crises before? What worked and what didn't?
- How can I be the best support to you and the school in a crisis?
- Do we have a list of the crisis team members? Do we know how to get a hold of them in the event of a crisis?
- How will you let me know when there is a crisis?

- What outside agencies might be available to assist in a crisis? Have they assisted before? Who will be responsible for coordinating efforts and follow up with them?
- Do we have a plan in place for dealing with media coverage? Are the staff trained on what to do if they are approached by the media to make a comment?
- What is the general plan of action in a crisis? How will we let students, teachers, and parents know about the crisis?

You may find when interviewing the principal that there is a formal, district-level plan for crises; you may instead find that there is no real comprehensive plan at all. In both circumstances, it is worth reviewing (or facilitating developing) a plan together during noncrisis moments. It may be an action item you can propose to add to a schoolwide intervention team meeting.

## TYPES OF CRISES

The types of crises that present themselves are unique, unpredictable, and often complex. However, there are two general types of crises that you may encounter: individual student crises, and school- or community-wide crises. Individual crises may not reach the level of implementation of a Psychological First Aid model, where many resources need to be mobilized; school- and community-wide crises may involve more coordination and resources. There are also situations in which an individual student's crisis can affect the whole school community. The first step in a crisis is to figure out how far the ripple effect may go, without assuming it will automatically require a full-team intervention. I remember a crisis at my school where two students were found inappropriately touching each other. The crisis with the two children could have been contained to the children and their families, but instead, there was a schoolwide assembly about touching, and the whole school community ended up knowing about the private crisis of the two children. In this circumstance, the response was bigger than the problem, and perhaps served to traumatize the two children by shining a schoolwide spotlight on the incident.

### Individual Student Crises: Danger to Self and Danger to Others

In general, individual student crises fall into two main categories: danger to self and danger to others.

#### *Danger to Self*

Crises where a student presents a possible danger to himself or herself come in many forms. At times, I get teachers showing me students' journal entries revealing suicidal ideation; at other times, I am working with a student already, and he or she reveals wanting to hurt himself or herself.

The first step is to gather all the facts by interviewing the student. In general, if you don't know the student, you will want to start with "warmup" questions and build some rapport before you launch into the direct questioning. Then you can move into how the student came to your attention (for example, "I wanted to chat with you today because your teacher told me that you've been having a hard time lately, and that you wrote in your journal that you wanted to die" or "I wanted to check in with you about what you told me earlier that sometimes you think about hurting yourself"). Then you can make an open-ended statement, such as, "Tell me more about that."

The goals of a suicide assessment are to determine the level of risk and develop a written intervention plan. In general, the level of worry about the student depends on his or her answers to questions about current status, prior status, plan, and access. Form 11.1 is a sample suicide assessment template that can be used to gain information about the level of risk in terms of each of these categories. You can also use this form as your documentation of your meeting with the student and your plan of response to the student's level of risk. It should also be noted that if you are new or untrained in suicide assessment, you will want to seek consultation or find another school support member (for example, counselor, social worker) with more training to conduct the assessment.

# Suicide Assessment

Date:

Name of Student:

Name of Assessor:

Description of Suicide Threat (verbal, drawings, writing):

| Assessment Area | Questions to Ask | Student Response |
|---|---|---|
| **Current status**: Does the student have current thoughts about hurting himself or herself? | I wanted to talk to you today because [insert description of threat]. Tell me more about that. | |
| **Prior status/attempts:** Has the student had prior thoughts about hurting himself or herself? | Have you thought about hurting yourself before? | |
| **Prior attempts**: Has the student made previous attempts or been hospitalized? | Have you ever tried to hurt yourself before? | |
| **Current plan:** Does the student have a plan, method, and access (for example, to pills, weapons, bridge)? | Do you have a plan to hurt yourself today? Have you thought about how you might do it? | |

Intervention plan and action items:

Parents notified on _____ (date). Notes about conversation.

In general, the level of risk increases if there is a past history, current plan, and current access. If a child has ideation but no history or plan, the intervention may be to contact the parents and the person who referred the child to you and let them know. A reasonable intervention may be to consult with the parents about monitoring or referrals to services, or to offer "check-ins" with the student periodically.

If a student presents as high risk (has made prior attempts and has a plan), the student should not be left alone for any period of time, nor released to go home or back to class. If the student is released, it should be to his or her parents' care or to a crisis intervention caseworker (for example, a law enforcement officer or paramedic). The first effort should definitely be to release the child to the parents' care with information about how to access emergency services. If possible, it is best to avoid calling emergency services and having the child removed from school to be hospitalized. This can be scary and traumatizing for the child, and it makes his or her experience very public. Calling emergency services also can end up slapping the parents with a giant bill for ambulance services. If possible, you can always coach the parents on how to get the child to emergency services first, and if they aren't available, aren't willing, or don't feel comfortable, then you can access emergency services.

If you are helping the parents go to emergency services, you will need to ensure that the child is supervised on the ride if he or she is actively suicidal (for example, have someone ride in the back of the car with him or her). You will then want to follow up with the family about whether the child was admitted or not, and develop a long-range plan for supporting the student as he or she returns to school.

### Danger to Others

The other individual crisis scenario arises when a child presents as a danger to others. This can happen when a student is having an aggressive outburst, makes a threat, or brings a weapon onto school property.

In the case of a student who is actively aggressive toward others, the crisis needs to be contained right away. If you have ever tried to move an aggressive student away from others, you probably know that it is a dangerous and rather fruitless intervention. Instead, move others away from the aggressive student first and then work your de-escalation skills. If you haven't been explicitly taught de-escalation skills, a great place to start is to talk to colleagues who have, or to request professional development in this area from your supervisor. In general, you want to first reduce the "audience" only to you and perhaps one other adult. I have seen students become more agitated as more adults try to join in on the de-escalation. Model calmness. Use a calm voice even if you are internally freaking out! You can make neutral statements, validate the student's experience, and give a directive: "I see you are very upset right now. It is okay to be upset. It's not safe to kick others, though. Let's figure out another solution together" or "I notice your hands are clenched into fists. Can you tell me what you're thinking about right now?" You can also provide alternatives and choices to give the student a sense of control: "You can sit in the library area until you are safe, take a walk with me, or talk to someone you trust. We can call someone if you think that would help. If you have another idea, I am open to hearing it as well." Do not follow the student around the room as you are talking. (I made this mistake just once, and it only escalated the situation.) Keep your distance and remain calm. Don't ask too many questions. If you are going to ask one question, it might be, "I see you are very upset. What do you need right now from us?"

The other type of crisis situation involving danger to others occurs when a student makes a threat against another student or a group of students, or makes a vague threat of danger or harm to others. As you did for the suicide assessment, you want to determine the severity of risk and threat. Every threat needs to be taken seriously, even if it is said in a supposedly "joking" manner. I had a horrible situation once where a teacher thought a kid was "just joking" about bringing a knife to school, and then the next day, he brought a knife to school with the intent to harm a classmate who had been bullying him. Train your teachers to take all threats seriously and to inform the principal so that you can do a threat assessment. Form 11.2 shows a sample threat assessment form you might use for documenting and developing an intervention plan when you have referred a student who has made a threat. As with the suicide assessment, if you are new or untrained in threat assessment, seek consultation first or locate a staff member who is trained in threat assessment to do the interview until you have had adequate training. A good resource for additional training and resources for threat assessment can be found on the Positive Environments, Networks of Trainers (PENT) website: http://www.pent.ca.gov/hom/bio/dianabw.html.

# *Threat Assessment*

Date:
Name of Student:
Name of Assessor:
Description of Threat (verbal, drawings, writing):

| Assessment Area | Questions to Ask | Student Response |
|---|---|---|
| **Information about threat:** | I wanted to talk to you today because [insert description of threat]. Can you tell me more about that? I'm not angry with you; I'm just trying to understand where you are coming from. | |
| **Context of threat:** What happened before the threat? | What has been going on for you that led you to say/draw/write that you wanted to [describe threat]? | |
| **Current plan:** Does the student have a plan, method, and access (for example, weapons)? Are there specific intended victims, a group of victims, or a vague threat (for example, "the school")? | Tell me what you have planned. When were you planning to do this? Where could you find a gun/knife/bomb [insert method]? | |

Intervention plan and action items:


Principal/law enforcement notified on _____ (date). Notes about conversations:


Parents notified on _____ (date). Notes about conversation:

The most important outcome of the threat assessment is that you leave the interview with a clear sense of the level of risk. If the student states that he or she was "just joking," you still want to notify the parents and the principal. The principal may have to take disciplinary action regardless of whether or not the student was joking. You may also have a duty to warn the intended victim, if the victim is specifically named. If possible, conduct the threat assessment and intervention planning with another staff member. Principals are also trained in threat assessment, and law enforcement sometimes needs to get involved. You can also consult with your supervisor or another school psychologist about the student if you are still left without a good sense of whether the threat is real or not.

### A Word About Consent and Child Protective Services

It is often the case that when a student presents as a danger to himself or herself or others, you do not need parental permission to speak with the child on a one-time basis. It is not considered "counseling," so you do not typically need permission. Whether or not you need permission to see a student in a crisis situation is something to ask your supervisor. You will of course want to involve the parents in the process, even though you may not need their consent to start the process of interviewing a student. It is also important to note that interviews about safety can sometimes lead to a need to contact Child Protective Services (CPS). You will need to follow the same procedures outlined in Chapter Nine on individual counseling. The only added factor in a crisis situation may be the timing of the call. You may be activating a higher level of care than CPS provides (for example, law enforcement, hospitalization), and you can postpone the call until you have stabilized the child. Typically, you have twenty-four hours to call, but check with your supervisor. In any case, you will want to make the call and report as soon as the child is stabilized.

## Schoolwide Crises: Determining the Ripple Effect and Implementing Psychological First Aid

Having a schoolwide crisis on your hands will, we all hope, be a rare event. In my years as a school psychologist, the most common crises that have presented are death of a student or teacher at my school, death of a popular student at another school, weapons on campus, and sexual misconduct (teacher-student or student-student). School psychologists across the country have likely also experienced dealing with crises related to the aftermath of a natural disaster.

The volume of crises you will encounter will vary by your school district and the demographics of your community. Unfortunately, in urban school districts, the dangers from the community frequently create crises at schools. In one district where I worked, we had eight crisis teams that rotated throughout the school year, and sometimes my crisis team was called up to respond several times in the year. Even one crisis is enough to be emotionally taxing, because we are expected to be the calm in the storm, so to speak. If you haven't had training or experience in crisis management, you might feel as though you are totally winging it, ill-equipped to give good advice about how to handle the crisis, or emotionally overwhelmed yourself. That is why having a model in your mind (in this case Psychological First Aid) is helpful for framing the question that the principal will inevitably ask you: What do we do?

### *Steps to Take in a Schoolwide Crisis*

In the event of a school- or community-wide crisis, there are several steps you can take or can consult with the crisis intervention team to take (in conjunction with previously established crisis plans).

**Step 1: Gather the information.** The first person to know about the crisis should notify the principal. The main task of the principal is to gather and verify the facts. Accurate information can be difficult to obtain, because rumors spread like wildfire in crises. People in crisis mode are also fairly distressed and disoriented. Your job is to tease out what is hearsay and what is fact by asking such questions as "Is that a fact we learned from [the police/the family/the hospital], or is that what we have heard happened from others?" I remember one case where I got a call that there was a "media frenzy" at my school over a sexual misconduct issue. It turns out that the so-called issue was just the *fear*, not the reality. I rushed to my school, and people were going about their regular school day.

**Step 2: Determine the level of response.** Meet with the school crisis team if you have one. If you don't have a team, then meet with principal to decide on the level of response together. Before you call in "the troops" and other resources (district crisis teams, outside agencies, and so on), evaluate the event and determine the degree of impact on the school. In general, the impact is higher if the students were emotionally or physically close to a victim, if there are ongoing concerns about safety, if a large number of individuals are affected by the event, and if the students and faculty are already having a strong reaction to the event. Once your crisis team has assessed the level of support needed, then you can start to mobilize additional resources.

**Step 3: Decide how much to disclose to the school community and how to disclose it; disseminate the information.** Once you gain the facts and determine the level of response, you will want to help the principal decide how much information to disclose. In general, you want to stop the rumor mill by reporting sufficient information to clarify the situation for the staff and students, while also respecting the wishes of the families of the victims, if applicable. It is important to disclose only the facts, and if there are facts that are as yet unknown, say so. In the event of a student death, avoid sharing any gory or unnecessary details.

There are several ways to disclose the information. You begin with the school staff and then disclose to the parents and community, typically in written form.

In general, when disclosing information to the staff, you will want to do so in a setting where students can get support right away. That rules out an announcement over the PA or an assembly. The preferred route is usually to have a faculty meeting, if possible, and give the teachers a script to read to their students and some sample activities they may do in class to support students. Mind you, not every teacher is equipped emotionally or practically to do this, so you can delegate crisis team members to classrooms where the teacher feels uncomfortable. Exhibit 11.1 is a sample handout you might distribute to help a teacher or crisis team member facilitate a discussion with the students regarding a death, along with some possible classroom activities. It can be adapted for other situations. Please note that in some crisis situations (for example, sexual misconduct or a confidential situation, a larger-scale disaster), a teacher-led discussion may not be appropriate. This is something that should be determined by your crisis team.

EXHIBIT 11.1. SAMPLE CRISIS INTERVENTION HANDOUT

*State the Facts*

Say, "As you may or may not know, [state the incident]. We do not have all the facts at this time. What we do know is . . ." Then describe the following:

- When incident occurred
- Where incident occurred
- What happened (omitting unnecessary detail)
- What is going to happen (for example, funeral, memorial service)

*Tips:* Keep to the facts. If you don't know a fact, say you don't know. Do not speculate about motives or the other people involved. Address rumors (for example, if a student says, "I heard that he was shot in the head," you can respond, "I do not know if that is true. What I know is that he was brought to the hospital and passed away last night").

*Acknowledge Feelings and Reactions*

Say, "It is normal for students to feel many different things when hearing about news like this. Students often react differently, and we all have different ways of dealing with our feelings. What are some of the feelings you have about hearing about this?"

*Tips:* Acknowledge feelings without judgment (for example, "Yes, some students feel sad"). At times, the feeling may seem odd to you, but acknowledge it anyway ("Some people do feel grossed out"). Let students know that if they aren't feeling anything, that is okay too (for example, "Some people feel sad right away, and some people aren't sure how they feel yet").

*Teach About Self-Care*

Say, "As we just discussed, feeling [insert feelings students mentioned] are normal feelings. It is also important to take care of our feelings and ourselves." Ask the students the following questions:

- What are some things you all do when you are feeling [insert feelings students mentioned]?
- Who can help you when you are feeling [insert feelings students mentioned]?

Throughout the discussion of self-care, remind students that feelings change over time. They usually start out strong and become less strong over time. Tell them that if they continue to have strong feelings, they need to tell someone they trust.

*Tips:* As students identify coping skills, write them on the board. If a student comes up with a coping skill that may not be adaptive (for example, "I hit my brother when I'm mad"), talk about an alternative coping skill ("It's okay to be mad, but hitting your brother is not okay. What is another way to get your 'mad' out that doesn't hurt anyone?"). If when identifying people they can turn to a student says "Nobody," provide him or her with some options (for example, "Sometimes it is hard to find the right person to talk to. You can always come to me or the principal if you need support").

## Conduct an Activity (If Appropriate)

Say, "When something tragic happens, we not only need to be kind to ourselves by taking care of our feelings and asking adults for support, but also be kind to others. What are some ideas for ways to support the friends and family members of [victim or victims of incident]?"

Take notes on the board of the ideas the students generated. If students are having difficulty coming up with activities, you can suggest some of the following:

- Making individual condolence cards for the family
- Making a group condolence card for the family
- Raising money for the family to take care of funeral expenses (in the event of a death)
- Making a memorial for the student (not appropriate in the case of suicide, however)

*Tips:* If the class members don't know the family or child, cue them to look out for friends who were close to the victim(s) who may be grieving, and to speak kindly about the victim and his or her family.

## Other Tips

- Model calmness and empathy. Your students will follow your lead.
- Watch for students having strong emotional or behavioral reactions. Both may be signs that they need additional support. Call the office or crisis room if you need support.
- Check in privately with students, perhaps during the activity. Do not offer counseling to the class in a public setting. If you feel that a student needs more support, then send him or her to the office with the crisis counseling pass. This will prevent students from wandering around campus in search of a counselor.
- In the weeks that follow, be on the lookout for delayed reactions, such as acting out, being "unmotivated," acting silly, or withdrawing from the group. Consult with your school psychologist if you are concerned about a delayed reaction.
- Take time to care for yourself too. School staff need support as much as students do in a time of crisis. Follow your own advice for your students and identify coping strategies and supports for yourself.

When you disseminate the handout to teachers, this is the opportunity to let teachers know of the support services you have made available (for example, a crisis counseling room) and who is appropriate to refer to counseling. Emphasize that not all students will require individual counseling. The students who most likely need counseling will be family members of a victim, close friends of a victim, students who have experienced a similar trauma that might be "triggered" by the event, emotionally vulnerable students, and younger students. It is important that teachers understand that the purpose of the intervention is to contain reactions to the event and triage support, not to send out every child who is having an emotional reaction. Form 11.3 is a sample crisis referral slip that teachers can use. It should not be shared with the child or used as a pass. It is for the purpose of informing the counseling staff of the referral concern. Teachers can place it in a sealed envelope, have a student who is coping well deliver the referrals, or call the crisis room to have a counselor pick up referrals.

# *Crisis Counseling Referral Form*

Referring Teacher: _____  Date: _____  Rm.: _____

Student Name: _____  Grade: _____

Area of concern:

____ Student is emotionally affected by the trauma.

____ Student was physically close to the trauma.

____ Student was well acquainted with the individuals involved

____ Student's past traumas seem reignited by the current situation

____ Other (please describe): _____

Notes: _____

_____

Once the staff and student body have been notified, the principal will want to write the letter to the parents and the community. It may be very similar to the one that was created for the school staff. Depending on the community, it may need to be translated into another language as well. Also, depending on the timing, you may have the parent letter ready to go to send with the teachers to disseminate when they make an announcement, or it may be sent home by the end of the day. If the crisis occurred at the end of the day, there may need to be a phone-tree notification of the incident with information about what will happen the following day and what resources are available; a follow-up letter would then be sent as soon as possible. Exhibit 11.2 is a sample parent letter that can be adapted to the needs of a specific crisis.

EXHIBIT 11.2. SAMPLE CRISIS LETTER TO PARENTS

Dear Parents/Guardians,

As you may or may not be aware, our school has recently experienced [specify event], which is a tragedy for our community. The facts as we know them are [give brief description of incident and known facts]. [If facts are still unknown or there is controversy about facts:] An investigation is under way, and until it is complete we will not have all the details about this tragedy.

Students and staff will react in different ways to tragedies such as this, so we will have counselors available at school [specify time frame of availability: today, all week] to help students cope with their reactions and feelings about [event]. If you feel your child is in need of special assistance or is having a great deal of difficulty coping with [event], please do not hesitate to call.

[If change in schedule is warranted:] Although it is important to deal with student and staff reactions, we believe it is essential to resume a normal school routine as soon as possible. The following modifications in our school's regular schedule will be in effect during [specify dates], and after that time, all regular schedules and routines will resume. [Specify needed information such as memorial services, possible changes in classroom locations, alterations to school operating hours, etc.]

Thank you for your support of our school as we work together to cope with [event]. Please observe your child closely over the next several days and weeks to watch for signs of distress that may indicate a need for additional support and guidance. Attached is a handout about how to help your child cope with traumatic events [insert resources about coping with death, dos and don'ts, and so on, available on the National Association of School Psychologists Web site: www.nasponline.com]. The following resources are also available for anyone who would like assistance in dealing with his or her reaction to this event:

*Local community mental health center [phone]:*

Please feel free to call if you have any concerns or questions regarding your child or steps being taken by the school to address this [tragedy, loss, event].

Sincerely,

*Sally Smith*

Sally Smith, Principal

(XXX)-XXX-XXXX

Ssmith@districtemail.edu

**Step 4: Provide needed support and coordinate mental health efforts.** Once you have set up your counseling room and have your support staff ready, your jobs may include both brief counseling with students and coordination of services. Depending on the volume of students referred to you, you may be doing individual or group counseling. In terms of materials needed, you will need a crisis referral tracking sheet (see Form 11.4) to make sure you are documenting your interactions with students as well as planning for short-term and long-term care. In your assessment of the student's coping, you will want to determine whether any follow-up is needed, and if it is, what type. For example, the student may need a check-in in a few days, or he or she may need to be connected to outside counseling resources for longer-term treatment. Before you refer out to an agency or add the student to your counseling caseload, check to see if the student already has a counselor. If he or she does, then your intervention may be to let that counselor know that the student needs follow-up care. And as always, inform the parents of the students who you think need a follow-up check-in or a referral.

# Crisis Referral Tracking Sheet

| Date/Time | Student Name | Seen Individually or in Group | Seen by (Counselor Name and Agency) | Notes/Status | Follow-up Plan (e.g., no follow-up needed, check in again in x days, refer to more intensive services) |
|---|---|---|---|---|---|
|  |  |  |  |  |  |
|  |  |  |  |  |  |
|  |  |  |  |  |  |
|  |  |  |  |  |  |

I have also found that having art supplies on hand is good for students. I would not, however, direct them to the materials and ask them to draw what happened or what they are feeling, as that might retraumatize them. I would leave the materials in proximity to the students if they spontaneously want to draw or to make a card for the family of the victim or victims (if appropriate to the crisis). In general, you want to contain and assess, not open up for a lengthy counseling process. You may also want to follow the handout for teachers in Exhibit 11.1 as a way to start the check-in. Being a good listener and source of emotional support, however, is more important than being a good question asker. In times of crisis, sometimes just consoling a crying child without a word is as healing as talking with him or her.

### After the Immediate Crisis

In times of crisis, school psychologists often jump into "psych-robot" mode, in which they put their feelings and reactions aside to help the students. At the end of the day, you may start to have your own feelings and reactions as well, and you are likely to be emotionally and physically exhausted. Like students, you may also experience a variety of your own emotions, ranging from anger to sadness to numbness. It is a good idea to debrief with your crisis team members about your experience in providing the crisis services and make sure you are using your coping skills too!

It is also important to debrief the experience with the whole school staff. Some principals hold a staff meeting at the end of school to debrief feelings and reactions, as well as get feedback on what worked and what didn't. This feedback is essential for your crisis team, so that you learn what to do and what not to do the next time a crisis comes your way. You will also be able to learn from the staff about any ongoing resources that may be needed so that you can provide follow-up care. Often, in a crisis, there is a slew of support on the first day or so, and then, even though there are lingering concerns, things return to "business as usual." You want to make sure that ongoing support is available for students, teachers, and staff who have delayed reactions.

## PULLING IT ALL TOGETHER

In times of crisis, whether it be an individual, schoolwide, or community-wide crisis, school psychologists are expected to have the skill set to facilitate the crisis response. You may or may not have had training in crisis response. Your level of experience with crises may also determine your comfort level with being a leader or participant on a crisis team. Preparing in advance for a crisis is one way to gain comfort in the role you will play in the process. Once a crisis arrives, you will also need a planned procedure to implement, as you and your staff may be distraught or disoriented by the crisis event. This chapter used the Psychological First Aid model and provided sample handouts that can be easily adapted to almost any crisis. It is important to note as well that you are one part of a crisis team: you are not expected to do it all alone. Your principal, district crisis team members, colleagues, school staff, and outside agencies are all potential sources of support. Part of your role may be to help coordinate crisis response efforts, deliver counseling services, and case-manage follow-up care.

## Key Points

- Crises are by definition unexpected, disorienting, and distressing. You can minimize the impact of crises by having a crisis plan and preparing your crisis team in advance. Consult and investigate with your principal and supervisor what the crisis plan model is, and identify the roles each member of the crisis team is expected to play.

- There are two general categories of crises that you may be asked to help with: individual student crises and schoolwide crises.

- In general, the two types of individual student crises arise when a student presents as a danger to himself or herself and when a student presents as a danger to others.

- When a student presents as a danger to himself or herself or others, your role is often to gather the facts, interview the student, determine the level of risk, develop a plan, follow up, and document your assessment and intervention.

- Schoolwide crises can vary in volume and type—you may have many ongoing crises, or only one every year or two. Schoolwide crises include the death of a student or staff member at your school, death of a student at another school, sexual misconduct, community violence, or a natural disaster.

- Psychological First Aid is recommended as the model to implement in a schoolwide crisis. The steps in the process include gathering information, determining the level of response, deciding how much to disclose to the school community and disseminating the information, and providing support and coordinating mental health efforts (short term and long term).

- Taking care of your staff and yourself is important following a crisis. You will want to set up a time to debrief the experience and process emotions about the crisis and the response efforts.

## DISCUSSION QUESTIONS

1. What is your school crisis response plan? Who is on your crisis team, and who is the leader of this team? What model does your school use? Does the school's current plan involve principles of Psychological First Aid?

2. If you don't know what your school's crisis plan is, what is your plan for gathering this information?

3. What is your experience, training, and comfort level with crisis intervention? What supports can you access if you feel you are not as equipped to handle a crisis as you would like to be?

4. If you have participated on a crisis intervention team, what was your experience? What did you learn about yourself or crisis management that you would share with others who have not been in a crisis?

5. How do you foster self-care among your school staff? How do you personally cope with the vicarious trauma that sometimes occurs when you are a crisis responder?

# chapter 12

# PUT ON YOUR OXYGEN MASK BEFORE HELPING OTHERS

## How to Manage the Stress of the Job

As helping professionals, school psychologists often burn out because they work under stressful conditions and do not always practice self-care. As "holders of trauma," we need practical strategies for managing vicarious trauma, dealing with the aftermath of emotionally charged situations, and keeping healthy work-life boundaries. Ironically, although we are the ones who can share great coping skills with others, we often don't use them on ourselves! You might keep in mind the familiar instruction you hear on airplanes: the flight attendant tells you that in the event of an emergency, you need to put on your own oxygen mask before assisting others. Whenever I hear this, I flash to a scene in my mind where I forget to do this, and pass out while trying to help someone else. The point is, if you don't take care of yourself, you will not be equipped to help others. Self-care and healthy work-life boundaries are the keys to survival in this profession.

## PRACTICING SELF-CARE

As school psychologists, we are trained in understanding the stress response in our students. However, when we get into stressful situations during our busy work days, it is often the case that we do not know exactly how to apply what we know to ourselves. Over the years, I have collected some self-care tools from wise school psychologists; I encourage you to try them out and see what works for you.

### Moments of Zen

A few years back, one of my school psychologist colleagues was discussing how she managed stress: "I finally learned to stop and smell the flowers instead of running over them to get to an IEP." She went on to explain that she had researched how just taking a few "Zen" private relaxation moments during the day increases dopamine production, which reduces stress. I tried to think of any Zen moments I had had during my school days, and came up blank. I was definitely a flower stomper. I made a new school year's resolution to take a few moments in the day to recharge my dopamine. I also surveyed readers of the Notes from the School Psychologist Blog Facebook page and collected some tips on how they recharge during the school day:

- Take lunch! Even if it is a fifteen-minute lunch, make sure you are doing nothing but eating during that time. We are masters of multitasking ("I'll just score this protocol while I eat"), and we are always trying to squeeze in consultation time ("I'll just check in with that teacher during lunch"). But just because we are good at it doesn't mean we should do it! Take some time to actually eat your lunch and relax a moment.
- Take a walk during your lunch or during a break time. Even if you just go outside and take one lap around the school, you are resetting for the afternoon. This can also help with your physical alertness—unlike going for that tempting donut and coffee in the teachers' lounge and crashing later!
- If you join your colleagues for lunch, try to keep the conversation social, not about work. Avoid teachers' lounge environments where the teachers just complain or spout negativity. Be selective about whom you have lunch with—the more positive your lunch crew is, the better you'll feel as you tackle the afternoon.
- Take a few moments to practice relaxation strategies, perhaps in between students. Breathing exercises take but a moment and can be rejuvenating.
- Take a few minutes to visit the classroom of an inspiring and positive teacher to remind yourself that not all children are suffering . . . only the ones who get referred to you!
- Take some time, even ten or fifteen minutes, just to be with kids, without an agenda. If you work with elementary kids, this might mean reading a book with a student or doing a read-aloud, coloring with students during their free time, or visiting them during playtime. I find that visiting a kindergarten classroom is often fun because those little ones are full of joy and energy, and they say the funniest things!
- After work, have an "unwinding" ritual. Go to the gym or for a walk, watch a mindless TV show, listen to music, "download" your day with your partner or

a friend (and then vow to be finished talking about work for the night!), or imagine when you close your car door that you are closing off all the stress of the day. It is important to note that you should not be downloading the specific details of your day to anyone, for confidentiality reasons. But you can always talk about the type of day you had (hectic, depressing, frustrating, satisfying).

## Flocking

The fact is, we work stressful jobs. Being a support to students, teachers, parents, and administrators in crisis can be exhausting and stress inducing. A groundbreaking study by researchers at UCLA (Taylor et al., 2000) helped me rethink the stress response and how to cope when stressed. The "traditional" model of stress response is "fight or flight." According to this model, when under stress, one prepares either to fight or to flee. Having only those two responses to stress didn't really fit for the researchers, nor did it fit for me. It's hard to imagine that during a contentious IEP meeting, my only options were to argue with the team members or leave the room! The researchers identified a common third response called "tending and befriending." They found that under stress, people actually nurture themselves or get support from others—and that, my friends, is what has kept me in this profession, not fight or flight. After that contentious IEP, the best way for me to let go of the stress is to talk with the special education teacher about it or to call up a school psychologist friend to debrief the stressful experience. I even told one of my teacher friends about this research, and she said, "Duh! It's not fight or flight for me either. It's *flocking* to others!"

There are many different forms of flocking that can be useful for self-care. What no one tells you about being a school psychologist is that it can actually be a fairly isolating experience. Even though you are around people all day, you are typically never around *your people*—other school psychologists. Other school psychologists are the ones who "get it" right away and have practical advice or comfort for you. You may even find you can "trade" assessment cases from time to time if you need to (for example, if you have a negative history with the parent or if your colleague has more expertise in the type of assessment needed). Knowing that you have that support is priceless.

Take time to connect with your colleagues. Even if you are in a small district with only one or two other school psychologists, try to connect with them on a regular basis, or advocate with district administration for monthly case consultation or staff meetings. I also have several school psychologists' cell phone numbers in my phone, ready to be dialed at a moment's notice when I need to flock to their advice or comfort. I also make time to see them socially after work, so I can feel a part of a larger community of helping professionals.

In the event that you don't have other school psychologist colleagues to flock to or you haven't really connected with your colleagues, you can also seek out online support. Read and subscribe to school psychologists' blogs. Join a school psychology forum or group to be part of an ongoing discussion and support team. Of course, I shall shamelessly plug my Notes from the School Psychologist Blog Facebook page, which has a wealth of school psychologists' information, insights, and humor to share. Go to www .facebook.com/pages/Notes-from-the-School-Psychologist-Blog/88305811218, or type in "Notes from the School Psychologist" in the Search function of Facebook.

Another great way to "flock" and gain inspiration from colleagues is to attend professional development activities and conferences. When you are in a rut and writing your fortieth psychoeducational report of the year, it's hard to be inspired. Finding a new and exciting way to describe phonological processing in a report doesn't really do the trick in the inspiration department. I find that signing up for and attending workshops and conferences boosts my inspiration and gives me fresh ideas. The other benefit of professional development is that you have a chance to connect with other school psychologists and learn from each other. If it's in your budget, I also recommend trying to go to new and exciting places for these conferences! A little travel over a weekend to a conference may feel a bit like a mini-vacation. You just might be able to relax and recharge during down times between presentations.

## MAINTAINING HEALTHY WORK-LIFE BOUNDARIES

I want you to go back to our analogy of putting on your oxygen mask in an emergency before assisting others. Imagine you have put your mask on (that is, you have good self-care techniques), and you look around and see a *whole plane of students* who need help. Yikes! What now? Help the students nearest to you? The ones who are most vulnerable? The ones who are crying out for help? Sometimes you have too many students to work with and not enough time.

One thing that was absolutely not taught in graduate school is how to cope in a situation where traditional time management techniques and coping skills alone are not sufficient for preventing burnout. As I've noted elsewhere, school psychologists can't practice the time management technique of "Do what's most important first" because all students are important. So what do you do? You change the way you think about your job. You use cognitive-behavioral therapy (CBT) techniques on yourself in order to have healthy boundaries about what is realistic and what is not.

### Your Role and Saying No

When I first started out as a school psychologist, I said yes to everything. I didn't know exactly what my role was because I was brand new, so I figured everything was part of my role. Can you check in with this student? Sure! Can you run a lunch group for angry students? Yep! Can you stay after school for leadership team meetings? Why not? Can you test so-and-so this week? No problem! I soon found out that saying yes to everything became a serious problem. I was so busy during the school day with all the extras, I didn't have time to work on any reports. So I took them home and worked on them at night and on the weekends. I told myself that I had to because of the legal timelines. I couldn't be late on a legal timeline, right? I told myself I had no choice.

Needless to say, that first year was the worst year of my career. I really burned myself out, and questioned why I had gone to graduate school for so long for such a horribly difficult job. I thought about quitting. Because I didn't have any boundaries, I ended up having no life after work, so I wasn't really using my "oxygen mask" either. I told myself that I *had* to keep working because the kids and the school were depending on me.

That's the cognitive trap I got myself into. I also discovered that this trap is very powerful because school psychologists have a never-ending to-do list. Kids are never "done" because they are always developing and changing. Furthermore, if your strategy for getting your work "done" is to work harder, faster, and longer, that will only take you so far. It is often the case that school psychologists have impossibly heavy caseloads. Working yourself to exhaustion to keep up doesn't really send a message to the district folks that you need more time at a school or that they need to hire new school psychologists to help. It sends the message, "I got this!" and there is no incentive to call in any more supports. Meanwhile, you are drowning in work, and you are in an unsustainable situation.

Saying no to extra work can be challenging. We are often naturally a "Yes!" kind of people, because we love to help. The first step to having appropriate boundaries with staff asking you to do extra things you don't have time for is for you to step back and look at your role. If your role is primarily assessment, you may not have time for other roles, and you will have to make assessment your top priority. If you are hired for counseling services or intervention support, you will have to think about your caseload and what is reasonable for you to handle. You want to do your job well, not a hundred little jobs poorly. Here is a sample of things you might say if someone asks you to do something you don't have time for:

- I would really like to help with that, but right now I have to give highest priority to my assessments because I have legal timelines to meet. If my referral rate slows down over the next few weeks, I will let you know.
- Can I get back to you on the amount of time I can dedicate to that? I need to look at my caseload and see if I can make enough time to do that job well.
- At the moment, I have ten spots for counseling, and they are full. However, I would be able to call the family and give them some community-based resources so they can access help that way.
- Right now, my schedule is such that I am not able to add a new commitment unless I let go of another. At this time, I have leadership team meetings on Tuesdays, RtI team on Wednesdays, and student study team meetings on Thursdays. I would like to serve on the school safety team as well. Which of these teams needs my presence the most?
- I would normally love to do yard duty, because it gives me a chance to see students in another context. However, I can't commit to it on a regular basis because I am often called away for meetings and emergencies. I would hate to have yard duty not covered because I am called away. Perhaps I can be available on an as-needed basis?
- I have ten signed assessment plans right now, which takes me to April 10th for finishing those up. If we add another, know that I will do my best to do it as quickly as possible, but I want you to be aware of the reality of my caseload at this time. I will do my best, though.

Also important: don't say "That's not my job!" or "I'm too busy." That goes over like a ton of bricks. It is better to explain your rationale with examples, so that people understand why you aren't able to help in that moment, and they don't think that you're just being unhelpful.

## Know When to Say When

In addition to learning how to say no to others, it is equally important to say no to yourself. Here is where you need to turn your CBT skills on yourself! If you find yourself writing reports, working on paperwork, or endlessly thinking about students after work hours or on the weekends, these tips are for you!

- At the end of the day, instead of running through all the things you need to do for tomorrow, run through all the accomplishments you achieved that day.
- Appoint a universal "stop time" for work. It may be when the last bell rings, at four in the afternoon, or before dinner. Tell yourself you must stop working at that time. Use self-talk like "My to-do list will never be done because kids are never done. Therefore, I need to stop so I am recharged for tomorrow." Recruit others (spouse, friends) to help you enforce the rule.
- If you *must* write a report after work hours, make it a rare occasion. I allow myself three "after-work reports" per year. Because let's face it: there are some cases you just have to get done. Limit yourself to only a certain number per semester or year.
- If you are ruminating about a student, tell yourself, "Worrying about the student is not going to change things." If you can't stop your worry, call a colleague to consult so that you can let it go.
- Continually focus on doing your personal best, and do not beat yourself up for your lack of superhuman powers. Instead of "I didn't get to X, Y, and Z today," tell yourself "I am doing my best under the circumstances."
- Ask for help! I know, this is a difficult one for folks in the helping professions, but if you are really not meeting timelines or are not able to "do it all," talk to your supervisor about what roles you should let go of, or to find out whether there are other school psychologists who can assist you for a time period until things are back to manageable levels.
- Seek professional guidance. Going to therapy yourself is one of the best things you can do to be a better school psychologist. Your therapist can help you with both self-care techniques and ways to maintain healthy work-life boundaries. Being on "the other side of the couch," so to speak, also gives you great empathy and a deeper understanding of what it might be like for your students.

## PULLING IT ALL TOGETHER

School psychologists are often experts at providing counsel and advice for others about stress management. In a stressful work environment, with time pressures, emotional stress, and a heavy workload, we can become burned out if we don't utilize our own coping skills. Practicing self-care is the first order of business for stress management. You can integrate self-care in your daily routines at work and also at home once you leave work. Tapping into your personal support network is another way to practice self-care. In addition, even if you use good self-care techniques, you may still experience challenges in juggling your multiple roles and divided time. Maintaining healthy work-life boundaries is key to preventing burnout. Learning to say no gracefully and challenging your own thoughts about your job are two techniques that will increase your odds of enjoying your work and staying in the profession.

It is my sincere hope that this book will also have given you some practical strategies and time-saving techniques to support you in one of the most rewarding and most challenging professions in education. School psychologists have much to offer students, teachers, parents, and administrators and, with support, can have a long and happy career knowing they made a difference.

---

## Key Points

- School psychologists tend to experience stressful working conditions, due to the nature of their jobs. They are often "holders of trauma" and need self-care tools to prevent burnout.
- There are two main strategies identified in this chapter for helping you feel energized, empowered, and successful in your job: practicing self-care and maintaining healthy work-life boundaries.
- Some strategies for self-care include finding "moments of Zen" (relaxing moments) during the school day and "flocking" (connecting with other school psychologists and support networks).
- Some strategies for maintaining healthy work-life boundaries include learning to say no to others, learning to say no to yourself, and rethinking your unrealistic expectations of yourself.

---

## DISCUSSION QUESTIONS

1. What do you do to practice "putting on your oxygen mask"? What are your self-care techniques and rituals to prevent burnout?
2. What are your "pitfall thoughts" that you fall into? (For example, "I *have* to write this report from home tonight" or "If I don't see this student, she will *never* get support.") How do you turn your pitfall thoughts into more adaptive thoughts?
3. What are the top stressors in your job? What tips from this chapter can you try this week to manage stress?

# Bibliography and Resources

## Web

AIMSweb: www.aimsweb.com/

Branstetter, R. Notes from the School Psychologist blog: www.studentsgrow.blogspot.com

Branstetter, R. Notes from the School Psychologist Blog Facebook page: www.facebook.com/pages/Notes-from-the-School-Psychologist-Blog/88305811218

DIBELS: https://dibels.uoregon.edu/

Greene, R. Lives in the Balance: www.livesinthebalance.org

Intervention Central: www.interventioncentral.org

National Association of School Psychologists: www.nasponline.org

National Center for Improving Student Learning and Achievement in Math and Science: http://ncisla.wceruw.org/

National Center on RtI: www.rti4success.org

National Child Traumatic Stress Network & National Center for PTSD. (2006). *Psychological first aid—field operations manual* (2nd ed.). Available at www.nctsn.org/content/psychological-first-aid

National Reading Panel: http://nationalreadingpanel.org/default.htm

National Research Center on Learning Disabilities: www.nrcld.org

Positive Environments, Network of Trainers: http://www.pent.ca.gov/hom/bio/dianabw.html

Wright, J. Intervention Central: www.interventioncentral.org/

Wright, J. RtI Wire: www.jimwrightonline.com/php/rti/rti_wire_5Jan06.php

## Print

Caplan, G., & Caplan, R. (1999). *Mental health consultation and collaboration.* Long Grove, IL: Waveland Press.

Drewes, A. A., & Schaefer, D. E. (Eds.). (2010). *School-based play therapy.* Hoboken, NJ: Wiley.

Johnson, E., Mellard, D. F., Fuchs, D., & McKnight, M. A. (2006). *Responsiveness to intervention (RTI): How to do it.* Lawrence, KS: National Research Center on Learning Disabilities.

Jones, A. (1998). *104 activities that build: Self esteem, teamwork, communication, anger management, self-discovery, and coping skills.* Richland, WA: Rec Room.

Landreth, G. (1991). *Play therapy: The art of the relationship.* Bristol, PA: Accelerated Development.

Landreth, G. (2002). *Play therapy: The art of the relationship* (2nd ed.). Muncie, IN: Accelerated Development.

Mannix, D. (2008). *Social skills activities for special children* (2nd ed.). Jossey Bass: San Francisco.

Murphy, J. (2008). *Solution-focused counseling in schools* (2nd ed.). Alexandria, VA: American Counseling Association.

Schaefer, C. E., & Drewes, A. A. (2009). The therapeutic powers of play and play therapy. In A. A. Drewes (Ed.), *Blending play therapy with cognitive behavioral therapy: Evidence-based and other effective treatments and techniques* (pp. 3–16). Hoboken, NJ: Wiley.

Siskind, D. (1999). *A primer for child psychotherapists.* Northvale, NJ: Aronson.

Taylor, S. E., Klein, L. C., Lewis, B. P., Gruenewald, T. L., Gurung, R. A., & Updegraff, J. A. (2000). Biobehavioral responses to stress in females: Tend-and-befriend, not fight-or-flight. *Psychological Review, 107,* 411–429.

Vernox, A. (2002). *What works when with children and adolescents: A handbook of individual counseling techniques.* Champaign, IL: Research Press.

# Index

Page references followed by *fig* indicate an illustrated figure; followed by *f* indicate a form; followed by *e* indicate an exhibit.

## A

"The ABCs of RtI" (NRCLD), 68

Academic consultation: being approach for, 130–131; step 1: setting the stage for collaboration with teacher, 131; step 2: allowing teacher to help you with curriculum, 131

Academic interventions: developing individual student plans and data-tracking tools for, 69–70, 71*e*–72*e*, 74; RtI data-based decision making for, 68–72*e*; Tier 1 interventions used as, 68–69; tips for facilitating, 56–57

ADHD (Other Health Impairment): group play for students with, 159; IEP meeting presentation on eligibility for, 114; providing parents with "preliminary results" on, 108; referral for, 102; school district policy on assessment of, 98

AIMSweb, 69

Assessment: ADHD, 98; autism, 99; completing within timelines, 34–39; managing your caseload, 32–34; problem statement and assessment data, 69; as school psychologist responsibility, 2–3; selecting tools for, 99; special education, 79–104; universal screening strategies, 73; when you are sent inappropriate referrals for, 61–62

Assessment audit of school: description of, 67; information required for, 67–68

Assessment caseload: checking for accuracy, 35; as half the battle of special education assessment, 79–80; managing your, 32–34; Master Assessment Log, 33*e*; time management tips for balancing, 40–45; timelines for, 34–39; what to do when you are overwhelmed by, 44–45

Assessment timelines: check your caseloads for accuracy, 35; issues related to keeping, 34; making your yearly assessment calendar, 35–39; Master Triennial Calendar, 35–39; special education assessment, 80, 83. *See also* Time management

Autism spectrum disorder: assessment of, 99; IEP meeting presentation on eligibility for, 116; providing parents with "preliminary results" on, 108–109

## B

Beginning-of-school logistics: considerations and opportunities of, 17–18; finding a work space at your school site, 22–23; during first few days and weeks, 18; getting needed materials, 23; of managing multiple sites, 18–22; the neighborhood and safety issues, 24; wardrobe choices, 24

Behavioral consultation: being approached about a, 124–125; step 1: evaluate if child is a danger to himself or others, 125; step 2: meeting with teacher, 125; step 3: identify what teacher has already done, 125–126; step 4: build empathy for the child, 126; step 5: offer to visit the classroom, 126; step 6: schedule a follow-up meeting to share observations, 126–127; step 7: developing an feasible action plan, 127; step 8: continue to follow up, 127–128; step 9: be available for future consultations, 128

Behavioral interventions: RtI data-based decision making for, 73–75; supporting students with, 57–58; tips for developing effective, 58–59; universal screening, 73

The Bureaucracy Monster: description of, 31–32; learning to tame the, 32–46. *See also* Documentation

## C

Caplan, G., 124, 134

Caplan, R., 124, 134

Check-ins: post-crisis management using, 188; social-emotional and crisis consultation and follow-up, 130; student crisis: danger to self, 182

Child abuse reports, 151–152

"Child crisis" telephone number, 152

Child-find clause (IDEA), 55

Child Protective Services (CPS): alleviating fears of parents about, 148; documenting calls and reports to, 40; individual counseling and need to call, 151–152; interviews about safety and need to contact, 185

Classroom observation: during behavioral consultation, 126; Classroom Observation Form, 88*f*; considerations for, 86–87

Classroom student study team (SST) meeting, 73

Cognitive-behavioral therapy (CBT), 142–143

Collaborative Problem Solving approach, 132

Confidential IEP Summary Form, 16

Confidentiality: explaining issue to parents, 148; individual counseling and, 152–153; in the teachers' lounge, 134

Consent for Individual Counseling Form, 146*f*

Consent for Small Group Counseling Form, 164

Consentimiento Para Consejería Individual Form, 147*f*

Consultation: academic, 130–131; behavioral, 124–128; consultee-centered model of, 124; during the IEP-writing process, 131–133; maintaining confidentiality in the teachers' lounge, 134; as school psychologist responsibility, 3–4, 123–124; social-emotional and crisis, 39–40, 128–130; working with teachers resistance to, 133–134

Consultee-centered consultation model, 124

Coping Cat program, 143

Counseling: Crisis Counseling Referral Form, 190*f*; documenting your, 39–40; group, 157–176; IEP plan stipulating services for, 59, 138; individual, 137–155; as school psychologist responsibility, 5–6

Counselors: building a relationship with other, 14; post-crisis, 187*e*–195

Crises: debriefing after the immediate, 195; individual student: danger to self and others, 179–185; schoolwide, 178–179, 185–189

Crises interventions: acknowledge feelings and reactions, 187; coordinating mental health efforts, 193–195; debriefing the entire staff, 195; decide how much to disclose and disseminate the information, 186, 189; determine the level of response, 186; gather the information, 186; providing information and support to parents, 191–192*e*; student referrals for counseling, 189–190*f*; teach about self-care, 187–188

Crises management: acknowledging feelings and reactions, 187; conducting appropriate activity, 188; Crisis Intervention Handout for, 187*e*–188*e*; danger to others, 182–185; danger to self, 179–182; debriefing component of, 195; post-crisis dissemination component of, 186–187; preparation component of, 178–179; Psychological First Aid approach to, 177–178, 185–189; teach about self-care, 187. *See also* Social-emotional and crisis consultation

Crises management forms: Crisis Counseling Referral Form, 190*f*; Crisis Intervention Handout, 187*e*–188*e*; Crisis Letter to Parents, 192*e*; Crisis Referral Tracking Sheet, 194*f*; Suicide Assessment, 181*f*; Threat Assessment, 184*f*

Crisis Counseling Referral Form, 190*f*

Cumulative and Special Education Review Checklist Form, 85*f*

Custodians: building a relationship with, 17; unlocking doors when there are no spare keys, 23

**D**

Daily Agenda for Talent Group, 171*e*

Daily schedule, 43–44

Danger to others: behavioral consultation to evaluate, 125; crisis management of, 182–183, 185; individual counseling and evaluating, 152; Threat Assessment, 184*f*

Danger to self: behavioral consultation to evaluate, 125; crisis management of, 179–182; individual counseling and evaluating, 152; Suicide Assessment, 181*f*

*Dangerous Minds* (film), 9, 24

Debriefing: following the immediate crisis, 195; parents and the IEP team following IEP meeting, 118–119

Designated Instruction and Service (DIS), 138

Developmental delays, 115–116

Developmental History Form, 90*f*–91*f*

"Discrepancy model" of SLD, 65, 111

Disseminating post-crisis information, 186–187

Documentation: assessment caseload and related, 32–39; Child Protective Services (CPS) calls and reports, 40; counseling and crisis counseling, 39–40; dealing with the continual paperwork and, 31–32; individual counseling and "SOAP notes" method, 149–151; intervention, 39. *See also* The Bureaucracy Monster; Forms and exhibits

Drewes, A. A., 140, 159

Dynamic Indicators of Basic Early Literacy Skills (DIBELS), 69

**E**

Eligibility: ADHD (Other Health Impairment), 114; autism, 116; emotional disturbance, 114–115; emotional reactions by parents and/or teachers to, 117–118; intellectual disability, mental retardation, developmental delays, 115–116; specific learning disability using discrepancy model, 111; specific learning disability using RtI model, 111, 114; when IEP team publicly disagrees with findings on, 118; when testing does not indicate, 117

Emotional disturbance: IEP meeting presentation of findings on, 114–115; referral on, 102

Emotional interventions: supporting students with, 57–58; tips for effective, 58–59

Empathy: behavioral consultation and role of, 1226; crisis management by modeling calmness and, 188

Exhibits. *See* Forms and exhibits

**F**

Families: introducing yourself to the, 27–28; providing Web sites on academic support for, 57. *See also* Parents/guardians

"Fight or flight" response, 199

Flocking practice: benefits and tips for, 199–200; description of, 199

Forms and exhibits: Classroom Observation Form, 88*f*; Confidential IEP Summary, 16; Consent for Individual Counseling, 146*f*; Consent for Small Group Counseling, 164; Consentimiento Para Consejería Individual, 147*f*; Crisis Counseling Referral Form, 190*f*; Crisis Intervention Handout, 187*e*–188*e*; Crisis Referral Tracking Sheet, 194*f*; Daily Agenda for Talent Group, 171*e*; Developmental History, 90*f*–91*f*; Group Counseling Permission Form (Spanish),

165*e*–166*e*; Group Permission Slip (English), 163*e*; Group Referral Form, 160*e*; Group Reminder Form, 168*e*–169*e*; Individual Intervention Plan and Tracking, 71*e*–72*e*, 74; Initial Referral List for HMS Talent Groups, 161*e*; Letter to Staff, 26*e*; Master Assessment Log, 33*e*; Psychological Services Memo: CONFIDENTIAL, 82*f*; School Psychologist Schedule, 20*e*–21*e*; School Year: 2012-2013, 37*e*–38*e*; Suicide Assessment, 181*f*; Survey/Rating Scale Memo to Parent(s), 97*f*; Survey/Rating Scale Memo to Teacher(s) Psychological Services Memo: CONFIDENTIAL, 93*f*; Teacher Feedback Survey, 94*f*–95*f*; Ten-Week Agenda for Talent Group, 170*e*–171*e*; Threat Assessment, 184*f*; Weekly To-Do List: September 5-9, 42*e*. *See also* Documentation

Friedberg, R., 143

Fuchs, D., 67

**G**

"Gatekeeping" role: changing your, 65–66; navigating your changing, 76; Response to Intervention (RtI) as solution to, 66

General education teachers: academic consultation role of, 130–131; behavioral consultation role of, 125–128; building a relationship with, 17; classroom observation of student and, 86–88*f*; classroom student study team (SST) meeting with each, 73; CPS-reportable information learned by, 152; Crisis Intervention Handout passed out to, 187*e*–189*e*; emotional reactions to child's disability or eligibility by, 117–118; feedback solicited during IEP meeting, 98; getting supplemental materials for curriculum from, 57; maintaining confidentiality in teachers' lounge with, 134; presenting developmental information during in-service meetings to, 60; social-emotional-behavioral evaluation role of, 92–96; working with those resistance to consultation, 133–134. *See also* Principal; Staff; Student referrals; Teacher surveys

Greene, R., 132

Group counseling: conducting needs assessment at your school, 158; how to handle problems that come up, 172–174; pulling it all together, 174; starting a group, 158–159, 162, 167, 169

Group counseling decisions: choosing a cofacilitator, 167; deciding who is in your group, 159, 162; level of structure in the group, 168–169; on what type of group to run, 158–159; when and where to hold your group, 167, 169

Group counseling forms: Consent for Small Group Counseling, 164; Daily Agenda for Talent Group, 171*e*; Group Counseling Permission Form (Spanish), 165*e*–166*e*; Group Permission Slip (English), 163*e*; Group Referral Form, 160*e*; Group Reminder Form, 168*e*; Initial Referral List for HMS Talent Groups, 161*e*; Ten-Week Agenda for Talent Group, 170*e*–171*e*

Group counseling problems: the group is out of control, 173; a group member does not participate, 174; group members "gang up" on another member or members, 172–173; a student leaves the group without permission, 173–174; a student wants to drop out of group, 172

Group Permission Slip (English), 163*e*

Group Referral Form, 160*e*

Group Reminder Form, 168*e*

Guardians. *See* Parents/guardians

**H**

History. *See* Student history

**I**

IEP (Individualized Education Plan): consultation during process of writing up the, 131–133; counseling services as part of the, 59, 138; developing behavior plans using information from the, 59; as part of special education assessment history, 55; SMART goals included in, 69, 132

IEP meeting: calculating legal timelines for, 80; changing your "gatekeeping" role during, 65–66, 76; dealing with rudeness during the, 118; handling irrational demands by parents during, 118; parent concerns regarding, 83; preparation before the, 106–110; presenting assessment report during, 101–102; recommended agenda during, 110–118; soliciting feedback from teachers and parents during, 98; what to do after the, 118–119; when parents present new information during the, 107. *See also* Special education assessment

IEP meeting agenda: advantages of creating a, 110; laying the groundwork for presenting results, 110–117; other helpful tips for presenting during meeting, 117–118

IEP meeting preparation: building consensus on your team, 106–108; collaborating with outside team members, 109–110; learn about your role and presentation style in meetings, 106; when to share results with parents before the meeting, 108–109

IEP meeting presentation: on ADHD (Other Health Impairment), 114; on autism, 116; on emotional disturbance, 114–115; on intellectual disability, mental retardation, developmental delays, 115–116; laying the ground for, 110–111; other helpful tips for making the, 117–118; on specific learning disabilities, 111–114

IEP teams: building consensus on your, 106–108; collaborating in the IEP with outside, 109–110; debriefing them after the IEP meeting, 118–119; when members publicly disagree with eligibility findings, 118

In-service meetings, 60

Individual counseling: beginning to undertake, 145–149; cognitive-behavioral therapy (CBT), 142–143; Consent for Individual Counseling Form, 146*f*; Consentimiento Para Consejería Individual Form, 147*f*; counseling roles taken during, 138–139; examining considerations for, 137–138; IEP plan stipulating services for, 59, 138; play and art therapy, 140–142; psychodynamic ("insight-oriented") therapy, 139–140; "SOAP notes" documentation used for, 149–151; solution-focused brief therapy, 143; sticky confidentiality issues of, 152–153; terminating, 153–154; when child is a danger to himself or others, 152; when to call Child Protective Services (CPS), 151–152

Individual Intervention Plan and Tracking Form, 71*e*–72*e*, 74

Individuals with Disabilities Education Act (IDEA) [2004]: child-find clause of the, 55; revision of the, 4, 5

Initial Referral List for HMS Talent Groups Form, 161*e*

Intellectual disability, 115–116

Intervention and prevention: academic, 56–57; being preventive when you have no time, 50–56; common pitfalls to avoid, 60–62; during crisis situations, 186–195; developing prevention activities and programs, 59–60; documenting, 39; remembering the importance of, 49–50; as school psychologist responsibility, 4–5; social, emotional, and behavioral, 57–59, 73–75. *See also* Response to Intervention (RtI)

Intervention Central Web site, 74

Intervention plans: data-tracking tools used with, 69; developing individual, 69–70; Tracking Form for, 71*e*–72*e*

## J

Johnson, E., 67

## L

Landreth, G., 140

Leadership teams, 51

Learning disabilities. *See* Specific learning disabilities

## M

Mannix, D., 159

Master Triennial Calendar: issues to consider when making your, 35–36; School Year: 2012-2013 Form, 37*e*–38*e*

Materials, gathering needed, 23

McKnight, M. A., 67

Mellard, D. F., 67

Mental health resources: providing parents with information on, 192; supporting post-crisis, 193

Mental retardation, 115–116

Multiple site management: practical considerations for, 18–19; School Psychologist Schedule form for, 20*e*–21*e*

## N

National Association of School Psychologists Web site: academic intervention resources on the, 57; social, emotional, and behavioral intervention resources on the, 58

National Center for Improving Student Learning and Achievement in Math and Science Web site, 76

National Child Traumatic Stress Network & National Center for PTSD, 177, 178

National Reading Panel Web site, 76

National Research Center on Learning Disabilities (NRCLD) Web site: "The ABCs of RtI" on the, 68; RtI resources available on the, 67

Neighborhood safety tips, 24

Notes from the School Psychologist blog, 3, 32

Notes from the School Psychologist Blog Facebook page, 5, 41, 66, 199

## P

PANDY program (Preventing Anxiety and Depression in Youth), 143

Paperwork. *See* Documentation; Forms and exhibits

Parental consent: Consent for Individual Counseling Form, 146*f*; Consent for Small Group Counseling Form, 164; Consentimiento Para Consejería Individual, 147*f*; during crisis situations, 185

Parents/guardians: alleviating fears regarding Child Protective Services (CPS) of, 148; conducting a developmental history with, 89–92; Crisis Letter to Parents, 192*e*; debriefing them

after the IEP meeting, 118–119; emotional reactions to child's disability or eligibility by, 117–118; explaining confidentiality issue to, 148; feedback solicited during IEP meeting, 98; handling irrational demands of, 118; IEP meeting concerns by, 83; offering preventive activities and programs to, 60; providing Web sites on academic support for, 57; special education assessment consent from, 80, 83; Survey/Rating Scale Memo to Parent(s) Form, 97*f*; tailoring discussion to best communication with, 118; tips for presenting IEP meeting findings to, 117–118; when new information is presented during IEP meeting by, 107; when to share testing results before the IEP meeting, 108–109. *See also* Families

Pfeiffer, Michelle, 9

Play and art therapy: description of, 140–141; recommendations on essentials for, 141–142

Positive behavioral intervention support (PSIS) teams, 51

Post-crisis dissemination, 186–187

Posttraumatic stress disorder (PTSD), 177

Preventive pitfalls: when only special education interventions are available, 60–61; when you are sent inappropriate referrals, 61–62

Preventive strategies: being effective in intervention teams, 50–51; developing your own activities and programs for, 59–60; RtI pyramid graphic on, 51–52*fig*, 58; schoolwide support teams, 51; student-focused support teams, 53–56

Principal: building a relationship with the, 12–13; going over crisis preparation with the, 178–179; key questions to ask during first meeting with, 13–14; questions to ask about finding a work space, 22. *See also* General education teachers; Schools; Staff

Problem statement and assessment data, 69

Progress monitoring tools, 74–75

Psychodynamic ("insight-oriented") therapy, 139–140

Psychological First Aid model: description of, 177–178; schoolwide crises and implementing, 185–189

Psychological Services Memo: CONFIDENTIAL Form, 82*f*

## R

Referrals. *See* Student referrals

Relationship building: beginning-of-school logistics and, 17–19; getting situated at new school site, 11; with key staff members, 12–15, 17; potential challenges to, 10–11

Response to Intervention (RtI): core principles of effective, 67; data-based decision making for academic, 68–72*e*; data-based decision making for behavioral, 73–75; description of, 4, 50; district requirements for eligibility reports, 86; "gatekeeping" solution through, 66, 76; NRCLD's Web site resources on, 67; promise and benefits of the, 66, 76–77; RtI pyramid graphic for schoolwide support teams, 51–52*fig*; school psychologists' roles in, 66–68; specific learning disability criteria under, 111, 114. *See also* Intervention and prevention

Response to Intervention (RtI) teams: navigating your role change within, 76; tracking individual student progress with your, 75–76

*Responsiveness to Intervention (RTI): How to Do It* (Johnson, Mellard, Fuchs, & McKnight), 67

RtI pyramid: graphic of the, 51–52*fig*; Tier 1 interventions of the, 68–69, 74; Tier 2 and Tier 3 interventions of the, 58, 74–75

RtI Wire Web site, 69

## S

Safety interviews. *See* Danger to others; Danger to self

Saying no: knowing when and how, 200–201; recommended tips on appropriate ways of, 201; to yourself, 202

Schaefer, C. E., 140, 159

Scheduling: tips for weekly, 41, 43; Weekly To-Do List: September 5-9, 42*e*; what to do when caseload is overwhelming, 44–45; your day, 43–44

*School-Based Play Therapy* (ed. Drewes and Schaefer), 159

School districts: ADHD assessment policy of, 98; managing multiple sites within the, 18–22; RtI eligibility report requirements by, 86. *See also* Schools

School psychologist "hats": assessment, 2–3; consultation, 3–4; counseling, 5–6; prevention and intervention, 4–5. *See also specific "hat"*

School Psychologist Schedule, 20*e*–21*e*

School psychologists: building relationships within their school, 9–29; dealing with paperwork, 31–47; four main "hats" and responsibilities of, 1–6; managing the stress of the job, 197–203; setting healthy work-life boundaries, 200–202

School secretary: building a relationship with the, 12; getting keys from the, 23

School sites: building relationships with key staff members at, 12–15, 17; considerations for managing multiple, 18–22; finding a work space at your, 22–23; getting needed materials at your, 23; getting situated at your new, 11

School support staff, building a relationship with, 14

School Year: 2012-2013 Form, 37*e*–38*e*

Schools: assessment audit of your, 67–68; beginning-of-school logistics, 17–24; building relationships within your, 9–29; group counseling needs assessment at your, 158; managing crisis at your, 177–196; what to do when inappropriate referrals are made by, 61–62. *See also* Principal; School districts

Schoolwide crises: Crisis Intervention Handout, 187*e*–188*e*; preparation for, 178–179; Psychological First Aid approach to, 177–178, 185–189; steps to take in a, 186–195

Schoolwide support teams, 51

Self-care: "flocking" practice for, 199–200; post-crisis teaching of, 187; stress management through, 197, 198–200; Zen moments as practice of, 198–199

SLD "discrepancy model," 65

SMART goals, 69, 132

"SOAP notes" documentation, 149–151

Social-emotional and crisis consultation: being approached for, 128; documenting your, 39–40; step 1: listen and reflect back concerns, 129; step 2: offer to "check in" with student, 129; step 3: follow up with consultee about the check-in, 130; step 4: follow up, 130. *See also* Crises management

Social-emotional-behavioral evaluation: deciding if one is necessary, 92; Survey/Rating Scale Memo to Parent(s) Form,

97*f*; Survey/Rating Scale Memo to Teacher(s) Psychological Services Memo: CONFIDENTIAL Form, 93*f*; Teacher Feedback Survey Form, 94*f*–95*f*

Social interventions: supporting students with, 57–58; tips for developing effective, 58–59

*Social Skills Activities for Special Children* (Mannix), 159

Socialization, 116

Solution-focused brief therapy, 143

Special education: how to frame with families and students, 27–28; when it is the only available intervention, 60–61

Special education assessment: beginning your testing with student, 100; case management component of, 79–80; deciding if full social-emotional-behavioral evaluation is needed, 92–98; determining timelines and informing all parties, 80, 83; differences between initial and triennials (reevaluations), 102–103; flowchart of the, 81*fig*; reviewing the history and gathering data, 83–92; selecting testing instruments, 98–99; selecting your testing tools, 99; writing quality reports, 101–102. *See also* IEP meeting; Students

Special educators, 14–15

Specific learning disabilities (SLDs): discrepancy model for identifying, 65, 111; normal curve in English and Spanish measuring, 112*fig*–113*fig*; parent reaction to diagnosis of, 108–109; referral on, 102; RtI model for identifying, 111, 114

Staff: building relationships with key members of, 12–15, 17; hosting professional development activities for, 60; introducing yourself to the, 24–27; letter for introducing yourself to the, 26*e*; post-crisis debriefing of, 195; potential challenges to building relationships with, 10–11; special education assessment notification to, 82*f*. *See also* General education teachers

Stress management: "flocking" practice for, 199–200; health work-life boundaries for, 200–202; Zen moments for, 198–199

Student-focused support teams, 53–56

Student history: classroom observation as part of, 86–88*f*; conducting a developmental history with parents/guardians, 89–92; Cumulative and Special Education Review Checklist, 85*f*; gathering environmental data and reviewing, 83–92

Student referrals: Crisis Counseling Referral Form, 190*f*; Crisis Referral Tracking Sheet, 194*fig*; Group Referral Form, 160*e*; Initial Referral List for HMS Talent Groups, 161*e*; top three types of, 102; when you are sent inappropriate, 61–62. *See also* General education teachers

Students: academic interventions for, 56–57; check-ins with, 130, 182, 188; developing individual academic intervention plans for, 69–70, 71*e*–72*e*; introducing yourself to the, 27–28; tracking individual progress with your RtI team, 75–76; when you are sent inappropriate referrals on, 61–62. *See also* Special education assessment

Suicide Assessment Form, 181*f*

Survey/Rating Scale Memo to Parent(s) Form, 97*f*

Survey/Rating Scale Memo to Teacher(s) Psychological Services Memo: CONFIDENTIAL Form, 93*f*

**T**

Taylor, S. E., 199

Teacher surveys: Survey/Rating Scale Memo to Teacher(s) Psychological Services Memo: CONFIDENTIAL Form, 93*f*; Teacher Feedback Survey Form, 94*f*–95*f*. *See also* General education teachers

Teachers' lounge confidentiality, 134

Teams: IEP (Individualized Education Plan), 106–110, 118–119; participation in leadership, 51; Response to Intervention (RtI), 75–76; schoolwide support, 51

Ten-Week Agenda for Talent Group, 170*e*–171*e*

Threat Assessment Form, 184*f*

Tier 1 interventions: applied for academic intervention, 68–69; behavioral intervention and reviewing effectiveness of, 74; RtI pyramid graphic on, 52*fig*

Tier 2 and 3 interventions: gathering baseline data using the, 74–75; referencing availability at your school, 58; RtI pyramid graphic on, 52*fig*

Time management: balancing assessment caseload with other roles, 40–41; scheduling your day, 43–44; scheduling your week, 41–43; what to do when your caseload is overwhelming, 44–45. *See also* Assessment timelines

**U**

Universal screening strategies, 73

**V**

Vernox, A., 159

**W**

Wardrobe choices, 24

Weekly schedule: tips for creating your, 41, 43; Weekly To-Do List: September 5-9 Form, 42*e*

Weekly To-Do List: September 5-9 Form, 42*e*

*What Works When with Children and Adolescents: A Handbook of Individual Counseling Techniques* (Vernox), 159

Work-life boundaries: knowing when to say no to yourself, 202; your role and saying no, 200–201

Work space: finding a confidential, 22–23; questions to ask the principal about your, 22

**Z**

Zen moments: description of, 198; list of recommended, 198–199